W9-AHM-067

The Grand-Slam Book of Canadian Baseball Writing

John Bell, editor

Pottersfield Press
Lawrencetown Beach
R.R. 2 Porters Lake, Nova Scotia

Printed in Canada

Copyright Pottersfield Press, 1993

Introduction, headnotes and "Further Reading" copyright John Bell, 1993.

All rights reserved. No part of this publication may be reproduced or transmitted in any form or by any means, electronic or mechanical, including photocopying, or by any information storage or retrieval system, without permission from the publisher.

Canadian Cataloguing in Publication Data

Main entry under title:

The Grand-Slam Book of Canadian Baseball Writing

ISBN: 0-919001-79-3

1. Baseball – Literary collections. 2. Canadian literature (English) – 20th century. I. Bell, John, 1952–

PS8237.B37G72 1993 C810.8′0355 C93-098606-7

PR9194.52.B37G72 1993

Cover artwork by Graham Pilsworth

Pottersfield Press gratefully acknowledges the ongoing support of the Nova Scotia Department of Tourism and Culture as well as the Canada Council.

Pottersfield Press
Lawrencetown Beach
R.R.2, Porters Lake
Nova Scotia B0J 2S0

CONTENTS

INTRODUCTION

In the beginning was the word, & the word was
"Play Ball!"

– George Bowering,

Baseball, a poem in the magic number 9

Canadians have probably played baseball as long as anyone; nevertheless, until recently our writers have seemed reluctant to embrace the game with the same degree of enthusiasm as their American counterparts. In fact, during the era prior to 1940, one is much more likely to find references in Canadian literature to cricket than to baseball.

There is, of course, some mention of the game in our literature before the Second World War. Perhaps the earliest baseball piece in nineteenth-century Canadian writing is Palmer Cox's narrative poem for children "The Brownies at Base-Ball," which is found in his collection *The Brownies, Their Book* (1887). (Interestingly, a few years before the appearance of Cox's poem, the first Canadian baseball cards, featuring caricatures of federal politicians playing ball, were issued by the Bain Wagon Company of Woodstock, Ontario.) Later, Ralph Connor – the pseudonym of Rev. Charles W. Gordon – had baseball play a pivotal role in his novel *The Sky Pilot* (1899). The novelist Nellie McClung also referred fondly to the game in her memoir *Clearing in the West* (1936).

The paucity of early baseball literature in Canada is such, however, that some of the strongest images of Canadian ball of the era are found in the American author Zane Grey's collection *The Red Headed Outfield and Other Stories* (1912), which includes an entertaining account of a U.S. team playing against a home team in Guelph. Apparently, Grey drew on the experiences of his brother Romer, who had played in Canada at the turn of the century.

Another famous foreign writer – and a contemporary of Grey's – Sir Arthur Conan Doyle, actually played a little ball in Canada but unfortunately did not leave a record of the experience. During the summer of 1914, Doyle was on a Canadian tour and had the honour of opening a game in Jasper, Alberta between Jasper Park and Edson. According to *Saturday Night* (July 11, 1914), Sherlock Holmes' creator "stepped to the plate and hit the first ball pitched – for a homer, had he run."

However, while there was some literary interest in the Canadian sport of baseball before the Great Depression, one gets the distinct impression that for many Canadian writers of the period baseball was a foreign game – worse yet, a Yankee game (according to "the annexationist," Goldwin Smith, it was "the game of the continent"). This bias was reinforced, perhaps, by the mythology of the Canada First group and those who followed in their footsteps. Within the context of this *weltanschauung*, baseball was viewed as an inferior republican game suited for southern climes. The manly sports of lacrosse, cricket, and later ice hockey were the proper diversions for the hardy Men of the North.

Accordingly, one suspects that the Atlantic-Canadian author Archibald MacMechan was speaking for more than a few of his compatriots when, in his controversial essay "Canada as a Vassal State" (*Canadian Historical Review*, December 1920), he decried the Americanization of Canadian sport: "Our native game, lacrosse, is dead. Cricket, which flourishes in Australia, is here a sickly exotic. But baseball is everywhere."

In 1926 the New Brunswick writer George Frederick Clarke acknowledged this Canadian bias against the game in his novel *The Best One Thing*, in which the protagonist's father echoes MacMechan's sentiments:

> Captain Fenwick was, as usual, not much enthused over the ball game. He took the opportunity to reiterate his belief that baseball was demoralising the youth of the land. If it was only cricket, now; a gentleman's game; a moulder of character...

Young Prang Fenwick is not convinced, however, by his father's outburst:

> Prang listened in silence. All very well for his father to run down baseball, he thought, but if cricket was such a wonderful game, why hadn't his parent made some effort to teach it to him?

Implicit in such criticism of baseball, of course, is more than a little class prejudice, since for many decades the game was perceived to be primarily a working-class sport. As MacMechan observed in an essay on Halifax in his *The Book of Ultima Thule* (1927), baseball was played by "the sons of the *commonalty* ... for the necessary apparatus is cheap, and neither uniform nor level ground is needed."

This Red Tory unease with the game has, to some degree, persisted to the present. One of the most recent expressions is found in a *Globe and Mail* "Cross Current" column (July 7, 1992) by Rick Salutin, who endeavours to strip baseball of its mythopoeic pretensions and expose it as an overrated game "in which nothing much happens."

Needless to say, the nationalist bias against baseball is founded not only on an elitist disregard for the longstanding attachment of the Canadian people to the game, but also on the fallacy that hockey and baseball are somehow mutually exclusive. The more rabid sports chauvinists conveniently ignore the fact that many hockey players, including some of the game's gods, also loved baseball. Lionel Conacher even died playing ball, but then that would only confirm nationalist suspicions about the game.

Although there is still some evidence of hostility to baseball in Canada, a change of attitude towards the game was apparent in the English-Canadian literary community in the 1930s and 1940s. Appropriately, perhaps, two of the first figures during this period to write about baseball are best described as Canadian-American writers: Mary Graham Bonner and Robert Fontaine.

Bonner, a native of Cooperstown who was raised and educated in Halifax, was for many years a popular juvenile writer. Starting in 1931, she published numerous books about baseball, including five young-adult novels. Fontaine was also born in the U.S., but grew up in Ottawa. His first and most famous book, *The Happy Time* (1945), contained the popular story "God Hit a Home Run," which provides a lively picture of baseball in Hull, Quebec, during the second decade of the twentieth century.

Not long after the appearance of Fontaine's story, the Canadian journalist Scott Young began contributing sports fiction, including several stories about baseball, to *Collier's* and other U.S. magazines. While Bonner, like most of the era's baseball-fiction authors, was writing for a juvenile audience, Fontaine and Young targeted adult readers, anticipating the shift in baseball writing that would begin in the fifties.

Prior to the early 1950s, baseball literature (at that time largely an American genre) consisted almost entirely of juvenile fiction. All that began to change, however, with the appearance of two classic American baseball novels: *The Natural* (1952) by Bernard Malamud and *The Southpaw* (1953) by Mark Harris. Suddenly, the game became a legitimate subject for adult literature; which is not to say that juvenile baseball fiction tailed off during the fifties. On the contrary, it experienced a boom, and Bonner, who saw the publication of four of her novels during the decade, was not the only Canadian to participate in this explosion of genre publishing. Between 1955 and 1958, the expatriate writer Charles Spain Verral, a noted contributor to the pulps and comics, also published several works of juvenile baseball literature in the U.S.

Even though the juvenile authors Bonner and Verral were undoubtedly the most prolific Canadian baseball writers of the fifties, the early years of the decade witnessed developments in the field of Canadian adult baseball literature that paralleled those in the U.S. Not only did one of Canada's greatest writers, the former sandlot pitcher Morley Callaghan, publish his classic story "A Cap for Steve" in *Esquire* in July 1952, but later that same year, Marshall McLuhan delivered a ground-breaking radio lecture entitled "Baseball Is Culture." Speaking a few weeks after CBC-TV in Montreal had begun broadcasting with test transmissions of Montreal Royals games, McLuhan, who had also briefly commented on the game in *The Mechanical Bride* (1951), argued that baseball was best understood as "a means of ritual or popular communication in a public place and collective way with the central, but abstract and specialized, financial and industrial drama." A little over a decade later, however, in *Understanding Media* (1964), he insisted that the game had, at least for a time, "lost its psychic and social relevance" as a result of the impact of television. (One has to wonder what McLuhan would have made of the sixth game of the 1992 World Series, when over 45,000 fans assembled at the Skydome to watch their beloved Blue Jays win the world championship on the stadium's JumboTron TV.)

While not even Marshall McLuhan could have been expected to speculate about the impact of television on baseball as early as 1952, it did not take very long for a Canadian writer to probe the connection between the game and the new technology. In 1954, *Maclean's* editor Ralph Allen published a near-future novel, *The Chartered Libertine*, which took a satirical look at the tension between public and private broadcasters. While not, strictly speaking, a work of baseball literature, the book is probably the first baseball-related adult novel by a Canadian, as it partly focusses on the efforts of a Toronto tycoon, whose prize possession is a signed Ty Cobb ball, to promote his new women's professional softball club – the Queens d'Amour – by arranging for television coverage of their games. The year 1954 also marked a turning point in the development of adult baseball poetry in Canada with the publication of Raymond Souster's first baseball poems in his collection *A Dream That Is Dying*.

In the decade and a half that followed, not only did Souster – like Callaghan, a former Toronto-area pitcher – continue to write about the game, but a number of other important writers addressed themselves to baseball themes. Among the most notable works of Canadian baseball literature to appear during the period were Gwen Pharis Ringwood's short story "Home Base" (*Family Herald*, September 27, 1962), Mordecai Richler's widely anthologized story "Playing Ball on Hampstead Heath" (*Gentlemen's Quarterly*, August 1966), and George Bowering's long poem *Baseball, a poem in the magic number 9* (1967), the first volume of baseball poetry published in Canada.

Despite the fact that a small but significant body of adult baseball literature by Canadians did appear through the 1950s and 1960s, the genre actually became established in Canada during the next two decades. This marked growth in fiction and poetry about the game can probably be attributed to two factors: the maturing of baseball literature in the U.S. – as evidenced by the work of writers like Mark Harris, Robert Coover, and Philip Roth – and the establishment of Canada's own major-league clubs: the Montreal Expos in 1969 and the Toronto Blue Jays in 1977. Increasingly, Canadian writers were becoming fans of baseball and of literature about the game. (See, for instance, the essays by Margaret Atwood and Elspeth Cameron in "The Season of '85," a special supplement to the October 19, 1985 issue of the *Globe and Mail*.) They were also becoming more willing to write about sports generally, as adult literature about other sports in Canada, especially hockey, also became more prevalent.

One of the most significant developments in Canadian baseball literature during the 1970s was John Craig's emergence as the country's first author of adult baseball novels. Although he received some recognition in Canada for his juvenile fiction, Craig was probably better known in the U.S., where he had established a reputation as a successful popular novelist. Before his death in 1981, he published two notable baseball books: the satire *All G.O.D.'s Children* (1975), in which a motley group of major-league rejects manages to make it to the World Series, and *Chappie and Me* (1979), an autobiographical novel about a young white player's experiences with a black barnstorming team during the 1930s.

The poets Raymond Souster and George Bowering also remained active during the 1970s. In fact, by 1976, Bowering, who wrote fiction and non-fiction about the game as well, had produced enough baseball poetry to publish the collection *Poem and Other Baseballs*. The decade also saw the publication of memorable baseball short stories by W.D. Valgardson and Hugh Hood.

The real breakthrough period for Canadian baseball literature, though, was the 1980s, and perhaps the dominant writer of the period, in both Canada and the U.S., was a former student of W.D. Valgardson's – W.P. Kinsella. Like Valgardson, Kinsella attended the University of Iowa's Writer's Workshop; something they both have in common with at least three other Canadian authors who have done some writing about the game: Kent Thompson, Robert Kroetsch, and Clark Blaise. In addition to emerging as one of the field's premier short-story writers, Kinsella has, since 1982, published three baseball novels, including two fantasies that are already considered classic works of baseball literature: *Shoeless Joe* (1982) and *The Iowa Baseball Confederacy* (1986).

By the time that Kinsella had established himself as a master of baseball fantasy fiction, another Canadian, the former American League beat writer Alison Gordon (the granddaughter of Ralph Connor/Rev. Charles W. Gordon), was beginning to earn a reputation as a leading baseball mystery writer. According to *Baseball by the Books* (1991), an exhaustive bibliographical survey of baseball fiction by the American specialist Andy McCue, Gordon's first novel, *The Dead Pull Hitter* (1988), "has the strongest baseball ambience and content of any of the baseball mysteries." Gordon has since published two more novels featuring her reporter-detective Kate Henry.

While Kinsella and Gordon, together with Hugh Hood and George Bowering, are probably the best-known contemporary contributors to baseball fiction in Canada, a number of other Canadian writers have also made their mark in the field, including Paul Quarrington, Jim Christy, Brian Fawcett, Robert Currie, and Steven Heighton. As well, a growing number of poets have followed the example of the veterans Souster and Bowering in celebrating the game in poetry. Among the most notable are Dennis Gruending, Gary Hyland, Ken Norris, Judith Fitzgerald, and Pat Jasper. Furthermore, baseball has become increasingly popular with Canadian juvenile and children's writers, as evidenced by recent works by Martyn Godfrey, Kathy Stinson, Roger Poupart, and Roch Carrier. (Interestingly, Canadian visual artists like William Kurelek, Michael Snow, Ted Harrison, Gerald McMaster, and Russell Yurisky have also produced baseball-related work during the past two decades.)

This same period also saw the publication of two important works by George Bowering that confirmed the genre's coming of age in Canada: the first essay on Canadian baseball literature, "Baseball and the Canadian Imagination" (*Canadian Literature*, Spring 1986), and the first baseball literary anthology edited by a Canadian, *Taking the Field* (1990).

It has been suggested that baseball's strong connection with adult literature (something which, curiously, coincides with television coverage of the game) derives to a large degree from the game's relationship with time. Presumably, baseball's special – detractors like Salutin would say boring – pace encourages contemplation, while its timelessness invites writers to exploit the game's potential for magic. This tendency towards fantasy and mythopoeism is probably reinforced by the game's seasonal cycles and by its pastoral nature. Perhaps more than any other sport, baseball illustrates McLuhan's point that our games "are a sort of artificial paradise."

McLuhan and other observers have also remarked on the ballpark's similarity to a theatre and on the ritualistic drama inherent in the game: the costumes, the crowds, the defined roles of the various players, the charged confrontations between the pitcher and batter. Another powerful attraction for some, of course, is baseball's rich mythology and its obsession with numbers and statistics.

Maybe the simplest explanation for the game's appeal is its uniqueness. As George Bowering observed, "Baseball is not like anything." Whatever the case, writing about this Canadian sport now forms a substantial body of first-rate prose and poetry. And with over a dozen anthologies of U.S. baseball literature (several of which include Canadian contributors) having appeared since 1980, the time is clearly overdue for a home-team collection, especially when one considers that our contributions to so many other literary genres have been extensively anthologized in recent years.

As the first anthology devoted to this relatively new field of English-Canadian literature, *The Grand-Slam Book of Canadian Baseball Writing* should be viewed more as a representative introduction to some of our best baseball fiction and poetry and less as an attempt to compile a definitive selection. Needless to say, a lot more work relating to the history of Canadian baseball literature remains to be done, and it is probable that additional contributors to the field – especially writers active prior to 1960 – will be identified by other researchers in the future. Nor does *The Grand-Slam Book* deal with French-language baseball writing. Despite the anthology's deliberately exaggerated title, then, the editor would be content if the book was viewed as the literary equivalent of a solid base hit.

In addition to representing different types of baseball fiction and a variety of poetic voices, the anthology is intended to reflect the development of English-Canadian baseball literature over the course of the past five decades. In so doing, the book touches on many different aspects and eras of the game, and brings together writing about men and women, parents and children, joy and pain, love and hate, life and death, and even more. Above all, though, *The Grand-Slam Book* is about fans and players, and the endless varieties, complexities, and seductions of a transcendent game.

Work began in earnest on the anthology at the mid-season point in 1992, but the project kept me particularly busy from October to the end of March, thus blunting the shock of the season's end and filling the void of late fall and winter with baseball reading and research. For this reason, the book has probably given me more pleasure than any of the previous anthologies or collections that I have worked on. In some respects, though, this project was also the most difficult, due to a problem that I should have anticipated: baseball inspires good writing. For this reason, making the final roster cuts for the book was no easy matter, as a number of fine stories and poems could not be included because of space limitations. (To speak of the anthology's contributors as a roster is more than just an obvious conceit, since several of them have displayed a kind of team spirit by dedicating work to each other, and a few have actually played ball together.)

It is hoped that the book's introduction and headnotes, combined with the note on further reading, will help readers to further explore this corner of Canadian literature. Contributors to the anthology were invited to comment in some way on the game, and while not all of them felt so inclined, a number took the opportunity to write about their connections with baseball. These pieces have been incorporated into the headnotes and provide readers, I think, with added insight into the appeal that the game holds for many of our writers.

A number of people – not all of them baseball fans – assisted in the compilation of *The Grand-Slam Book*. In particular, I would like to thank the staff of the National Library and the following individuals: John Barton, Bob Belvin, Laszlo Buhasz, Jim Burant, Barry Callaghan, John Robert Colombo, Luc Couture, Ed Dahl, David Fraser, Margaret Giacomelli, Anne Goddard, Charles Gordon, Sandra Gwyn, Phil Jenkins, Christopher Levenson, Gerald Lynch, Nadine McGinnis, Sue Rogers, Rena Van Dam, Corrie Van't Haaff, Ron Verzuh, and Bruce Walton. As always, my friend and publisher Lesley Choyce was extremely supportive.

As I complete work on the anthology, the season's opening is just a few days away. This year, here in Ottawa, an important part of baseball for many of us will be the inaugural season of the Lynx, the Expos' new Triple-A affiliate. As I sit there, especially on summer evenings, amidst the splendour of the capital's new ballpark (I can already smell the grass), I know that I will find echoes not only of the game's glorious past and my own baseball experiences (not nearly so glorious), but also of the players, fans, and events that I have encountered in the writings of authors like Callaghan, Souster, Richler, Bowering, Kinsella, and Gordon. In going the distance to explore baseball and its verities, our writers have inevitably shaped the way in which we perceive the game. They have shown that the diamond contains a multitude of realities; that it might, in fact, contain them all.

John Bell
Ottawa
April 1993

ROBERT FONTAINE

* * * * * * *

Robert Fontaine was born at Marlboro, Massachusetts in 1911, but grew up in Ottawa. A prolific contributor to American and Canadian periodicals during the 1930s and 1940s, he died in 1965. "God Hit a Home Run," which has been widely anthologized, is taken from The Happy Time *(1945), one of three books that draw on Fontaine's childhood experiences in Ottawa. Fontaine wrote at least one other memorable baseball story – see "Roman Catholics vs. All-Stars" in* Hello to Springtime *(1955).*

* * * * * * *

God Hit a Home Run

Long ago when I was very young my mother and father and I moved to Canada, to the lovely city of Ottawa.

We settled down in one half of a double house, next door to my several unusual uncles, my grandfather, and my aunt Felice, all of whom spoke, as we did ourselves, a strange language. It was a mixture of corrupt French, literally translated idioms, and, in time, the salt of French-Canadian patois.

There are but few memories of the first years in Ottawa. They are only bright fragments, like the little pieces of colored glass in the small hallway window at the stair landing.

The time, however, that God hit a home run is very clear.

My father played the violin and conducted an orchestra for a two-a-day vaudeville theater, so he had little time for diversion. In what spare moments he had, he turned to baseball. In spite of his sensitive, debonair temperament, he loved the game. It refreshed him, perhaps, because it was so far from his métier

I remember well how many times he begged my mother to go with him to the twilight games at Strathcona Park. There was just time for him to see a game between the end of the *matinée* and the beginning of the evening performance.

My mother seemed always too busy.

"I must get the dinner, you know," she would say, with the faint, calm, resigned, Presbyterian air she often assumed.

"Dinner!" my father would exclaim. "We will stuff our pockets with apples and cheese."

"What about the Boy?" my mother would ask.

My father would look at me.

"The Boy is already too fat. Regard him!"

"It is only," my mother would smile, "because he has his cheeks full of shortbreads."

If it was not dinner she had to cook, it was socks she had to darn or blouses she had to make for me, or the kitchen floor she felt the need of shining.

All this made my father quite sad, even though, at each invitation, my mother promised to accompany him "some other time." Still, he never abandoned the hope that he would, in time, have the warm joy of explaining the principles of the intricate game to her. I suppose he knew that she was proud of his artistic talents and he wanted her to be pleased with his athletic knowledge, too.

One warm Sunday in the summer, when I was five or six (who can remember precisely those early times of coming-to-life when every week is as a year?), my mind was occupied with the American funny papers and the eccentric doings of one Happy Hooligan, he of the ragged, patched coat and the small tin can on the side of his head.

My father came into the room where my mother was dusting the china on the mantel and shining the golden letters on the sign that proclaimed: *Jesus Christ Is the Unseen Guest in This House*.

There was, by the way, nothing else to do in Ottawa on a Sunday in those days but to dust religious signs and plates on the mantel or to read the papers. All stores were closed. All theaters were closed. There was prohibition, too, as I recall, so there was not even a bar where one could sit and dream. True, one could go across the Inter-Provincial Bridge to Hull, in Quebec province, and return with a secret bottle of wine, but it could not be served in public.

No, Sunday was the Sad Day in Ottawa.

But to return to my father. He spoke to my mother with some hesitation: "The Boy and I...we...we go to a game of baseball."

My mother turned from the plates and regarded my father coldly.

"On Sunday?" she inquired.

My father ran his finger the length of his nose, a gesture which always indicated an attempt at restraint. Then he removed the band from his cigar as nonchalantly as possible.

"But naturally," he replied. "Do I have some other time to go?"

"You can go, as usual, to the twilight games."

My father bit off the end of his cigar.

"Bah!" he exclaimed. "Baseball for seven innings only is like a dinner without cognac at the end. It is like kissing the woman you love good night by blowing it from your fingers. No. Baseball in the shadows, when the stars are appearing, is not in the true spirit of the game. One must have the bright sun and the green grass."

My mother looked at my eager, shining face and then looked back at my father.

"What is wrong," she asked, smiling faintly, "with kissing a woman you love good night by blowing it from your fingers?"

My father put his arm around her and laughed.

"The same thing that is wrong," he said, "with making from sour cherries an apple pie."

"You can't make an apple pie from sour cherries."

"*Eh, bien*, you can't kiss a woman good night this way...you can only kiss your fingers."

He touched his lips to the back of my mother's neck.

I coughed impatiently at this dallying. My mind was fastened firmly on baseball.

"Papa," I said anxiously, "we go now? Yes?"

"You come with us," my father said to my mother. "Eh? We will stuff our pockets with apples and cheese and make a picnic. Red wine, too, perhaps."

"And an onion," I said, loving onions.

"Some other time," my mother said hastily. "Certainly not on Sunday."

"Ah!" my father cried. "Always some other time. Do you promise some time soon?"

"Yes," my mother replied without much conviction. I suppose the thought of sitting on a hard bench for hours, watching that of which she knew nothing, frightened her. I felt, though, that in time my father's plaintive eagerness would win her over.

"Why," she questioned, as if to soften the blow, "do you not ask Uncle Louis or Uncle Felix?"

"Uncle Louis will be full and will chase butterflies across the diamond. Uncle Felix will wish to measure the speed at which the baseball arrives at the catcher. Besides, they are gone up the Gatineau to bring back the Boy's grandfather."

"Grandpa is coming?" I asked happily.

"Yes. He will stay next door as usual and sleep here."

I laughed. "Why is it that Grandpa stays next door and sleeps here?"

My father shrugged.

"When you are old you sleep where you wish."

My mother was at the window, fixing the small jars of ivy that stood there.

"It looks like a thunderstorm coming," she said. "Grandpa and the uncles will get wet. You and the Boy, too, should not go out in a thunderstorm."

Our entire family was frightened to death of thunderstorms. At the first deep roll in the Laurentian Hills or up the Gatineau we huddled together in one room until the sun broke through, or the stars.

My father spoke bravely, though, on this occasion: "It will probably follow the river."

He did not mention the fact that there were three or four rivers it might follow, all of which came, in the end, almost to our back yard.

"Look!" my mother exclaimed, as a white flash lit the horizon's dark clouds.

"Bah!" my father said nervously. "Heat lightning."

"To me," my mother countered solemnly, "it looks like chain lightning."

"Chain lightning...heat lightning...it is miles away, *n'est-ce-pas*? It is not here is it?"

"*Maman*," I begged, "let us go please, before the storm begins."

"*Voilà*, a smart boy!" my father said proudly, patting me on the head.

My mother sighed and adjusted the tiebacks of the curtains.

"Very well," she said sadly, "but you know what Louis says – he pays too dear a price for honey who licks it off thorns!"

"Honey...thorns," my father repeated, rolling his eyes unhappily. "It is baseball of which we speak now."

"All right," my mother said. "All right. Only, just be careful. Don't stand under trees or near cows."

"No," my father agreed, "no cows and no trees."

He kissed my mother gently on the lips, and I naturally understood there would be no further discussion. I put on my best straw sailor, a white hat with the brim curled up and with a black elastic under the chin to keep the bonnet from the fury of any possible gales.

My mother regarded me with sadness, tucking in the string of my blouse. It was as if I were soon to be guillotined.

"It just doesn't seem right," she said slowly, "on Sunday."

My father lit his cigar impatiently.

"We must be going," he announced hastily. "The game will commence before we arrive."

My father took me by the hand. My mother put her arms around me and hugged and kissed me. It was as if I were going away forever to become a monk.

"Be careful," she said.

"Yes, *Maman*," I said dutifully.

"And pull up your stockings," she added.

On the trolly car going up Rideau Street I was happy. The wind blew through the open, summer seats and the sun was not too warm.

It is true I should have been in Sunday school at my mother's Presbyterian church, learning about the Red Sea turning back. Instead, I was on my way to the very brink of hell. For Hull, where my father whispered confidentially we were going, was well known to be a place of sinful living, and the sulphur that drifted daily from the match factories was enough to convince me of the truth of the report.

"Papa," I asked, "is it true Hull is wicked?"

"Not in the part where they play baseball," my father assured me.

A faint flash of lightning startled me a little.

"Papa. I have fear Uncle Louis and Uncle Felix and Grandpa will be struck by lightning."

My father smiled.

"Louis and Felix are too fast for the lightning."

"And Grandpa?" I plucked nervously at the tight elastic under my warm chin.

"Grandpa is too close a friend of the Lord to suffer from such things."

I felt better after this. I reasoned that if the Lord was a friend of Grandpa, then Grandpa would no doubt see that nothing happened to Papa and me.

We changed cars presently and were soon crossing the bridge into Hull and the province of Quebec.

I looked down the dirty, roaring falls that ran the factories.

"No sulphur," I observed.

"Not on Sunday," my father said.

This pleased me a great deal. On the one hand, Grandpa and the Lord were good friends. On the other hand, the Devil did not work on Sunday. I was in a splendid strategic position to deal with Evil.

We descended from the trolley on the main street of Hull.

"We can walk from here," my father informed me. "At the theater, they say it is not far out on this street."

Soon we found ourselves in the midst of hundreds of jabbering French-Canadians, all speaking so quickly and with such laughter and mockery that I could not follow them. The patois, too, was beyond my young understanding. What is more, every other building on the main street of Hull was one of swinging doors from which came the strong smell of ale, making my head dizzy.

"What do they say, Papa? What do they all say so fast?"

My father laughed.

"They say that Hull will beat Ottawa like a hot knife enters the butter! The pitcher of Hull will fan every batter of Ottawa. The batters of Hull will strike the ball every time into the Lachine Rapids, which is many, many miles away. In the end, they say, everybody will become full as a barrel of ale except the people from Ottawa. They will return home crying and drink lime juice and go to bed ashamed."

I clapped my hands happily at this foolishness which sounded like a fairy tale – the white balls flying by the hundreds, like birds, up the Lachine Rapids.

A man reeled by from a bar as I was pondering the flight of the baseballs. He began to shout loudly: "Hooray for Ottawa! Hull is full of pea soups. Down with Hull and the pea soups!"

The crowd picked him up and tossed him on high from group to group, laughing all the while, until, at last, he admitted Hull was the fairest city in all Canada and pea soup the most delicious dish.

I laughed joyfully. "It will be a good game, no?" I asked happily.

"*Mais oui*," my father chuckled. "With the Hull and the Ottawa it is like with David and Goliath."

It had become quite cloudy and dark when we made our way through the grounds to the ancient wooden stand. In the gray distance the lightning continued to dance.

My father patted my head gently. "Heat lightning," he said uneasily.

"I know," I said. In spite of the fact that I knew Grandpa was a friend of the Lord and that the Devil had taken the day off, I nevertheless felt a little nervous. After all, I *had* skipped Sunday school for the first time. And we *were* so far from home!

My attention turned from the storm for a time as the Hull team began field practice amid great roars of approval that drowned out the rumbling thunder. The crowd began to chatter happily and proudly like many birds screaming in our back yard.

"All the world," I said, "speaks French here."

"*Mais oui*," my father agreed. "In Hull all the world is French. In Ottawa it is mostly English. That is why there is so much desire to fight with each other."

"And we," I asked curiously, "what do we speak, you and me?"

"Ha!" my father exclaimed, patting my knee, "that is a problem for the French Academy!"

Since I did not know what the French Academy was, I placed my small chin in my hands and watched the Ottawa team as it came out on the field.

Groans and jeers now filled the air. Bottles, legs of chairs, programs, and bad fruit were thrown on the field like confetti at a wedding.

Two umpires and several groundkeepers cleared away the debris. One of the umpires announced through a megaphone:

"*Mesdames et messieurs*, we are the hosts. They are the guests. They are from Ottawa, but that is not a sin. We cannot always help where we live. It is requested not to throw bottles while the game proceeds as this is not the fair way we shall win. I am born in Hull and also my wife and four children and I am proud of it. But I do my honest duty to make a fair game. God save the King! *Play ball!*"

The game went on evenly and colorlessly for five or six innings. The darkness of the afternoon turned a sulphur yellow and the air became filled with tension.

The rumble of thunder grew louder.

In the seventh inning the Ottawa pitcher singled and stood proudly on first base. The bat boy ran out with a sweater. This is, of course, the custom in the big leagues, so that the pitcher will not expose his arm to possible chills.

To Hull, however, it was a fine opportunity to start something.

"Sissy!" someone shouted.

"Si...sssssssssyyyyyyyyyy!" The crowd made one long sound as if the wind were moaning. Most of them probably did not know what the word meant, but it had a pleasant sound of derision.

The pitcher, O'Ryan, stepped far off first base in an attempt to taunt the Hull pitcher to throw, which he did.

O'Ryan darted back safely, stood arrogantly on the white bag, and carefully thumbed his nose.

The crowd jeered.

O'Ryan removed his cap and bowed from the waist in sarcasm.

Once more bottles, legs of chairs, programs, and overripe fruit came down on the field like hailstones.

Again the umpire picked up his megaphone and spoke:

"*Mes amis,*" he begged, "they are the guests...we are the hosts."

A tomato glanced off the side of his head; a cushion landed in his face. He shrugged his shoulders, brushed himself off, and ordered wearily: "Play ball!"

The next pitch was hit and it was accompanied by a violent peal of thunder which almost coincided with the crack of the bat.

O'Ryan started for second base and was forced to slide when the Hull second baseman attempted to force him out. The second baseman, with his spiked shoes, jumped on O'Ryan's hand.

The Ottawa pitcher was safe by many seconds, but the crowd shouted insistently: "Out! *Out!*" with such anger that the umpire hesitated but a moment and then waved the astonished and stunned Irishman off the field.

Two thousand French-Canadian noses were instantly thumbed.

O'Ryan stood up dazedly and regarded his maimed hand. He brushed the dust from his uniform and strode quietly to the Ottawa bench. There he picked up several bats, swung them together for a while, and selected his favorite.

He pulled down his cap firmly, walked calmly to second base, and, with only a slight motion, brought the bat down solidly on the head of the Hull second baseman.

This was the signal for a riot. Spectators, umpires, players, peanut vendors – all swarmed across the field in one great pitched battle. In the increasing darkness from the oncoming storm they were as a great swarm of hornets, moving around the diamond.

My father and I, alone, remained seated. We did not speak for a long time.

I began to wish I had gone to Sunday school to have the Red Sea divided, or that I had stayed home with *Maman* and Happy Hooligan. I was coming to believe that Grandpa was not so good a friend of the Lord as he pretended and that if the Devil did not work on Sunday he had assistants who *did*.

My father spoke, at length, with the hollow sound of sin: "Poor *Maman* would be angry if she knew, eh?"

"*Mais oui*," I mumbled, fearfully watching the lightning tear the sky.

Papa tried to be calm and to talk lightly.

"Ah, well," he remarked, "it is not always so simple, eh, to tell the heat lightning from the chain lightning?"

"*Mais non*," I muttered.

"Also, in this case, one can see the storm did not follow the river."

"It followed *us*," I replied nervously, almost to myself.

"Well, we are safe here, no? We are, thank the good Lord, not in the melee. Here we are safe. When the fight is ended we will go home. Meanwhile we are safe. *N'est-ce pas*?"

"And the storm, Papa?" I queried, pulling my sailor hat down over my head as far as it would go.

"The storm," my father announced, as thunder sounded so loudly it shook the flimsy stand, "is mostly wind. It will blow itself away in no time."

I sighed. I will pray, I told myself. I will ask to be forgiven for going to the city of the Devil on Sunday. I will pray the good Lord forgive me, in the name of my grandfather, for forgetting to attend the opening of the Red Sea, also.

I had but managed to mutter: "Dear Lord..." when the sky, like the Red Sea, divided in two and there was hurled at us a great fiery ball, as if someone in heaven had knocked it our way.

Before I could get my breath, the dry, wooden stand was in flames.

"Dear Lord," I began again, breathlessly and hastily, "we are not so bad as all this...we only..." But my father had me by the hand and was dragging me swiftly on to the field.

By this time, the rioters had stopped banging heads and were wistfully watching their beloved stand disappear with the flames.

By the time we arrived home the storm was over and even the rain had stopped. We had been at a restaurant to eat and rest and had recovered a little when we faced *Maman*.

In fact I did not feel bad at all. I reasoned that the Lord had not been after my destruction but after the rioters who profaned his Sabbath with fighting. For if the Lord had been after me, He could, in His infinite wisdom, have made the ball come even closer.

"I told you we would have a thunderstorm," my mother said angrily.

"To me," my father replied meekly, "it looked like heat lightning."

"You know I don't like the Boy out in thunderstorms!"

"Ah, well, he is safe now. Eh, *bibi*? And Louis and Felix and Papa?"

"They are here."

"Good."

"A baseball game on Sunday is just not right," my mother went on, refusing to be deflected from the subject. "Look how pale and sick-looking you both are!"

My father coughed uneasily.

"Let us call down Grandpa and have some wine and shortbreads. Let us forget the rest. No?" He kissed my mother. She turned to me, relented a bit, and smiled.

"Was it a good game?"

I clapped my hands together excitedly. "It was wonderful *Maman*! Everything happened!"

"Wine and shortbreads," Papa interrupted nervously.

"What do you mean, everything happened?" my mother asked, glancing sidelong at Papa.

"I must go up and see my poor father," said Papa. "It is now many months..."

"One moment," my mother cautioned. She turned and motioned for me to sit on her knee. My father sank wearily into a chair.

"Well," my mother urged.

It was too wonderful and exciting to keep!

"*Maman*," I exclaimed, "God hit a home run!"

My father groaned. My mother's eyes widened.

"He what?" she asked, pale.

The words came rushing out: "He hit a home run and He struck the grandstand with His powerful lightning and then the grandstand burned to very small pieces, all of a sudden, and this was because everybody was fighting on the Sabbath and..."

My mother let me down slowly from her knee.

"Is this true?" she said to my father.

My father shrugged and waved his delicate hands helplessly.

"A small fire. The stand in Hull is made of..."

My mother jumped to her feet.

"*Where?*"

My father lowered his eyes.

"Hull," he admitted slowly. "After all, they do not permit baseball on Sunday in Ottawa. If they permit you to breathe it is something. All the world knows that."

"Hull!" my mother whispered, as if it were a dreadful name. "Hull! No wonder! To take the Boy from Sunday school to Hull! And on Sunday! Hull!"

"*Maman*," I said, tears coming into my eyes, "I will speak to the Lord..."

"Go," said my mother, and she sounded like a voice from the heavens, "and wash your dirty face."

"*Ma chère*," my father said, trying to be pleasant, "does one always know where a storm will travel?"

"You," my mother ordered, "go wipe your shoes. Look at the mud you have tracked in!"

As Papa and I went our respective ways, heads bowed, we heard her whisper once more: "Hull!"

I knew then that she would never go to a baseball game with Papa. The memory of the Lord's home run which so barely missed us would remain, I thought, forever in her mind. She would know one of the places the Lord was going to strike and she would know now that His aim was very good, if not perfect.

SCOTT YOUNG

* * * * * * *

Scott Young was born in 1918 and grew up in Manitoba and Saskatchewan. He now lives in Ireland. For several decades he was one of Canada's leading journalists, working for the Winnipeg Free Press, *Canadian Press, the* Toronto Globe and Mail, *and the* Toronto Telegram. *Since the forties he has also been active as a writer and has published more than two dozen books, primarily in the fields of sports biography and juvenile sports fiction. "Seven Parts of a Ball Team" first appeared in* Collier's *(May 6, 1950) and was subsequently collected in Young's* We Won't Be Needing You, Al *(1968). Most of the stories in the latter collection, including a number about baseball, are now available in two paperback volumes:* Seven Parts of a Ball Team and Other Sports Stories *(1990) and* The Pinch Hitter and Other Sports Stories *(1991).*

Young offered the following account of the origin of "Seven Parts of a Ball Team" in his preface to We Won't Be Needing You, Al: *"The story...came almost intact, word for word, from a talk I had one afternoon with my Uncle Milt in Cypress River, Manitoba, while my Uncle Billy threw in his laughter. Six of the seven brothers in the story were my uncles and the other, Percy, my father."*

* * * * * * *

Seven Parts of a Ball Team

The Old Man was scowling around the barn, as he always did on the day of a baseball tournament, when he would be left with the women and grandchildren to do the chores. In the barn, his seven sons worked with unusual intentness. Three milked. One cleaned the boxstall of the tempestuous Clydesdale stallion. The other three cleaned the horse barn, sending out a loaded stoneboat with a quick slap to a bay mare's flank, harnessing another team for the light work of the day, turning the other horses out to pasture. All this was done in a race against the sun, showing low and red in the delicate blue behind maples to the east.

The sons left the barns separately. Little Hughie, the center fielder, strode quickly across the farmyard to start the gasoline motor in the pump house and fill the water trough. The milkers came next – Matt, the shortstop; and young Nels, the catcher; and Milt, the pitcher – each swaying from the weight of two full pails. The three from the horse barn were close behind: Perce, the second basemen, dapper and compact; Herb, the third baseman, a great hitter, at thirty the oldest of them all; and Billy, who couldn't play baseball for sour apples but said there was no other right fielder in the world going to play on the team that his brothers played on, no one except him.

The Old Man stood small and strong before the big barn. He and his sons farmed the four full sections of Manitoba wheatland that had grown from his original homestead. He watched his sons walking toward the big brick house and pulled at his full white mustache and talked to himself. "About time they got whopped," he said. "Gettin' too big for their britches. About time they got whopped and this'll be the time."

A little boy child ran after a squawking rooster along the side of the barn. He was in bare feet, his shirt buttoned tightly against the morning chill. The Old Man thoughtfully snapped the boy's behind with the heavy end of a broken leather trace, and the boy went howling after Billy, his father, who didn't so much as turn his head. On no account would the seven sons become involved this morning in an argument with the Old Man, who had never played baseball himself and who had never said he approved his sons' playing it.

The boys lined up the milk pails by the cream separator, where Billy's wife was winding the handle to get the machine going and Herb's wife stood by to pour in the first pail.

"Good morning, wife," said Billy, touching the shoulder of the small fair-haired woman he'd brought ten miles from her own father's farm to be his bride.

"Was that the boy crying?" she asked him, searching his face.

"Stubbed his toe on his grandpa," Billy said with a grin.

"Morning, Beatrice," said Herb to his wife, who had been a schoolteacher at Indian Leg until Herb took her away from all that.

"Morning, Herbert," Beatrice said, smiling at him fondly.

The sons passed through the milk shed to the huge kitchen where Mary, the mother, black-haired and black-eyed and handsome, stood over the range. As her sons pumped water into the kitchen basin, washed, then filed to the long oilcloth-covered table, she poured oatmeal into the plates in front of them. They poured cool milk from jugs on it and sweetened it with coarse brown sugar, and they buttered white bread warm from the oven to eat along with it.

The Old Man came in and, without a word, began to eat. The mother placed a platter of fried eggs alongside another of fresh pork chops and brought a bowl of boiled eggs for Hughie and Matt, who liked them better boiled. Some of them had one egg, some had five. At the end, they ate a lot more fresh bread and butter and drank coffee and spooned preserved saskatoon berries into fruit dishes to finish off their breakfast.

There was still little talk as they changed, upstairs, into their baseball uniforms, bought from the catalogue with prize money they'd won in the first of three victories in small tournaments last year. Before that, they had played in their overalls. Carrying their baseball shoes, they went down the back stairs through the kitchen. Their mother kissed each as he passed, and each kissed and hugged her in return.

"Be careful, now, Herbert," she instructed her eldest. "You'll break my ribs, Perce. Milton look after young Nelson. I don't know that he should be going out so often. This playing ball...."

"Heck, Maw," Nels said. "They want me."

"Sixteen's old enough," Billy said. "Anyhow, who'd catch?"

Matt, who had been a company sergeant major in the war just past, the one which ended in 1918, said, "We'll be all right, Mother. Don't you worry."

The talk so far had not included the Old Man, who sat in an old black leather rocker and rattled his copy of the *Free Press Prairie Farmer*, glaring into its pages as if he had suddenly sighted an old enemy.

But finally Hughie brought the Old Man into it. He put the dipper back into the water pail and stepped up to his father and grabbed one hand away from the paper and said in his high drawl, "Farewell, fair friend, we go but to return," and while the seven boys and their mother laughed at Hughie's audacity, the Old Man let Hughie pump his hand and even let out a dry chuckle or two himself. But the Old Man was professionally ornery and he didn't like being forced into looking otherwise, although Hughie could always make him laugh. He didn't go out with the mother and the daughters-in-law when they stood on the back porch and waved good-by as the old touring car, top down, circled the barnyard and wheeled down the leafy lane, bound for the Carberry Fair and the richest baseball tournament the seven sons had ever entered.

On a corner a mile away, they picked up Jack Whitman, who was forty-two years old. He wore his baseball cap backward and morosely clutched a catcher's mitt in his right hand. He was the first baseman. He climbed up behind the back seat and sat on the rolled-down top cover. Two miles farther on, they waited for Oxford Anderson to run down the lane from his father's farm. Oxford, known as Fangs because of the remarkable shape of his teeth, was excited as he climbed up beside Whitman, full of the rumor that for this baseball tournament today Carberry's ball club was so interested in the one thousand dollars first money that it had brought in six players from the semipro Minot Colts.

"Say," said Billy, "if they've brought in anybody they've probably brought in that catcher, Agnew. They say he's something to watch."

"Somebody was sayin' on that team we beat in the final at Cypress River that they'd played against him and he's an awful mean-mouthed man," said Hughie.

"Used to be in organized ball, I heard," Anderson said. "Got tossed out for something he done in a training camp, something like that."

They talked about Agnew as they rolled north toward the Assiniboine river. Nels, squeezed between Matt and Milt in the front seat, said, "He better not try anything on us."

Matt laughed, looking down fondly at the youngest brother, squeezing the boy's solid shoulder with one hand. "Don't get too tough, there, Junior," he said.

There was a short silence until Hughie called from the back. "Nice of the Old Man to give us his usual blessing when we took off this morning."

His brothers laughed. Whitman made one of his infrequent contributions to the conversation. "Guess old John doesn't like it too much, you boys going off to play ball."

"Heck," Milt called back. "I don't think he really minds so much. One time Herb hit a homer, over there at Cypress, the Old Man jumped right up in the air."

"I saw him," Hughie said. "But he came down awful fast and tried to look as if he hadn't done a thing."

"It's just Father's way," Herb said.

Perce said, "It just galls him to think anything's happened in this family that he hasn't done all by himself."

Billy laughed. "Well, not many men in the country have sired seven parts of a baseball team, at that."

Milt, driving, was the only one silent, piloting the cumbersome car over the first sandy ruts of the river hills. He was always the only one of the seven who worried, and that's why his father let him drive.

He reflected now that each one of them had something the Old Man particularly let him do – he lets me drive, he laughs at

Hughie when it seems nothing can make him laugh, he respects Matt because Matt was the only one of the four of us in the Army who got past being a private, he gives Herb most responsibility because Herb is the oldest, he lets Perce do the bookwork on the farm because nobody can do it as well, and he always takes Billy along any time he makes a deal because Billy can deal the pulpit right out from under a preacher when he sets his mind to it. And he seems to have chosen Nels as the one who'll keep on at school, all the way through, something he never gave the rest of us a chance to do.

Milt rolled the high-wheeled car down the steep sand track to the ferry. The sleepy ferryman came out of his hut and shoved off, and the current took the cable-held ferry across.

The ferryman didn't even ask where they were going. He knew.

"Hope you win, boys," he said, as they hit the other shore. "But with that Carberry team packed I don't suppose you will."

They had to pile out to push the car up the bank of the river, and then they were bowling along on the dry dirt road, and at nine in the morning they drove through the shady streets of Carberry to the fair grounds and Milt laid the twenty-five-dollar entry fee on the line.

"Say," Milt said to the fat, friendly man who was taking the money, "is it true that Carberry hired six men from Minot for this tournament?

"No," the man said.

"Well, good," said Hughie.

"They only hired five," the fat man said, laughing. "Battery and three infielders." Some others around the entry tent laughed, too, looking at this baseball team.

"Don't need to worry about Carberry unless you're drawed agin us first," a man said. "You probably won't last more'n one draw."

"Hey," said another, pointing at Nels, "ain't there no age limit in this tournament?"

Milt spoke back to him, mildly. "That boy's my brother," he said. "I don't like to hear any kidding of him, since he's the best catcher you'll see in this tournament."

All the loiterers laughed at that. "With Agnew, from Minot, catching, you say that kid is the best in the tournament?"

"I say it," Milt said. He turned back to the fat man. "When do we play our first game?"

The fat man looked down at their entry. "Probably on the first draw, at eleven," he said. "Say, where is this town, Indian Leg, anyway? I never heard of it."

"It isn't a town," Milt said. "It's a school district. T'other side of the river."

"No town there at all."

"None at all."

"Where do you haul your wheat?"

"Holland."

"How far away's that?"

"Eight miles."

"We'll call you Holland, then, so people'll know where you're from."

"You'll call us Indian Leg, mister," Milt said. "Because that's where we're from."

The two men gazed at each other steadily and finally the fat man shrugged and tossed the entry slip, unaltered, on top of the others beside him.

Ordinarily, if the men around the entry tent hadn't kidded Nels, he'd have been left there to bring back the news when the draw was made, because he was youngest, but now Billy offered to stay behind.

The eight others walked around the fair grounds. For a time they watched the half-dozen trotters and pacers limbering up around the half-mile track surrounding the two baseball diamonds. Behind the grandstand they saw a small boy win fifty-five cents on a wheel game. They passed a rakish old man and a studious young man standing together near an empty booth, already taking a few advance bets on the races, which would be run intermittently all day. They saw no one they knew among the throngs of red-faced men with purple arm bands and white shirts and blue serge trousers and boots that shone dully under a film of dust. They walked through the animal barns, threaded through the women looking at the exhibits of pies and cakes and sewing, dodged children who ran like hares in the forest of legs.

They were not conscious of the looks they got – five men and a boy in cheap white mail-order uniforms and one, Whitman, the first baseman, in a gray-blue uniform his wife had made, and Fangs Anderson in a red flannel uniform that was too small for him. All had the name Indian Leg sewed across their backs.

Matt and Milt led them now to warm up. Matt, three or four inches shorter than Milt, took short steps to Milt's long ones, pounding his hand every once in a while into his glove. People already were lining up around the main diamond in front of the grandstand. The Indian Leg team picked the other diamond, fairly confident that this would be where they would play. They pitched an old ball around and warmed up slowly.

Milt didn't warm up. If they got to the final round, he'd be pitching three or four games today, depending on how many teams were entered. He didn't feel like warming up, although he knew he could pitch thirty or more innings any day of his life and still be up the next morning before dawn to work on the farm.

Then they saw Agnew, the catcher Carberry had brought in from Minot. He came onto another part of the field to warm up a tall southpaw pitcher. Agnew was a heavily built man, close to six feet tall. He noticed their stares and yelled out to them in a strong, carrying voice. "Who's doing the milking with all you hicks away?"

The gathering crowd, mostly farmers themselves, chuckled half-heartedly.

Nels turned to Perce beside him and said, "I wonder how he knew we were from a farm."

"Just guessed," Perce said.

Hughie yelled back, "You'll be wishing later we'd stayed and done the milking ourselves."

The crowd laughed.

Agnew tossed the ball back to his pitcher and walked out into the outfield and looked down at Hughie. "It won't pay you to get fresh with me, shorty," he said. "I eat farm boys for breakfast."

Matt came up beside him. "On our farm," he said, "we feed slops to the hogs."

Milt moved closer, thinking Agnew was going to swing on Matt. But Nels, young and as quick as Matt to anger, got there first and said in his half-man, half-boy voice, "Get the heck away from here!"

Agnew turned. "Well, baby-doll!" he said.

"Better go, Agnew," Milt said mildly. "This isn't getting you or us anywhere."

Agnew stared around at them all silently. Finally, turning away, he sneered, "I hope there's some chance we'll be playing you plowboys today."

"When you do, you'll wish you hadn't," Hughie called, tossing a ball to Herb.

As Agnew walked away, Perce said, "Now, what the heck do you suppose is eating that guy?"

Matt stared after Agnew. "I don't think anything's eating him, particularly," he said. "He's just one of those rough, tough bully types. Lots of them in the world."

About five past ten Billy crossed the diamond with his rolling stride, and the others clustered about. "Eight teams in," he said. "Our first game's at eleven. If we win, we play again at three, and if we win that, we're in the final at five-thirty. All games seven innings until the final."

"Where's Carberry in the draw?" Matt asked.

"At the other end from us. Their first game's at one o'clock. If we last and they last, we'll play them in the final."

"Can't meet before?"

"No."

When the word went around that the ball games were just about to start, the crowd converged on the two diamonds, with the smaller part of the crowd gathering to watch Indian Leg face its first adversary, a team from Wawanesa.

Wawanesa won the toss and took the field. Hughie was first up and beat out a bunt for an infield hit. Perce singled to center and Hughie got to third in a reckless headfirst slide, and stood on the bag and dusted himself off and smiled broadly, and when Matt was choosing from the three bats owned by the team, the most concentrated cheering in the fairgrounds was coming from the other brothers. They danced and shouted and grimaced on the side lines, raking the Wawanesa pitcher with abuse, and Matt hit the first pitch over the center fielder's head and under the rail onto the race track. Hughie trotted slowly from third. Perce sprinted around to catch up, with Matt close behind him. As they crossed home plate in lock step, each one raised his baseball cap to the crowd and showed a shaven head, for all the unmarried brothers shaved their heads on the first of each July. The crowd laughed, and from that time on, Indian Leg had the full support of every farmer and his family watching, except, naturally, the few who had come from Wawanesa.

Milt wasn't a thoughtful pitcher. He didn't consider whether he had it today or didn't have it, but with this three-run lead, he saved himself from the first pitch. He had good control, and mostly he pitched for the inside corners, with an occasional curve thrown in.

He struck out the first two. The third man up hit a hot one to Matt at shortstop.

As the ball hopped once in the infield, Whitman, on first base, his right hand in its catcher's mitt out in a target while he toed the bag, gave passionate advice. Before Matt touched the ball Whitman roared, "E-e-e-asy, Matt!" As Matt made the catch: "Lots of time, Matt!" As Matt's arm came back for the throw that was like a whip, straight and true: "Ma-a-tt, e-e-asy, boy!"

And as the ball hit his mitt, he yelled, "Damn it!" pulling his mitt back to lessen the impact. After each tournament Whitman's hand was swollen from catching Matt's throws from shortstop. After the first time he played with Matt, he had traded his first baseman's mitt for this catcher's mitt, and now, despite all the ribbing, he would wear no other.

He trotted to the bench, swearing, while the others kidded him and Matt told him as he always did that he'd throw it easier next time.

They won that game, 9-4, and walked in a group to the car, jesting casually with the friendly crowds. They got out the cream can full of lemonade and the box of thick sandwiches and hard-boiled eggs.

"We'd best carry some of this grub with us to the next game," Milt said. "We won't have much time between it and the final, if we keep winning."

"We'll keep winning," said Hughie. "What'll we do with that thousand dollars?"

"With my share," Whitman said, "I'm going to buy a hundred dollars' worth of sponges to catch Matt with."

"We could buy a farm and scare hell out of the Old Man," Perce said.

"We could buy something nice for Mother with some of it," said Herb.

Nels stood up. "That Carberry game's started," he said. "I'd like to see that Agnew catch." Milt packed away the sandwiches and put the lid on the lemonade.

They couldn't get very close to the Carberry game, the crowd was so thick along the side lines. Some families sat in groups, eating their lunches while they watched, and keeping up a constant stream of insults at the enemy and encouragement to their friends. The support for the Carberry team was little more than perfunctory, because many of the spectators resented the way the team had been packed. Agnew talked constantly to the batters, and some of them snapped back at him, but what was being said couldn't be heard in the crowd.

Agnew batted cleanup for the Carberry team. He hit each time up. Going into second one time, he slammed into the second baseman. The crowd yelled at him, and the single umpire, who stood behind the plate when the bases were empty and behind the pitcher when there was anyone on, warned him. Agnew spat in the dust.

The big southpaw import had a blazing fast ball. He allowed only three hits, and Carberry won the game, 10-0.

Milt felt good in the three-o'clock game, again on the second-best diamond, but this time the crowd was almost as big there as it was for the second Carberry game, played simultaneously in front of the grandstand. The trotters and pacers whirled in the background, the goggled drivers yelling and cursing on the turns, and Whitman swore his way through the same agonized routine each time Matt threw to first base. Hughie went deep into Billy's position in right field to cut off a liner, and miraculously held the runner to one base. Milt saved his arm, never bearing down except when men were in scoring position. Once he glanced over and saw that the Carberry southpaw was throwing as hard as ever.

Milt hoped the man would wear himself out, because he was afraid of what those imports might do to his pitching, and he wanted his brothers to be able to hit a few and get him some runs because he felt sure he'd need them.

Indian Leg won that game, 6-3, while Carberry won, 12-4, and each was finished in time for a half-hour rest before the final. The brothers and Whitman and Anderson moved from one diamond to the other, carrying their food. The races were over, and, while everyone gathered for this final game, the Indian Leg team ate beef sandwiches and drank lemonade and finished off with dozens of the thick sugar-coated cookies that Mary, their mother, could make better than anyone else in the world.

Agnew and Milt and the umpire met at home plate for the toss. Milt won. He walked back toward the Indian Leg bench and picked up his glove and waved the others into the infield, and they all ran except Whitman, who walked to first base with the air of a man afraid of his fate. The grandstand was filled with nearly a thousand people, but the greater part of the crowd was behind the chicken-wire backstop and stretched along the first and third base lines and around the outfield at a respectful distance from home plate.

Even before the first pitch, the Carberry team started to ride young Nels, the catcher. Someone yelled to the umpire that he'd have to call the game at seven because it would be the kid's bedtime. Agnew rode him hardest, with references to safety pins and diapers and related subjects, and Milt could see the boy's discomfort.

He found the inside corner for two called strikes on the first batter and then blazed in his fast ball, for this was the last game and his arm was fine. The batter swung and missed, and Milt could feel the whole team lift behind him; and when the batter was walking in disgust from the plate, Nels was on his feet, yelling after him.

But the next two men singled cleanly to center, Hughie holding them each to a single base, and Agnew came up with only one out and two men on. He was left-handed, and Milt fed him a curve that broke to the inside, and Agnew lashed at it and hit it on the handle and it bounced slowly at Perce, the second baseman, who tossed it to Matt, covering at second, and above the yells of the crowd came Whitman's pleading roar, "Easy, Matt! Matt, easy boy!" and his groaning curse as he caught the ball for the double play.

But as Whitman made the catch, Agnew hit him hard and rolled him over and over, and Milt had to grab Matt as he came across the diamond on the dead run to attack Agnew, who outweighed him by forty pounds. The umpire lectured Agnew, and three tournament officials restrained Whitman's groggy efforts to get at him. Agnew turned away from the umpire in the middle of the lecture and got into his catching gear.

The southpaw struck out Hughie, Agnew riding him from his crouch. Perce turned and told Agnew he'd kill him with his bat if he said another word, but Perce struck out, too. Matt said that went for him, too, but Agnew kept on riding him and Matt got whiter and whiter and struck out, too.

In the fourth, Agnew caught Milt's fast ball for a home run to put Carberry one up. Matt stood on the base line between second and third when he came around, daring the big man to push him out of the way, and Agnew did, and Matt threw out a hip that missed.

They were scoreless again through the fifth and sixth; and in the seventh, when Agnew came to bat with two out, Milt heard Nels' voice from behind the plate.

"You can't be lucky twice, you bum."

Agnew seemed not to hear. Called strike one.

"I got six brothers who can play better ball than you," Nels said.

No reply. Ball one.

On the next pitch, Agnew, seemingly swinging back to get ready for the pitch, hit Nels on the mask with his bat and laid him out in the dust.

When the brothers came in on the run, some of the Carberry team got up, ready to fight, but the brothers gathered around Nels on the ground, Milt holding his head up while Perce ran for water. Matt bent over him, speaking in a low voice, asking him how he was, telling him he'd be all right.

It was five minutes before Nels got to his feet again, pale and dogged, mumbling over and over an unaccustomed swearword. He shook off the hands of his brothers and tried to help Herb straighten the mask. Then he stood alone behind the plate until Milt pitched again. He didn't get too close to Agnew's bat this time, but he stayed close enough to catch well. Agnew hit cleanly to center field.

Hughie fielded it on the first bounce and threw it to second. From the pitcher's mound, Milt saw Matt's set, angry glance at Agnew who was rounding first, and then he saw in amazement that Matt was backing away from second toward the mound. Hughie's fine throw was allowed to bounce once, and then Matt seemed to have it and then dropped it. Agnew had paused for an instant, but when the ball rolled through Matt's legs, Agnew sprinted for second. And then Milt, backing up Matt, was bending for it, and Matt yelled, "No! No, Milt! I want him on second!" And although Perce was covering second and a toss would have had a fair chance to catch Agnew as he slid in, spikes high, Matt picked it up, with no chance to catch him, and trotted over to where Agnew stood, grinning, on the bag.

"Yah, ya dumb farmer!" Agnew yelled, and his yell ended in a protesting bellow as Matt tagged him hard with the ball.

Matt turned and tossed the ball back to Milt. Milt rubbed the ball slowly, tense and angry, suddenly knowing, waiting. When Matt yelled for a throw, Milt threw and, at second, Matt swung and slugged Agnew again with the ball, although the catcher hadn't moved off the bag.

The beginning of a chuckling murmur rose from the crowd.

Agnew swore and shoved Matt violently, but Matt tossed the ball back to Milt. Then Perce streaked in behind Agnew to take another throw from Milt and hammer the big catcher in the ribs. Agnew stood on the bag and roared at the umpire, at the shouting crowd, at the brothers; and Perce tossed the ball back again to Milt.

"Again, Milt!" Matt yelled.

When he slugged Agnew this time, the catcher tried to protect himself with his arms and then swung a glancing blow at Matt.

Matt said in a calm voice, "The next time you swing at me I'll tag you in the teeth!"

The rest of the Carberry team crowded around the umpire, who kept yelling, "Play ball!" and betweentimes shook his head and repeated there was nothing in the rules said you couldn't tag a man, whether he was standing on the base or not. If the Indian Leg team wanted to waste time that way, the umpire couldn't stop them.

Milt looked at the sun. It was near the horizon, and they were one run down. But the bump on young Nels' head still wasn't quite paid for, and he threw again to Matt, when Matt called, and this time Agnew winced with pain.

The umpire stood behind Milt, and said, "I've been umpiring that guy all summer. I was wondering when somebody would finally give it to him. But you better stop now."

Milt walked from the mound toward second base. Perce and Matt came in toward him and the three of them stood a few feet away and looked at Agnew. The big man stared silently at them, an apprehensive question in his face. He looked more vulnerable than defiant.

Milt took the ball from Matt's hand and walked back to the mound and looked down past home plate to young Nels, who crouched, waiting. Milt read his signal and glanced at the runner and threw up his leg and pitched.

The batter slapped the pitch toward second. Perce charged it and ignored the easier play to first and threw to third. When Agnew saw Herb waiting with the ball he made a halfhearted, limping attempt to slide under the hard, swinging tag. But he failed, and the side was retired.

When the team came off the field, the umpire looked at the rosy glow where the sun had been and shouted to the crowd that this would be the last half-inning.

Agnew had enough left to curse Herb when he came to bat, saying they'd lost the game by stalling.

Herb hit the ball over the race-track fence to tie the score.

Whitman walked. Anderson struck out and so did Nels, and Billy got his first hit in three baseball tournaments, a ball that disappeared into the dusk of the outfield, scattering the crowd. He chased Whitman all the way around to win the game....

It was midnight when the boys got home. The Old Man came down in his flannelette nightgown. He stalked in his bare feet to the kitchen table, where his sons were eating warmed-up beef and gravy and potatoes and bread, and he looked at the pile of bank notes in the middle of the table.

"How much in that pile?" he asked.

"About seven hundred and seventy, something like that," Hughie said.

"What you going to do with it?"

"Look at it for a while," Hughie said.

The Old Man rubbed his face and looked at all the money. "Didn't get whopped yet," he muttered. Then he noticed the bump on Nels' forehead. "What happened to you?"

"Got hit by a bat."

"Hit the fella back?"

"Matt did. And Perce and Herb."

The Old Man looked around at his grinning sons, and half grinned in return. "I suppose I'll have hell's own time gettin' you all up in the morning," the Old Man said. "Get to bed."

MORLEY CALLAGHAN

* * * * * * *

Morley Callaghan (1903-1990) was born and raised in Toronto, where, during his teens and early twenties, he distinguished himself as a star pitcher in the city's sandlot leagues (for more on his baseball career see chapter two of his 1963 memoir, That Summer in Paris*). Educated at the University of Toronto and Osgoode Hall Law School, Callaghan began publishing stories in Paris in the late 1920s. His first novel,* Strange Fugitive*, appeared in 1928 and was soon followed by the collection* Native Argosy *(1929). After a visit to Paris in 1929, he continued to publish fiction, although with several intervals of relative silence. Among his many renowned novels are* Such Is My Beloved *(1934),* They Shall Inherit the Earth *(1935),* More Joy in Heaven *(1937),* The Loved and the Lost *(1951, Governor General's Award),* A Fine and Private Place *(1975),* A Time for Judas *(1983), and* A Wild Old Man on the Road *(1988). An important collection of his short fiction,* The Lost and Found Stories of Morley Callaghan*, appeared in 1985. "A Cap for Steve" was originally published in* Esquire *(July 1952) and was later reprinted in* Morley Callaghan's Stories *(1959). The story has appeared all over the world, in many languages.*

* * * * * * *

A Cap for Steve

Dave Diamond, a poor man, a carpenter's assistant, was a small, wiry, quick-tempered individual who had learned how to make every dollar count in his home. His wife, Anna, had been sick a lot, and his twelve-year-old-son, Steve, had to be kept in school. Steve, a big-eyed, shy kid, ought to have known the value of money as well as Dave did. It had been ground into him.

But the boy was crazy about baseball, and after school, when he could have been working as a delivery boy or selling papers, he played ball with the kids. His failure to appreciate that the family needed a few extra dollars disgusted Dave. Around the house he wouldn't let Steve talk about baseball, and he scowled when he saw him hurrying off with his glove after dinner.

When the Phillies came to town to play an exhibition game with the home team and Steve pleaded to be taken to the ball park, Dave, of course, was outraged. Steve knew they couldn't afford it. But he had got his mother on his side. Finally Dave made a bargain with them. He said that if Steve came home after school and worked hard helping to make some kitchen shelves he would take him that night to the ball park.

Steve worked hard, but Dave was still resentful. They had to coax him to put on his good suit. When they started out Steve held aloof, feeling guilty, and they walked down the street like strangers; then Dave glanced at Steve's face and, half-ashamed, took his arm more cheerfully.

As the game went on, Dave had to listen to Steve's recitation of the batting average of every Philly that stepped up to the plate; the time the boy must have wasted learning these averages began to appal him. He showed it so plainly that Steve felt guilty again and was silent.

After the game Dave let Steve drag him onto the field to keep him company while he tried to get some autographs from the Philly players, who were being hemmed in by gangs of kids blocking the way to the clubhouse. But Steve, who was shy, let the other kids block him off from the players. Steve would push his way in, get blocked out, and come back to stand mournfully beside Dave. And Dave grew impatient. He was wasting valuable time. He wanted to get home; Steve knew it and was worried.

Then the big, blond Philly outfielder, Eddie Condon, who had been held up by a gang of kids tugging at his arm and thrusting their score cards at him, broke loose and made a run for the clubhouse. He was jostled, and his blue cap with the red peak, tilted far back on his head, fell off. It fell at Steve's feet, and Steve stooped quickly and grabbed it. "Okay, son," the outfielder called, turning back. But Steve, holding the hat in both hands, only stared at him.

"Give him his cap, Steve," Dave said, smiling apologetically at the big outfielder who towered over him. But Steve drew the hat closer to his chest. In an awed trance he looked up at big Eddie Condon. It was an embarrassing moment. All the other kids were watching. Some shouted. "Give him his cap."

"My cap, son," Eddie Condon said, his hand out.

"Hey, Steve," Dave said, and he gave him a shake. But he had to jerk the cap out of Steve's hands.

"Here you are," he said.

The outfielder, noticing Steve's white, worshipping face and pleading eyes, grinned and then shrugged. "Aw, let him keep it," he said.

"No, Mister Condon, you don't need to do that," Steve protested.

"It's happened before. Forget it," Eddie Condon said, and he trotted away to the clubhouse.

Dave handed the cap to Steve; envious kids circled around them and Steve said, "He said I could keep it, Dad. You heard him, didn't you?"

"Yeah, I heard him," Dave admitted. The wonder in Steve's face made him smile. He took the boy by the arm and they hurried off the field.

On the way home Dave couldn't get him to talk about the game; he couldn't get him to take his eyes off the cap. Steve could hardly believe in his own happiness. "See," he said suddenly, and he showed Dave that Eddie Condon's name was printed on the sweatband. Then he went on dreaming. Finally he put the cap on his head and turned to Dave with a slow, proud smile. The cap was way too big for him; it fell down over his ears. "Never mind," Dave said. "You can get your mother to take a tuck in the back."

When they got home Dave was tired and his wife didn't understand the cap's importance, and they couldn't get Steve to go to bed. He swaggered around wearing the cap and looking in the mirror every ten minutes. He took the cap to bed with him.

Dave and his wife had a cup of coffee in the kitchen, and Dave told her again how they had got the cap. They agreed that their boy must have an attractive quality that showed in his face, and that Eddie Condon must have been drawn to him – why else would he have singled Steve out from all the kids?

But Dave got tired of the fuss Steve made over that cap and of the way he wore it from the time he got up in the morning until the time he went to bed. Some kid was always coming in, wanting to try on the cap. It was childish, Dave said, for Steve to go around assuming that the cap made him important in the neighbourhood, and to keep telling them how he had become a leader in the park a few blocks away where he played ball in the evenings. And Dave wouldn't stand for Steve's keeping the cap on while he was eating. He was always scolding his wife for accepting Steve's explanation that he'd forgotten he had it on. Just the same, it was remarkable what a little thing like a ball cap could do for a kid, Dave admitted to his wife as he smiled to himself.

One night Steve was late coming home from the park. Dave didn't realize how late it was until he put down his newspaper and watched his wife at the window. Her restlessness got on his nerves. "See what comes from encouraging the boy to hang around with those park loafers," he said. "I don't encourage him," she protested. "You do," he insisted irritably, for he was really worried now. A gang hung around the park until midnight. It was a bad park. It was true that on one side there was a good district with fine, expensive apartment houses, but the kids from that neighbourhood left the park to the kids from the poorer homes. When his wife went out and walked down to the corner it was his turn to wait and worry and watch at the open window. Each waiting moment tortured him. At last he heard his wife's voice and Steve's voice, and he relaxed and sighed; then he remembered his duty and rushed angrily to meet them.

"I'll fix you, Steve, once and for all," he said. "I'll show you you can't start coming into the house at midnight."

"Hold your horses, Dave," his wife said. "Can't you see the state he's in?" Steve looked utterly exhausted and beaten.

"What's the matter?" Dave asked quickly.

"I lost my cap," Steve whispered; he walked past his father and threw himself on the couch in the living-room and lay with his face hidden.

"Now, don't scold him, Dave," his wife said.

"Scold him. Who's scolding him?" Dave asked, indignantly. "It's his cap, not mine. If it's not worth his while to hang on to it, why should I scold him?" But he was implying resentfully that he alone recognized the cap's value.

"So you are scolding him," his wife said. "It's his cap. Not yours. What happened, Steve?"

Steve told them he had been playing ball and he found that when he ran the bases the cap fell off; it was still too big despite the tuck his mother had taken in the band. So the next time he came to bat he tucked the cap in his hip pocket. Someone had lifted it, he was sure.

"And he didn't even know whether it was still in his pocket," Dave said sarcastically.

"I wasn't careless, Dad," Steve said. For the last three hours he had been wandering around to the homes of the kids who had been in the park at the time; he wanted to go on, but he was too tired. Dave knew the boy was apologizing to him, but he didn't know why it made him angry.

"If he didn't hang on to it, it's not worth worrying about now," he said, and he sounded offended.

After that night they knew that Steve didn't go to the park to play ball; he went to look for the cap. It irritated Dave to see him sit around listlessly, or walk in circles, trying to force his memory to find a particular incident which would suddenly recall to him the moment when the cap had been taken. It was no attitude for a growing, healthy boy to take, Dave complained. He told Steve firmly once and for all he didn't want to hear any more about the cap.

One night, two weeks later, Dave was walking home with Steve from the shoemaker's. It was a hot night. When they passed an ice cream parlour Steve slowed down. "I guess I couldn't have a soda, could I?" Steve said. "Nothing doing," Dave said firmly. "Come on now," he added as Steve hung back, looking in the window.

"Dad, look!" Steve cried suddenly, pointing at the window. "My cap! There's my cap! He's coming out!"

A well-dressed boy was leaving the ice cream parlour; he had on a blue ball cap with a red peak, just like Steve's cap. "Hey, you!" Steve cried, and he rushed at the boy, his small face fierce and his eyes wild. Before the boy could back away Steve had snatched the cap from his head. "That's my cap!" he shouted.

"What's this?" the bigger boy said. "Hey, give me my cap or I'll give you a poke on the nose."

Dave was surprised that his own shy boy did not back away. He watched him clutch the cap in his left hand, half crying with excitement as he put his head down and drew back his right fist: he was willing to fight. And Dave was proud of him.

"Wait now," Dave said. "Take it easy, son," he said to the other boy, who refused to back away.

"My boy says it's his cap," Dave said.

"Well, he's crazy. It's my cap."

"I was with him when he got this cap. When the Phillies played here. It's a Philly cap."

"Eddie Condon gave it to me," Steve said. "And you stole it from me, you jerk."

"Don't call me a jerk, you little squirt. I never saw you before in my life."

"Look," Steve said, pointing to the printing on the cap's sweatband. "It's Eddie Condon's cap. See? See, Dad?"

"Yeah. You're right, Son. Ever see this boy before, Steve?"

"No," Steve said reluctantly.

The other boy realized he might lose the cap. "I bought it from a guy," he said. "I paid him. My father knows I paid him." He said he got the cap at the ball park. He groped for some magically impressive words and suddenly found them. "You'll have to speak to my father," he said.

"Sure, I'll speak to your father," Dave said. "What's your name? Where do you live?"

"My name's Hudson. I live about ten minutes away on the other side of the park." The boy appraised Dave, who wasn't any bigger than he was and who wore a faded windbreaker and no tie. "My father is a lawyer," he said boldly. "He wouldn't let me keep the cap if he didn't think I should."

"Is that a fact?" Dave asked belligerently. "Well, we'll see. Come on. Let's go." And he got between the two boys and they walked along the street. They didn't talk to each other. Dave knew the Hudson boy was waiting to get to the protection of his home, and Steve knew it, too, and he looked up apprehensively at Dave. And Dave, reaching for his hand, squeezed it encouragingly and strode along, cocky and belligerent, knowing that Steve relied on him.

The Hudson boy lived in that row of fine apartment houses on the other side of the park. At the entrance to one of these houses Dave tried not to hang back and show he was impressed, because he could feel Steve hanging back. When they got into the small elevator Dave didn't know why he took off his hat. In the carpeted hall on the fourth floor the Hudson boy said, "Just a minute," and entered his own apartment. Dave and Steve were left alone in the corridor, knowing that the other boy was preparing his father for the encounter. Steve looked anxiously at his father, and Dave said, "Don't worry, Son," and he added resolutely, "No one's putting anything over on us."

A tall, balding man in a brown velvet smoking-jacket suddenly opened the door. Dave had never seen a man wearing one of these jackets, although he had seen them in department-store windows. "Good evening," he said, making a deprecatory gesture at the cap Steve still clutched tightly in his left hand. "My boy didn't get your name. My name is Hudson."

"Mine's Diamond."

"Come on in," Mr. Hudson said, putting out his hand and laughing good-naturedly. He led Dave and Steve into his living-room. "What's this about that cap?" he asked. "The way kids can get excited about a cap. Well, it's understandable, isn't it?"

"So it is," Dave said, moving closer to Steve, who was awed by the broadloom rug and the fine furniture. He wanted to show Steve he was at ease himself, and he wished Mr. Hudson wouldn't be so polite. That meant Dave had to be polite and affable, too, and it was hard to manage when he was standing in the middle of the floor with his old windbreaker.

"Sit down, Mr. Diamond," Mr. Hudson said. Dave took Steve's arm and sat him down beside him on the chesterfield. The Hudson boy watched his father. And Dave looked at Steve and saw that he wouldn't face Mr. Hudson or the other boy; he kept looking up at Dave, putting all his faith in him.

"Well, Mr. Diamond, from what I gathered from my boy, you're able to prove this cap belonged to your boy."

"That's a fact," Dave said.

"Mr. Diamond, you'll have to believe my boy bought that cap from some kid in good faith."

"I don't doubt it," Dave said. "But no kid can sell something that doesn't belong to him. You know that's a fact, Mr. Hudson."

"Yes, that's a fact," Mr. Hudson agreed. "But that cap means a lot to my boy, Mr. Diamond."

"It means a lot to my boy, too, Mr. Hudson."

"Sure it does. But supposing we called in a policeman. You know what he'd say? He'd ask you if you were willing to pay my boy what he paid for that cap. That's usually the way it works out," Mr. Hudson said, friendly and smiling, as he eyed Dave shrewdly.

"But that's not right. It's not justice," Dave protested. "Not when it's my boy's cap."

"I know it isn't right. But that's what they do."

"All right. What did you say your boy paid for the cap?" Dave said reluctantly.

"Two dollars."

"Two dollars!" Dave repeated. Mr. Hudson's smile was still kindly, but his eyes were shrewd, and Dave knew the lawyer was counting on his not having the two dollars; Mr. Hudson thought he had Dave sized up; he had looked at him and decided he was broke. Dave's pride was hurt, and he turned to Steve. What he saw in Steve's face was more powerful than the hurt to his pride; it was the memory of how difficult it had been to get an extra nickel, the talk he heard about the cost of food, the worry in his mother's face as she tried to make ends meet, and the bewildered embarrassment that he was here in a rich man's home, forcing his father to confess that he couldn't afford to spend two dollars. Then Dave grew angry and reckless. "I'll give you the two dollars," he said.

Steve looked at the Hudson boy and grinned brightly. The Hudson boy watched his father.

"I suppose that's fair enough," Mr. Hudson said. "A cap like this can be worth a lot to a kid. You know how it is. Your boy might want to sell – I mean be satisfied. Would he take five dollars for it?"

"Five dollars?" Dave repeated, "Is it worth five dollars, Steve?" he asked uncertainly.

Steve shook his head and looked frightened.

"No, thanks, Mr. Hudson," Dave said firmly.

"I'll tell you what I'll do," Mr. Hudson said. "I'll give you ten dollars. The cap has a sentimental value for my boy, a Philly cap, a big-leaguer's cap. It's only worth about a buck and a half really," he added. But Dave shook his head again. Mr. Hudson frowned. He looked at his own boy with indulgent concern, but now he was embarrassed. "I'll tell you what I'll do," he said. "This cap – well, it's worth as much as a day at the circus to my boy. Your boy should be recompensed. I want to be fair. Here's twenty dollars," and he held out two ten-dollar bills to Dave.

That much money for a cap, Dave thought, and his eyes brightened. But he knew what the cap had meant to Steve; to deprive him of it now that it was within his reach would be unbearable. All the things he needed in his life gathered around him; his wife was there, saying he couldn't afford to reject the offer, he had no right to do it; and he turned to Steve to see if Steve thought it wonderful that the cap could bring them twenty dollars.

"What do you say, Steve?" he asked uneasily.

"I don't know," Steve said. He was in a trance. When Dave smiled, Steve smiled too, and Dave believed that Steve was as impressed as he was, only more bewildered, and maybe even more aware that they could not possibly turn away that much money for a ball cap.

"Well, here you are," Mr. Hudson said, and he put the two bills in Steve's hand. "It's a lot of money. But I guess you had a right to expect as much."

With a dazed, fixed smile Steve handed the money slowly to his father, and his face was white.

Laughing jovially, Mr. Hudson led them to the door. His own boy followed a few paces behind.

In the elevator Dave took the bills out of his pocket. "See Stevie," he whispered eagerly. "That windbreaker you wanted! And ten dollars for your bank! Won't Mother be surprised?"

"Yeah," Steve whispered, the little smile still on his face. But Dave had to turn away quickly so their eyes wouldn't meet, for he saw that it was a scared smile.

Outside, Dave said, "Here, you carry the money home, Steve. You show it to your mother."

"No, you keep it," Steve said, and then there was nothing to say. They walked in silence.

"It's a lot of money," Dave said finally. When Steve didn't answer him, he added angrily, "I turned to you, Steve. I asked you, didn't I?"

"That man knew how much his boy wanted that cap," Steve said.

"Sure. But he recognized how much it was worth to us."

"No, you let him take it away from us," Steve blurted.

"That's unfair," Dave said. "Don't you dare say that to me."

"I don't want to be like you," Steve muttered, and he darted across the road and walked along the other side of the street.

"It's unfair," Dave said angrily, only now he didn't mean that Steve was unfair, he meant that what happened in the prosperous Hudson home was unfair, and he didn't know quite why. He had been trapped, not just by Mr. Hudson, but by his own life. Across the road Steve was hurrying along with his head down, wanting to be alone. They walked most of the way home on opposite sides of the street, until Dave could stand it no longer. "Steve," he called, crossing the street. "It was very unfair. I mean, for you to say..." but Steve started to run. Dave walked as fast as he could and Steve was getting beyond him, and he felt enraged and suddenly he yelled, "Steve!" and he started to chase his son. He wanted to get hold of Steve and pound him, and he didn't know why. He gained on him, he gasped for breath and he almost got him by the shoulder. Turning, Steve saw his father's face in the street light and was terrified; he circled away, got to the house, and rushed in, yelling, "Mother!"

"Son, Son!" she cried, rushing from the kitchen. As soon as she threw her arms around Steve, shielding him, Dave's anger left him and he felt stupid. He walked past them into the kitchen.

"What happened?" she asked anxiously. "Have you both gone crazy? What did you do, Steve?"

"Nothing," he said sullenly.

"What did your father do?"

"We found the boy with my ball cap, and he let the boy's father take it from us."

"No, no," Dave protested. "Nobody pushed us around. The man didn't put anything over us." He felt tired and his face was burning. He told what had happened; then he slowly took the two ten-dollar bills out of his wallet and tossed them on the table and looked up guiltily at his wife.

It hurt him that she didn't pick up the money, and that she didn't rebuke him. "It is a lot of money, Son," she said slowly. "Your father was only trying to do what he knew was right, and it'll work out, and you'll understand." She was soothing Steve, but Dave knew she felt that she needed to be gentle with him, too, and he was ashamed.

When she went with Steve to his bedroom, Dave sat by himself. His son had contempt for him, he thought. His son, for the first time, had seen how easy it was for another man to handle him, and he had judged him and had wanted to walk alone on the other side of the street. He looked at the money and he hated the sight of it.

His wife returned to the kitchen, made a cup of tea, talked soothingly, and said it was incredible that he had forced the Hudson man to pay him twenty dollars for the cap, but all Dave could think of was Steve was scared of me.

Finally, he got up and went into Steve's room. The room was in darkness, but he could see the outline of Steve's body on the bed, and he sat down beside him and whispered, "Look, Son, it was a mistake. I know why. People like us – in circumstances where money can scare us. No, no," he said, feeling ashamed and shaking his head apologetically; he was taking the wrong way of showing the boy they were together; he was covering up his own failure. For the failure had been his, and it had come out of being so separated from his son that he had been blind to what was beyond the price in a boy's life. He longed now to show Steve he could be with him from day to day. His hand went out hesitantly to Steve's shoulder. "Steve, look," he said eagerly. "The trouble was I didn't realize how much I enjoyed it that night at the ball park. If I had watched you playing for your own team – the kids around here say you could be a great pitcher. We could take that money and buy a new pitcher's glove for you, and a catcher's mitt. Steve, Steve, are you listening? I could catch you, work with you in the lane. Maybe I could be your coach...watch you become a great pitcher." In the half-darkness he could see the boy's pale face turn to him.

Steve, who had never heard his father talk like this, was shy and wondering. All he knew was that his father, for the first time, wanted to be with him in his hopes and adventures. He said, "I guess you do know how important that cap was." His hand went out to his father's arm. "With that man the cap was – well it was just something he could buy, eh Dad?" Dave gripped his son's hand hard. The wonderful generosity of childhood – the price a boy was willing to pay to be able to count on his father's admiration and approval – made him feel humble, then strangely exalted.

RAYMOND SOUSTER

* * * * * * *

One of Canada's most distinguished poets, Raymond Souster still lives in his native city of Toronto. During the 1930s, he pitched for the West Toronto Nationals and other Toronto teams (for more on his baseball career see "Getting on with It" in Contemporary Authors Autobiographical Series; Volume 14, *issued in 1991). The recipient of a Governor General's Award in 1964, Souster has published nearly forty books of poetry, including seven volumes of his* Collected Poems *(1980-1992). He has also written two novels and has edited a number of anthologies and collections. Baseball has been a constant theme throughout his career, as evidenced by the titles of several of his works:* Change-up *(1974),* Double-Header *(1975),* Extra Innings *(1977), and* Going the Distance *(1983). "The Opener" first appeared in his* A Dream That Is Dying *(1954).*

* * * * * * *

The Opener

From where I was sitting
it looked like an easy double-play.

But at that precise moment
a sloppy-looking freighter
(slipping out through the Western Gap
with a clothesline of washing
half the length of her deck)
glided past the stadium,

and the runner going into second
took one look at that ship
and yelled, "Hey, look, they got
my old lady's black pants
flying up at the masthead."

And when all the infield
turned around to get a gape,
he made second, stole third,
then scored standing up
the winning run in what otherwise
was one of the cleanest-played openers
in a Toronto ballpark.

MORDECAI RICHLER

* * * * * * *

Montreal writer Mordecai Richler is one of Canada's leading literary figures. The recipient of two Governor General's Awards (1968, 1969) and numerous other honours, he is the author of nine novels, including The Apprenticeship of Duddy Kravitz *(1959),* St. Urbain's Horseman *(1971), and* Joshua Then and Now *(1980). His other works include a short-story collection, two books for children, several volumes of essays, a number of anthologies, and the book-length essay* Oh Canada! Oh Quebec! *(1992). A longtime fan of baseball, he has written several notable essays on the game. "Playing Ball on Hampstead Heath," which is one of his most widely anthologized stories, originally appeared in* Gentlemen's Quarterly *(August 1966) and was later incorporated into* St. Urbain's Horseman.

* * * * * * *

Playing Ball on Hampstead Heath

Summer.
Drifting through Soho in the early evening, Jake stopped at the Nosh Bar for a sustaining salt-beef sandwich. He had only managed one squirting mouthful and a glance at the unit trust quotations in the *Standard* (S&P Capital was steady, but Pan Australian had dipped again) when he was distracted by a bulging-bellied American in a Dacron suit. The American's wife, unsuccessfully shoehorned into a mini-skirt, clutching a *London A to Z* to her bosom. The American opened a fat credit-card-filled wallet, briefly exposing an international medical passport which listed his blood type; he extracted a pound note and slapped it into the waiter's hand. "I suppose," he said, winking, "I get twenty-four shillings change for this?"

The waiter shot him a sour look.

"Tell your boss," the American continued, unperturbed, "that I'm a Galicianer, just like him."

"Oh, Morty," his wife said, bubbling.

And the juicy salt beef sandwich turned to leather in Jake's mouth. It's here again, he realized, heart sinking, the season.

Come summer, American and Canadian show business plenipotentiaries domiciled in London had more than the usual hardships to contend with. The usual hardships being the income tax tangle, scheming and incompetent natives, uppity *au pairs* or nannies, wives overspending at the bazaar (Harrod's, Fortnum's, Asprey's), choosing suitable prep schools for the kids, doing without real pastrami and pickled tomatoes, fighting decorators and smog, and of course keeping warm. But come summer, tourist liners and jets began to disgorge demanding hordes of relatives and friends of friends, long (and best) forgotten schoolmates and army buddies, on London, thereby transmogrifying the telephone, charmingly inefficient all winter, into an instrument of terror. For there was not a stranger who phoned and did not exude warmth and expect help in procuring theater tickets and a night on the town ("What we're really dying for is a pub crawl. The swinging pubs.

Waddiya say, old chap?") or an invitation to dinner at home. ("Well, Yankel, did you tell the Queen your Uncle Labish was coming? Did she bake a cake?")

The tourist season's dialogue, the observations, the complaints, was a recurring hazard to be endured. You agreed, oh how many times you agreed, the taxis were cute, the bobbies polite, and the pace slower than New York or, in Jake's case, Montreal. "People still know how to enjoy life here. I can see that." Yes. On the other hand, you've got to admit...the bowler hats are a scream, hotel service is lousy, there's nowhere you can get a suit pressed in a hurry, the British have snobby British accents and hate all Americans. Jealousy. "Look at it this way, it isn't home." Yes, a thousand times yes. All the same, everybody was glad to have made the trip, it was expensive but broadening, the world was getting smaller all the time, a global village, only next time they wouldn't try to squeeze so many countries into twenty-one days. "Mind you, the American Express was very, very nice everywhere. No complaints in that department."

Summer was charged with menace, with schnorrers and greenhorns from the New Country. So how glorious, how utterly delightful, it was for the hard-core show biz expatriates (those who weren't in Juan-les-Pins or Dubrovnik) to come together on a Sunday morning for a sweet and soothing game of softball, just as the Raj of another dynasty had used to meet on the cricket pitch in Malabar.

Sunday morning softball on Hampstead Heath in summer was unquestionably the fun thing to do. It was a ritual.

Manny Gordon tooled in all the way from Richmond, stowing a fielder's mitt and a thermos of martinis in the boot, clapping a sporty tweed cap over his bald head and strapping himself and his starlet of the night before into his Aston-Martin at nine A.M. C. Bernard Farber started out from Ham Common, picking up Al Levine, Bob Cohen, Jimmy Grief and Myer Gross outside Mary Quant's on the King's Road. Moey Hanover had once startled the staff at the Connaught by tripping down the stairs on a Sunday morning, wearing a peak cap and T-shirt and blue jeans, carrying his personal Babe Ruth bat in one hand and a softball in the other. Another Sunday Ziggy Alter had flown in from Rome, just for the sake of a restorative nine innings.

Frankie Demaine drove in from Marlow-on-Thames in his Maserati. Lou Caplan, Morty Calman, and Cy Levi usually brought their wives and children. Monty Talman, ever mindful of his latest twenty-one-year-old girlfriend, always cycled to the Heath from St. John's Wood. Wearing a maroon track suit, he usually lapped the field eight or nine times before anyone else turned up.

Jake generally strolled to the Heath, his tattered fielder's mitt and three enervating bagels filled with smoked salmon concealed under the *Observer* in his shopping bag. Some Sundays, like this one, possibly his last for a while, Nancy brought the kids along to watch.

The starting line-up on Sunday, June 28, 1963 was:

AL LEVINE'S TEAM	LOU CAPLAN'S BUNCH
Manny Gordon, *ss.*	Bob Cohen, *3b.*
C. Bernard Farber, *2b.*	Myer Gross, *ss.*
Jimmy Grief, *3b.*	Frankie Demaine, *lf.*
Al Levine, *cf.*	Morty Calman, *rf.*
Monty Talman, *1b.*	Cy Levi, *2b.*
Ziggy Alter, *lf.*	Moey Hanover, *c.*
Jack Monroe, *rf.*	Johnny Roper, *cf.*
Sean Fielding, *c.*	Jason Storm, *1b.*
Alfie Roberts, *p.*	Lou Caplan, *p.*

Jake, like five or six others who had arrived late and hung over (or who were unusually inept players), was a sub. A utility fielder, Jake sat on the bench with Lou Caplan's Bunch. It was a fine, all but cloudless morning, but looking around Jake felt there were too many wives, children, and kibitzers about. Even more ominous, the Filmmakers' First Wives Club or, as Ziggy Alter put it, the Alimony Gallery, was forming, seemingly relaxed but actually fulminating, on the grass behind home plate.

First Al Levine's Team and then Lou Caplan's Bunch, both sides made up mostly of men in their forties, trotted out, sunken bellies quaking, discs suddenly tender, hemorrhoids smarting, to take a turn at fielding and batting practice.

Nate Sugarman, once a classy shortstop, but since his coronary the regular umpire, bit into a digitalis pill, strode onto the field, and called, "Play ball!"

"Let's go, boychick."

"We need a hit," Monty Talman, the producer, hollered.

"*You* certainly do," Bob Cohen, who only yesterday had winced through a rough cut of Talman's latest fiasco, shouted back snidely from the opposite bench.

Manny, hunched over the plate cat-like, trying to look menacing, was knotted with more than his usual fill of anxiety. If he struck out, his own team would not be too upset because it was early in the game, but Lou Caplan, pitching for the first time since his Mexican divorce, would be grateful, and flattering Lou was a good idea because he was rumored to be ready to go with a three-picture deal for Twentieth; and Manny had not been asked to direct a big-budget film since *Chase*. *Ball one, inside.* If, Manny thought, I hit a single I will be obliged to pass the time of day with that stomach-turning queen Jason Storm, 1b., who was in London to make a TV pilot film for Ziggy Alter. *Strike one, called.* He had never hit a homer, so that was out, but if come a miracle he connected for a triple, what then? He would be stuck on third sack with Bob Cohen, strictly second featuresville, a born loser, and Manny didn't want to be seen with Bob, even for an inning, especially with so many producers and agents about, K-nack! *Goddammit, it's a hit! A double, for Chrissake!*

As the players on Al Levine's bench rose to a man, shouting encouragement –

"Go, man. Go."

"Shake the lead out, Manny. Run!"

– Manny, conscious only of Lou Caplan glaring at him ("It's not my fault, Lou."), scampered past first base and took myopic, round-shouldered aim on second, wondering should he say something shitty to Cy Levi, 2b., who he suspected was responsible for getting his name on the blacklist years ago.

Next man up to the plate, C. Bernie Farber, who had signed to write Lou Caplan's first picture for Twentieth, struck out gracefully, which brought up Jimmy Grief. Jimmy swung on the first pitch, lifting it high and foul, and Moey Hanover, c., called for it, feeling guilty because next Saturday Jimmy was flying to Rome and Moey had already arranged to have lunch with Jimmy's wife on Sunday. Moey made the catch, which brought up Al Levine, who homered, bringing in Manny Gordon ahead of him. Monty Talman grounded out to Gross, ss., retiring the side.

Al Levine's Team, first inning: two hits, no errors, two runs.

Leading off for Lou Caplan's Bunch, Bob Cohen smashed a burner to center for a single and Myer Gross fanned, bringing up Frankie Demaine and sending all the outfielders back, back, back. Frankie whacked the third pitch long and high, an easy fly had Al Levine been playing him deep left instead of inside right, where he was able to flirt hopefully with Manny Gordon's starlet, who was sprawled on the grass there in the shortest of possible Pucci prints. Al Levine was the only man on either team who always played wearing shorts – shorts revealing an elastic bandage which began at his left kneecap and ran almost as low as the ankle.

"Oh, you poor darling," the starlet said, making a face at Levine's knee.

Levine, sucking in his stomach, replied, "Spain," as if he were tossing the girl a rare coin.

"Don't tell me," she squealed. "The beach at Torremolinos. Ugh!"

"No, no," Levine protested. "The civil war, for Chrissake. Shrapnel. Defense of Madrid."

Demaine's fly fell for a homer, driving in a panting Bob Cohen.

Lou Caplan's Bunch, first inning: one hit, one error, two runs.

Neither side scored in the next two innings, which were noteworthy only because Moey Hanover's game began to slip badly. In the second Moey muffed an easy pop fly and actually let C. Bernie Farber, still weak on his legs after a cleansing, all but foodless, week at Forest Mere Hydro, steal a base on him. The problem was clearly Sean Fielding, the young RADA graduate whom Columbia had put under contract because, in profile, he looked like Peter O'Toole. The game had only just started when Moey Hanover's wife, Lilian, had ambled over to Al Levine's bench and stretched herself out on the grass, an offering, beside Fielding, and the two of them had been giggling together and nudging each other ever since, which was making Moey nervy. Moey, however, had not spent his young manhood at a yeshiva to no avail. Not only had he plundered the *Old Testament* for most of his winning *Rawhide* and *Bonanza* plots, but now that his Lilian was obviously in heat again, his hard-bought Jewish education, which his father had always assured him was priceless, served him splendidly once more. Moey remembered his *David ha'Melech: And it came to pass in the morning, that David wrote a letter to Joab, and sent it by the hand of Uriah. And he wrote in the letter, saying, Set Uriah in the forefront of the hottest battle, and retire ye from him, that he may be smitten, and die.*

Amen.

Lou Caplan yielded two successive hits in the third and Moey Hanover took off his catcher's mask, called for time, and strode to the mound, rubbing the ball in his hands.

"I'm all right," Lou said. "Don't worry. I'm going to settle down now."

"It's not that. Listen, when do you start shooting in Rome?"

"Three weeks tomorrow. You heard something bad?"

"No."

"You're a friend now, remember. No secrets."

"No. It's just that I've had second thoughts about Sean Fielding. I think he's very exciting. He's got lots of appeal. He'd be a natural to play Domingo."

As the two men began to whisper together, players on Al Levine's bench hollered, "Let's go, gang."

"Come on. Break it up, Moey."

Moey returned to the plate, satisfied that Fielding was as good as in Rome already. May he do his own stunts, he thought.

"Play ball," Nate Sugarman called.

Alfie Roberts, the director, ordinarily expected soft pitches from Lou, as he did the same for him, but today he wasn't so sure, because on Wednesday his agent had sent him one of Lou's properties to read and – Lou's first pitch made Alfie hit the dirt. That settles it, he thought, my agent already told him it doesn't grab me. Alfie struck out as quickly as he could. Better be put down for a rally-stopper than suffer a head fracture.

Which brought up Manny Gordon again, with one out and runners on first and third. Manny dribbled into a double play, retiring the side.

Multi-colored kites bounced in the skies over the Heath. Lovers strolled on the tow paths and locked together on the grass. Old people sat on benches, sucking in the sun. Nannies passed, wheeling toddlers with titles. The odd baffled Englishman stopped to watch the Americans at play.

"Are they air force chaps?"

"Filmmakers, actually. It's their version of rounders."

"Whatever is that enormous thing that woman is slicing?"

"Salami."

"On the Heath?"

"Afraid so. One Sunday they actually set up a bloody folding table, right over there, with cold cuts and herrings and mounds of black bread and a whole bloody side of smoked salmon. Scotch. *Ten and six a quarter, don't you know?*"

"On the Heath?"

"Champagne *in paper cups*. Mumm's. One of them had won some sort of award."

Going into the bottom of the fifth, Al Levine's Team led 6-3, and Tom Hunt came in to play second base for Lou Caplan's Bunch.

Hunt, a Negro actor, was in town shooting *Othello X* for Bob Cohen.

Moey Hanover lifted a lazy fly into left field, which Ziggy Alter trapped rolling over and over on the grass until – just before getting up – he was well placed to look up Natalie Calman's skirt. Something he saw there so unnerved him that he dropped the ball, turning pale and allowing Hanover to pull up safely at second.

Johnny Roper walked. Which brought up Jason Storm, to the delight of a pride of British fairies who stood with their dogs on the first base line, squealing and jumping. Jason poked a bouncer through the infield and floated to second, obliging the fairies and their dogs to move up a base.

With two out and the score tied 7-7 in the bottom half of the sixth, Alfie Roberts was unwillingly retired and a new pitcher came in for Al Levine's Team. It was Gordie Kaufman, a writer blacklisted for years, who now divided his time between Madrid and Rome, asking a hundred thousand dollars a spectacular. Gordie came in to pitch with the go-ahead run on third and Tom Hunt stepping up to the plate for the first time. Big black Tom Hunt, who had once played semi-pro ball in Florida, was a militant. If he homered, Hunt felt he would be put down for another buck nigger, good at games, but if he struck out, which would call for rather more acting skill than was required of him on the set of *Othello X*, what then? He would enable a bunch of fat, foxy, sexually worried Jews to feel big, goysy. Screw them, Hunt thought.

Gordie Kaufman had his problems too. His stunning villa on Mallorca was run by Spanish servants, his two boys were boarding at a reputable British public school, and Gordie himself was president, sole stockholder, and the only employee of a company that was a plaque in Liechtenstein. And yet – and yet – Gordie still subscribed to the *Nation*; he filled his Roman slaves with anti-apartheid dialogue and sagacious Talmudic sayings; and whenever the left-wing *pushke* was passed around he came through with a nice check. I must bear down on Hunt,

Gordie thought, because if he touches me for even a scratch single I'll come off a patronizing ofay. If he homers, God forbid, I'm a shitty liberal. And so with the count 3 and 2, and a walk, the typical social-democrat's compromise, seemingly the easiest way out for both men, Gordie gritted his teeth, his proud Trotskyite past getting the best of him, and threw a fast ball right at Hunt, bouncing it off his head. Hunt threw away his bat and started for the mound, fist clenched, but not so fast that players from both sides couldn't rush in to separate the two men, both of whom felt vindicated, proud, because they had triumphed over impersonal racial prejudice to hit each other as individuals on a fun Sunday on Hampstead Heath.

Come the crucial seventh, the Filmmaker's First Wives Club grew restive, no longer content to belittle their former husbands from afar, and moved in on the baselines and benches, undermining confidence with their heckling. When Myer Gross, for instance, came to bat with two men on base and his teammates shouted, "Go, man. Go," one familiar grating voice floated out over the others. "Hit, Myer. Make your son proud of you, *just this once*."

What a reproach the first wives were. How steadfast! How unchanging! Still Waiting For Lefty after all these years. Today maybe hair had grayed and chins doubled, necks had gone pruney, breasts drooped and stomachs dropped, but let no man say these crones had aged in spirit. Where once they had petitioned for the Scotsboro Boys, broken with their families over mixed marriages, sent their boy friends off to defend Madrid, split with old comrades over the Stalin-Hitler Pact, fought for Henry Wallace, demonstrated for the Rosenbergs, and never, never yielded to McCarthy...today they clapped hands at China Friendship Clubs, petitioned for others to keep hands off Cuba and Vietnam, and made their sons chopped liver sandwiches and sent them off to march to Aldermaston.

The wives, alimonied but abandoned, had known the early struggling years with their husbands, the self-doubts, the humiliations, the rejections, the cold-water flats, and the blacklist, but they had always remained loyal. They hadn't altered, their husbands had.

Each marriage had shattered in the eye of its own self-made hurricane, but essentially the men felt, as Ziggy Alter had once put it so succinctly at the poker table, "Right, wrong, don't be silly, it's really a question of who wants to grow old with Anna Pauker when there are so many juicy little things we can now afford."

So there they were, out on the grass chasing fly balls on a Sunday morning, short men, overpaid and unprincipled, all well within the coronary and lung cancer belt, allowing themselves to look ridiculous in the hope of pleasing their new young wives and girlfriends. There was Ziggy Alter, who had once written a play "with content" for the Group Theatre. Here was Al Levine, who used to throw marbles under horses' legs at demonstrations and now raced two horses of his own at Epsom. On the pitcher's mound stood Gordie Kaufman, who had once carried a banner that read *No Pasarn* through the streets of Manhattan and now employed a man especially to keep Spaniards off the beach at his villa on Mallorca. And sweating under a catcher's mask there was Moey Hanover, who had studied at a yeshiva, stood up to the committee, and was now on a sabbatical from Desilu.

Usually the husbands were able to avoid their used-up wives. They didn't see them in the gaming rooms at the White Elephant or in the Mirabelle or Les Ambassadeurs. But come Brecht to Shaftesbury Avenue and without looking up from the second row center they could feel them squatting in their cotton bloomers in the second balcony, burning holes in their necks.

And count on them to turn up on a Sunday morning in summer on Hampstead Heath just to ruin a game of fun baseball. Even homering, as Al Levine did, was no answer to the drones.

"It's nice for him, I suppose," a voice behind Levine on the bench observed, "that on the playing field, with an audience, if you know what I mean, he actually appears virile."

The game dragged on. In the eighth inning Jack Monroe had to retire to his Mercedes-Benz for his insulin injection and Jake Hersh, until now an embarrassed sub, finally trotted onto the field. Hersh, thirty-three, one-time relief pitcher for Room 41, Fletcher's Field High (2-7), moved into right field, mindful of his disc condition and hoping he would not be called on to make a tricksy catch. He assumed a loose-limbed stance on the grass, waving at his wife, grinning at his children, when without warning a sizzling line drive came right at him. Jake, startled, did the only sensible thing: he ducked. Outraged shouts and moans from the bench reminded Jake where he was, in a softball game, and he started after the ball.

"Fishfingers."

"Putz!"

Runners on first and third started for home as Jake, breathless, finally caught up with the ball. It had rolled to a stop under a bench where a nanny sat watching over an elegant perambulator.

"Excuse me," Jake said.

"Americans," the nurse said.

"I'm a Canadian," Jake protested automatically, fishing the ball out from under the bench.

Three runs scored. Jake caught a glimpse of Nancy, unable to contain her laughter. The children looked ashamed of him.

In the ninth inning with the score tied again, 11-11, Sol Peters, another sub, stepped cautiously to the plate for Lou Caplan's Bunch. The go-ahead run was on second and there was only one out. Gordie Kaufman, trying to prevent a bunt, threw right at him and Sol, forgetting he was wearing his contact lenses, held the bat in front of him to protect his glasses. The ball hit the bat and rebounded for a perfectly laid down bunt.

"Run, you shmock."

"Go, man."

Sol, terrified, ran, carrying the bat with him.

Monty Talman phoned home.

"Who won?" his wife asked.

"We did. 13-12. But that's not the point. We had lots of fun."

"How many you bringing back for lunch?"

"Eight."

"Eight?"

"I couldn't get out of inviting Johnny Roper. He knows Jack Monroe is coming."

"I see."

"A little warning. Don't, for Chrissake, ask Cy how Marsha is. They're separating. And I'm afraid Manny Gordon is coming with a girl. I want you to be nice to her."

"Anything else?"

"If Gershon phones from Rome while the guys are there please remember I'm taking the call upstairs. And please don't start collecting glasses and emptying ashtrays at four o'clock. It's embarrassing. Bloody Jake Hersh is coming and it's just the sort of incident he'd pick on and joke about for months."

"I never coll..."

"All right, all right. Oh, shit, something else. Tom Hunt is coming."

"The actor?"

"Yeah. Now listen, he's very touchy, so will you please put away Sheila's doll."

"Sheila's doll?"

"If she comes in carrying that bloody golliwog I'll die. Hide it. Burn it. Hunt gets script approval these days, you know."

"All right, dear."

"See you soon."

GEORGE BOWERING

* * * * * * *

British Columbia writer George Bowering was born at Okanagan Falls and now lives in Vancouver, where he teaches English at Simon Fraser University. The author of more than forty books, he has won the Governor General's Award for both poetry (1969) and fiction (1980). His extensive baseball writings encompass three decades worth of poetry, fiction, essays, journalism, radio pieces, songs, and more. "Baseball, a poem in the magic number 9" was written during the 1965 baseball season and was first published by Coach House Press in 1967, in a pennant-shaped chapbook with a green felt cover. ("People complained," notes Bowering, "that it was hard to shelve. The Montreal poet and collector Artie Gold solved the problem by putting it on his wall.") The poem was later included in a collection of Bowering's baseball poems, Poem and Other Baseballs *(1976).*

Bowering, who recently edited an anthology of baseball fiction, Taking the Field *(1990), still plays ball: "I play first base now for a team called the Paperbacks, in the TwiLight League, a league of softball teams made up of word handlers, book sellers, reporters, writers, etc. We will have nothing to do with the US abomination slo-pitch, but we do not allow windmill pitching. In 1992 I had my worst hitting slump ever, but my best fielding average. My favourite ML teams since my childhood have been the Red Sox and the Dodgers. My favourite park is Briggs Stadium (Tiger Stadium) in Detroit. I know all there is to know about baseball. I hate the designated hitter and the fake cheese on nachos found everywhere now, even in Anaheim."*

* * * * * * *

Baseball, a poem in the magic number 9

for Jack Spicer

1.
The white sphere
turns, rolls
in dark space

the far side of one destroyed galaxy,
a curve ball
bending thru its long arc
past every planet of our dream.

A holy spectre of a curve ball,
dazzling white, brand new
trademark still fresh:
"This is a regulation Heavenly League Baseball"

O mystic orb of horseshoe stitching!
Hurled from what mound in what Elysian field,
        from what mound, what
        mystical mount,
                        where what life-bringing stream?

God is the Commissioner of Baseball
Apollo is the president of the Heavenly League.
The Nine Muses, his sisters
            the first all-girls baseball team.
Archangel Michael the head umpire.
Satan was thrown out of the game
            for arguing with the officials.

In the beginning was the word, & the word was
"Play Ball!"

                Now that white sphere
                cools,
                & the continents
                rise from the seas.

                There is life on Baseball.

The new season is beginning.
Zeus winds up to throw out
the first ball
like a thunderbolt.

Take me out

to the ball

game.

2.
July in Oliver, cactus drying
in the vacant lots.

in the ball park, the Kamloops Elks
here for a double header, Sunday

baseball day in Oliver, day of worship
for me.

At the park an hour early,

scribbler full of batting averages,

sometimes I got a steel basket
& sold hotdogs, peanuts, sometimes

I pickt up a broken bat, lugged it home
& taped it, not so much for batting

as for my collection. Louisville Slugger.
My father was official scorer,

high in the chicken wire box
on top of the grandstand, he was tough

on the hitters, as later I was,
pens & pencils in front of me. Oliver

nearly always won, the cars parkt
around the outfield fence honking

for a hometown rally, me quieter,
figuring out the percentage, a third the age

of the players, calculating chances
of the hit & run play.

Later,
I was official scorer, they knew

I had the thick rule book memorized.
Sweat all over my face, eyes squinting

thru the chicken wire, preparing
batting averages & story for

the Oliver Chronicle.

3.
Manuel Louie, old Manuel Louie
is chief of the Indians around Oliver.
1965 now, he is 94, but looks 55.
He's still got big black mustache, shoots pool
with his belly hanging over the rail.

Age 80, he was still playing Indian baseball games,
the chief, bowlegged running bases with turkey feather
in his hat.

The Wenatchee Chiefs, class A,
were spring training in Oliver then,
letting Manuel Louie work out at shortstop, weird Sitting Bull
Honus Wagner,

in exchange for his steam bath, that's how he lookt 40
at age 80, a creek beside his house, mud hut full of steam.

That year the Wenatchee Chiefs finisht fifth.

4.
The New York Yankees
are dying this year, the famous pinstripe uniform
covered with dust of other ballparks.

Mickey Mantle is a tired man with sore legs,
working at a job. Roger Maris forgotten
on the sports pages, a momentary spark
turned to wet ash.

> A beanball on the side of the skull
> killed a ballplayer
> when I was a kid,
> it was violence
> hidden behind the grace of base-
> ball.

Now Warren Spahn is trying
to win a few more games
with his arm 44 years old,
in the National League
where no pitcher's mound
is Olympus.

& Willie Mays is after all
sinew & flesh
as a baseball
is string & leather,

& when baseballs get old
kids throw them around,
torn horsehide flapping
from that dark sphere.

I was in love with Ted Williams.
His long legs, that grace,
his narrow baseball bat
level-swung, his knowledge of art,
it has to be perfect, as near
as possible, dont swing
at a pitch seven centimeters
wide of the plate.

I root for the Boston Red Sox.
Who are in ninth place.
Who havent won since 1946.

It has to be perfect.

5.
In the nineteenth century
baseball came to the Pacific Northwest.

Mustache big muscled ballplayers of beer barrels
among bull lumberjacks & puffsteam train engines,
mighty trees of rainforest, pinstripe uniforms,
those little gloves of hurt hand, heavy bats of yore,
baseball in Seattles & Vancouvers of the past when Victoria
was queen of Canada, Manifest Destiny of the ballpark
cut into swathe of rainy fir trees.

Now still there – I go to see the Vancouver Mounties
of minor league green fence baseball playing
Hawaii of the Pacific, Arkansas Travelers of gray visitors garb,
I sit in warm sun bleachers behind first base
with Keep-a-movin Dan McLeod, bleach head poet of the Coast

gobbling crack shell peanuts — he's sitting beside me,
gadget bag full of binoculars & transistor radio, tape recorder,
cheering for the Mounties, nuts, they are Dominicans of the North,
dusky smiling on the lucky number souvenir program,
where I no longer write mystic scorekeeper numbers in the
        little squares,
sophisticate of baseball now, I've seen later famous players here.

        What are you doing, they ask,
        young esthete poet
        going to baseball games,
        where's your hip pocket
        Rimbaud?

I see the perfect double play, second baseman in the air legs tuckt
over feet of spikes in the dust, arm whipping baseball
on straight line to first baseman, plock of ball,
side's retired, the pitcher walks head down quiet from the mound.

6.
The herring-
bone stitching
takes one last
turn
till Louisville Slugger
        cracks
        & the spin
        changes, a cleat
                turns in the
                sod, digs earth,
                brown showing
                under green,
                bent knee takes
                pressure.

Lungs fill
with air,
pump-
action legs, foot
pounds on narrow
corner of the bag, rounding
                    the body leans
                    inward, eyes
                    flick up once
                    under cap, head
                    down, legs running,
                    buckle!

& the fire that breaks from thee then told a million
times
      since 1903.
      the first
      World Series, white sphere
      turns, the world again
      spun around once, the sun
      in October again sinking
      over the pavilion roof
      in left field.

This story is for you, Jack, who had eyes to see
a small signal
from the box
            more than 90 feet
            away.

7.
When I was 12 years old I had a baseball league
made of a pair of dice, old home-made scorebooks,
National Leagues, American Leagues, Most Valuable Players!

The St. Louis Browns played the Chicago Cubs in the World Series!
The Yankees finisht in seventh place, the batting championship
went at .394. It was chance, roll of dice, blood doesnt tell
in that kid's bedroom season –
I was afraid to try out
for the Oliver junior league team,
I would strike out
every time

till I was sixteen,
oldest you could be, & played
one game before my summer job,

& hit a bases loaded single
in the first inning. I was the
tallest kid on the team.

But I bought Sport magazine & Baseball Digest, & knew all
the numbers. Ty Cobb's lifetime batting average was .367, I
remember now,
Rogers Hornsby's lifetime batting average was .354. In 1921
Babe Ruth hit
59 home runs.

Ty Cobb was better than Babe Ruth.
Ted Williams was better than Joe DiMaggio.
I like the Boston Red Sox who are in 9th place.

I still play that game, I think.
I'm sitting at my desk in my bedroom right now.

8.
Nine.
Is a baseball number.
Nine innings.
Nine players.
Ted Williams was the best hitter of all time.
& the number on his back was nine.

Here is today's lineup:

lf	Terpsichore
2b	Polyhymnia
rf	Clio
1b	Erato
3b	Urania
cf	Euterpe
ss	Thalia
c	Melpomene
p	Calliope

A lineup like that is enough to inspire
the faithfulness of any fans of the good art
of baseball.

I have seen it happen
to the best poets
of this summer
& last.

9.
Long shadows
fall across the infield

in the ninth inning.
Sometimes ball players

look like they're dying
as they walk off the field

in the dusk.

I knew an old man in San Francisco
came to life
when the Dodgers were in town.
Now he is dead, too,
& Jack is dead,

& the solders play baseball
in Asia,
where there is no season,
no season's end.

"It's just a game,"
I used to be told,

"It isnt whether you win or lose,
but how you

play the game."
In baseball
that is how you say
the meek shall inherit
the earth.

September 30, 1965,

Willy Mays has 51 home runs,
gray hair
at his temples,
he says he has been
getting tired
for six years.

I know I feel my own body
wearing down,
my eyes watch
that white ball
coming to life.
Abner Doubleday
lived in the nineteeth century,
he is dead,
but next spring
the swing of a
35 ounce bat
is going to flash with sunlight,
& I will be a year
older.

My nose was broken twice
                    by baseballs.
My body depends on the game.
                    My eyes
see it now on television.
                    No chicken wire –
it is the aging process.

                    The season
can't help but measure.

                    I want to say only
that it is not a
          diversion of the intelligence,
a man breathes differently
                    after rounding the bag,
history is there such a thing,
                    does not
choose, it waits & watches,
                    the game
isnt over till the last man's
                    out.

September, 1965

W.D. VALGARDSON

* * * * * * *

William Dempsey Valgardson grew up in Winnipeg and is presently a professor of Creative Writing at the University of Victoria. A frequent contributor to literary magazines and anthologies, he is the author of eight books. His latest novel is The Girl with the Botticelli Face *(1992). "The Baseball Game" appeared in the anthology* Winnipeg Stories *(1974) edited by Joan Parr. Valgardson notes that the story was written and published before he met and taught his most famous student, W.P. Kinsella.*

"Baseball," Valgardson recounts, "was an integral part of my childhood. As a child I lived across the street from the 'big field' where baseball was played regularly during the summer. Baseball was taken seriously, with players from various small towns coming to play the local team and each other. As well, during the long summer evenings there were pickup teams. There was some softball but hardball was the game we all aspired to. There were local heroes. To be the best batter, the best pitcher, the best infielder, etc. was something that mattered because, before the appearance of television, local heroes did not compete against the professionals. We could all aspire to be the best in our district.

"Later, when I went to Iowa City to graduate school, there were the long summer evenings, the local teams playing softball, the magic of this slow ritual. It is the perfect cure for ulcers, for getting the world into balance, for contemplation, for admiration."

* * * * * * *

The Baseball Game

"My name's Jenkins," he said. "I came to see a baseball game tonight. There is a game, isn't there?"

He was an old man with a red nose and white hair that stood out like wings from the sides of his head. His face was soft and slack with skin that hung heavily around his jaw.

Agnes had seen him before but they had never spoken. He attended every game. Sometimes he came with two or three cronies but tonight he was alone. His white shirt was soiled and his pants, cast-offs from an old suit, were so much too small that he had to use a safety pin to keep up the zipper of his fly.

Agnes pretended not to have heard him. She kept her little finger extended as she took a sip from her tin of root beer. To her annoyance Allan said the game would start at eight o'clock. She wished her husband would be more discriminating about the people to whom he talked. He was kneading his thigh muscles with his thumbs.

Jenkins sidled closer. "Who's playing?"

"City against the medical school."

"That so!" Jenkins exclaimed as though having just been given information of great importance. He tucked his thumbs into his belt loops and added, "You playing tonight?"

Agnes scowled and nudged Allan in the back with her toe. She was sitting two steps above him.

Jenkins pretended he had not seen her. "You played ball long?" he asked, but he did not wait for an answer. "I used to play all the time. Played one game with a fever of a hundred and five. Saw two balls everytime. But that was all right. I had lots of help. I had four hands." He laughed loudly at his own joke.

Flattered by the attention Allan answered, "Twenty years. I played at college and got scouted twice. I nearly got a contract for semi-pro."

"Well, I'll be!" His exclamation was full of admiration. He leaned back on his heels to get a better perspective on Allan. He shook his head in disbelief. "They threw away some good talent there, all right. But that's the way of the world. You can't expect a fair shake. You've got to have pull to get ahead."

Jenkins shifted his body slyly and insinuated himself onto the edge of the seat. He moved like a self-conscious guest who is not sure of his welcome but is determined to stay. From where she sat, Agnes could see that his neck hair needed trimming and his collar was dirty.

Unable to stop the conversation, Agnes pretended to be uninterested. She let her eyes roam across the ball park, over the slope that rose gently to the highway half-a-mile away, to the passing cars, the Esso station and the blank sky. The three of them were alone. Allan had pulled a muscle in his right arm two weeks before and had missed one game and four practices.

Obstinately, he had refused to go to a doctor and had been treating it at home with liniment and hot cloths. Although his arm had not improved, he was so determined not to sit out any more games that as soon as he had arrived home from work, he had changed into his sweat suit and begun doing warm ups in the middle of the living room.

His playing ball always caused tension between them. On the way to the park, they had nearly had a fight. Allan had starting praising Dubie, the captain of the team. Agnes had no use for Dubie and, irritated that she was going to spend another evening in the bleachers, snapped, "I don't know why you want to have anything to do with someone like that. Dubie's disgusting. He's got a belly on him bigger than his wife's and she's six months gone."

"He's a good pitcher," Allan had retorted. Allan had voted for Kennedy because he had seen a picture of him playing softball with some kids.

"A good pitcher," she had replied indignantly. His reply had made her so annoyed that she forgot she was driving and jerked the wheel to one side. For a second, it seemed their Volkswagen was going to plunge off the road and slice through a group having a back yard barbecue. With another jerk, she rescued eight people, a grill and a table of steaks from immediate destruction. "Is that," she had asked bitterly, "all there is to life?"

If she had stopped there it would have been all right but she made the mistake of saying, "Gerald's started playing golf." Gerald lived in the townhouse next door. He was a junior executive on the way up. A week previously he had bought a plum colored Cadillac.

Allan had fallen into an ominous silence. She wished she had bitten her tongue. She had plans for Allan. One more promotion would make him an executive but he had been passed over twice already and she was sure that it was because his spare time was spent wearing a sweat suit and playing baseball. From what she had read in the newspapers, promotions came to those who worked for charity and belonged to the right clubs and made the right connections at the 18th hole.

Jenkins made a sudden movement and her eyes flicked protectively toward her purse. He pulled out a package of makings and papers and began to roll himself a cigarette. He offered the package to Allan but Allan shook his head.

"Don't blame you." Jenkins looked relieved as he stuffed the package back into his pocket. "An athlete mustn't pollute his tissues. A man's tissues have to breathe and smoking clogs them. That's what makes smokers slower. Their tissues can't get air." He paused, then asked with careful casualness, "You drink much beer?"

"No," Allan replied flatly.

Jenkins looked disappointed but he said, "I don't blame you. It's not a good habit for a semi-pro. Not unless he needs to build up his red-blood count. Of course, lots don't care." Allan did not reply so Jenkins added, "That's the trouble with the world. The ones who know best aren't the ones who are listened to."

Allan started kneading his left calf. Jenkins' comment had struck a tender spot. "At least sport's better than business. There, no matter what you do, somebody else takes the credit."

"Ain't it the truth. The world is corrupt," Jenkins intoned solemnly as he twisted the ends of his cigarette to hold the dried out tobacco in place.

Agnes' face felt like it was made of wood and that if she said what she thought it would split as if it had been struck by an axe.

Allan, at times, was a burden, but after fourteen years of marriage she still believed she could make something of him. He had wasted most of his time in college by playing sports but had still managed to get a good job in research and development in plastics. College had been hard on him. He had been sensitive about his background and instead of trying to blend in had defied his classmates by exaggerating his deficiencies. He still spoke of himself as The Boor and The Barbarian and he delighted in relating how, once, when a group of his wealthy Eastern classmates were at an adjoining table in the school cafeteria, he bought an entire serving bowl of salad and ate it with his hands.

He felt the same way about the executives who from time to time wandered into his lab. Today, when he had come through the door, the first thing he had said was, "Boy, were the Morons stupider than usual. This is the only company where the criteria for being an executive is to be too dumb to work on the assembly line." Brownlee, the manager of sales, had no technical background and Allan regarded him as his own personal cross. He described Brownlee as being the only person he knew who thought a cubic foot was a birth defect.

The sound of the car door slamming made Agnes turn around. Joe Boy was lifting cases of soft drinks from the trunk of his car. He had on a green satin shirt with a yellow stripe on the sleeve and Joe's Garage painted on the back in Gothic letters. His black slacks were cut off at the knees. His wife was lifting boxes of candy out the other side. Her hair was piled so high that it looked like it would topple her onto her face.

Allan and Jenkins both went to help Joe Boy carry cases of soft drinks. Agnes wished that Allan would show some of the same independence around the ball park that he showed at work. Instead, he was pathetically eager to help out. He was always hurrying to carry equipment, hit fly balls or lay out base lines. That much effort to please at the factory would long ago have earned him a front office.

That evening, just as they had arrived at the park, he had broken his silence by suddenly saying, "You'd better take me home. You're right. I'm too old to be playing baseball. When you're thirty-nine, you've got to admit you're finished."

Agnes had quietly sighed. She knew from past experiences that if she did take him home, he would chip away at her until he provoked her into saying something really nasty. Then, justified, he would retreat into hurt silence, refusing her peace offerings of food. Lying on his back in the middle of the living room floor with his head propped comfortably on their red leather hassock, he would determinedly watch television and ignore the green grapes, the salami, even the bowls of feta cheese.

Rather than face a week-long fight, she flattered him. "Who is going to play third base if you don't?" she asked. "They need you."

"They'll get someone," he replied stiffly. "The guy who's been taking my place. Maybe Dubie will take it himself and let someone else pitch."

"Dubie," she snorted. "Dubie can't touch his toes, never mind field grounders. Nobody can pick up grounders like you. If they want double plays, they've got to put you on third."

Mollified, Allan had said no more about going home.

Other cars began arriving and Allan helped carry equipment to the dugout. After that he returned for his red baseball cap which he snugged down backwards over his closely cropped head. He jogged back and forth along the cinder path in front of the stands. In the quiet, his feet made a soft crunching sound like someone eating peanut brittle. Watching him, she realized that, although he was not fat, some day he would be. There were no angles to his body. His legs and thighs arced smoothly upward in a nearly perfect ellipse so he looked, in outline, like an elongated egg.

She grimaced internally as Allan jogged by. His grey sweat suit was obscenely intimate, as if it were dirty long underwear.

The pants bagged in back, flopping with every movement. He stopped beside the pale green cinder block dugout and bending down, disappeared inside as Dubie strolled arrogantly up to home plate to join the captain of the other team and the umpire. The umpire took a whisk broom out of his pocket and vigorously swept the plate. Dubie walked flat-footed, swinging his stomach proudly before him. He had on a blue cap, white shorts, a T-shirt embroidered in blue with Harry's Pizza and a white glove on his left hand. The fingers of the glove had been cut off at the second knuckle. His legs were noticeably bowed and were covered in thick, black hair. The umpire flipped a quarter, letting it land in the dust. Dubie lost the toss and the other team took the field.

The medical team wore green operating room shirts and caps. The pitcher had mutton chop whiskers and his blond hair was held back with a piece of red string. His windup was short and he fired the ball low and fast.

The pitcher had no flair but Agnes reluctantly admitted he was good. He struck out the first three batters. To Agnes' surprise Allan did not take the field with his team. Normally, the regular team member started and, then, if he did not play well, his substitute took over. Instead, a young kid with taped wrists jogged to third. Agnes leaned forward to peer at the dugout but she could not see Allan.

She wondered if the other wives had noticed. Normally, she sat by herself for she had nothing in common with them. They were younger and they all had one or two kids crying or whining and they came in slacks and curlers, not caring what they looked like. She always dressed up just in case she might bump into someone from the plant. She regularly wore a white blouse and blue skirt because blue went well with her red hair. Her only concession to the sport was that instead of wearing panty hose which snapped on the plank benches, she wore ankle socks with her high-heeled shoes.

All through the second half of the inning, she could not believe that Dubie had benched Allan. That, she knew, was the beginning of the end. She felt a momentary sense of indignation but it was quickly smothered by a feeling of relief.

Taped Wrists on third looked good. He was lithe, with square shoulders and long arms. As he picked up a hard line drive, he moved with the easy grace of a young animal.

Allan did not leave the dugout until the end of the seventh inning. The score was one to one so there was no chance of his being put into the game as an act of charity. He lay his duffle bag between them and sat down.

"Arm's not as good as I thought," he explained, avoiding her eyes.

There was the soft thunk of a tip and the ball flew over their heads and disappeared. She saw Jenkins start after it. Joe Boy's wife would credit Jenkins five cents for every retrieved ball and when he had six, would give him a free beer.

The light had faded so gradually that at no particular moment would it have been possible to say that it was darker than the moment before but when, without warning, the high, overhead lights flashed on, the darkness was suddenly heavy and complete. In that moment, the signs along the back fence, advertising Miller High Life, AAMCO, SuperValue, Food Giant, Shell and Schlitz, glowed with the deep intensity of red and yellow gems. Distances were newly defined. Before, the focal point had been the infield. Now, it was the back fence and the players were magically diminished. Beyond the fence was a deep, purple darkness in which the Esso station floated serenely in its own neon world.

Agnes tried to get Allan to talk, but he refused to answer, focusing all his attention on the figures on the other side of the wire screen. Unable to obtain a response, she drifted into a silence of her own.

Jenkins appeared again from under the stands. "Too bad you didn't get to play tonight," he murmured sympathetically. "I was looking forward to seeing you. It's not often you get to watch a semi-pro play ball around here."

"My arm's still not ready," Allan explained. He held his arm out, tensed the muscle and gave an exaggerated wince. "I don't want to do it any permanent damage."

"That's right," Jenkins quickly agreed. "Sometimes you've got to make sacrifices. Somebody like you doesn't want to take a chance with their arm." He reached into his pocket, looked puzzled, searched the other pocket, then said, "Would you believe that? I forgot my wallet at home. Can you loan me thirty cents for a beer?"

Agnes was so affronted that she drew herself up to her full five feet and tilted back her chin. *Cadging money for a beer*, she thought with contempt. *He was so transparent.*

Allan never carried any money to the games because his sweat suit had no pockets. "Give me a dollar," he said. She hesitated, her hand resting protectively on her purse. Finding a dollar bill, she shoved it at Allan. He took it and held it out to Jenkins. Jenkins snatched it from him and shuffled away at a near run.

Because the others could hear, Agnes kept silent. Jenkins returned triumphantly with two beers and made a production of returning the forty cents change. He sucked greedily at the can. The lumpy ridge of his esophagus jerked up and down inside the loose skin of his throat. Allan pulled off his tab and took a sip.

With dignified casualness, Agnes rose and, after taking her purse and blanket, descended to the cinder path. She walked to the car without looking back. Beyond the artificial brightness of the lights, the darkness was so thick that she imagined herself wading at the bottom of a deep river.

As she sat in the car waiting for Allan to come, she admitted that he had suffered a hard lesson, but that it was one which had to be learned. The only unfortunate part of the whole affair was that it had taken so long to come. That made it harder. Most people were forced to face reality much sooner. Now, perhaps, he would focus his energies on getting a promotion.

She watched the stands in her rear view mirror, but Allan, to her surprise, did not appear. Even when the game was over and the other players flowed briefly about her and drove away, there was still no sign of him. With a rising feeling of panic, she got out of the car and hurried with short, choppy steps toward the field. Her high heels slipped in the gravel so that she staggered and nearly lost her balance. Just as she reached the entrance, Joe Boy turned off the floodlights.

Unable to see because of the sudden change, she called, "Allan." Her voice rose tremulously as from a broken or imperfect reed, then faded so quickly that it seemed it could carry no more than a few feet.

Straining forward, she was able to see that someone was standing behind home plate and someone else was in the pitcher's box. She knew instinctively that the two players had to be Allan and Jenkins and though they did not look anything the same, she realized with an awakening sense of fear, that from where she stood, she could not tell them apart.

DENNIS GRUENDING

* * * * * * *

Dennis Gruending was raised in Saskatchewan and now lives in Ottawa. A former newspaper and television reporter, he has also worked as a radio producer and host. His most recent book is Promises to Keep: A Political Biography of Allan Blakeney *(1990). "Chucker Chatter" was originally published in* Grain *(June 1978) and has since been reprinted in various publications, including the anthologies* The Best of Grain *(1980) edited by Caroline Heath, Don Kerr, and Anne Szumigalski;* Draft: An Anthology of Prairie Poetry *(1981) edited by Dennis Cooley; and* 100% Cracked Wheat *(1983) edited by Robert Currie, Gary Hyland, and Jim McLean.*

"I grew up," Gruending notes, "throwing sinkers and rising fastballs in rural Saskatchewan. Between ages 15 and 22, I spent most Sundays in spring and summer pitching baseball in senior men's tournaments. My arm didn't last, but I still talk a good game."

* * * * * * *

Chucker Chatter

hudda buddy
hudda buddy
now you gonowyou go
fireball fireball
righthander
shoot to me buddy
shoot to me buddy buddy
fireball now fireball
righthander
ohhh
now you smoke
now you smoke buddy now you smoke buddy
buddy
now you hot
now you hot shot ohhh
now you hot
buddy
c'mon babe c'mon babe
c'mon shooter
c'mon shooter buddy buddy
you'n me honey
all they is
honey
all they is honey honey
buddy buddy
way to mix
way to mix now righthander
now you work
now you work buddy
now you hot buddy
you push to me buddy
push to me buddy
push ball
push ball
you'n me honey
all they is honey honey
all they is honey
buddy buddy
buddy buddy

HUGH HOOD

* * * * * * *

Born and educated in Toronto, Hugh Hood has taught English at the University of Montreal since the early sixties. In addition to a number of volumes of short stories, he has published over a dozen novels, nine of which belong to his The New Age *series. Among his other works are* Strength Down Centre *(1970),* Scoring: Seymour Segal's Art of Hockey *(1979), and* Unsupported Assertions *(1991). "Ghosts at Jarry" first appeared in* 78: Best Canadian Stories *(1978) edited by John Metcalf and Clark Blaise and was subsequently collected in Hood's* None Genuine Without This Signature *(1980). Other baseball stories by Hood can be found in the collections* Dark Glasses *(1976) and* August Nights *(1985). For more of his observations on the game, see his contribution to* Contemporary Authors Autobiographical Series; Volume 17 (1993).

* * * * * * *

Ghosts at Jarry

Mario at the big O, a man who likes company. Squeezed into the 400 level up and in and remote from the *voltigeur de gauche*, not too many people near him in the four dollar seats, filling for a cement sandwich, like being on a slab. Cold concrete. The 400 level is indeterminate space, neither a good seat nor a bad, too far away to hear the cries of the infielders like lonely birds swooping over green, too near to shave the price. That April afternoon he saw *les boucaniers de Pittsburgh* take the Expos as the home forces booted the ball repeatedly. Fresh from Florida the unmeshed infield found the home weather too cold for fumbling fingers, baseballs rolling hither and yon, none penetrating the 400 level. No *fausse balle* enlivened the narrow precinct. Mario decided not to sit there again; it would have to be *le niveau 200, Section 18, Section 20*, or nothing, and it would cost.

He looked for friends, found none, though they were there for sure. They had told him they were coming, Ti-cul, Kurt, Silvo, present but invisible. After the fourth inning he went in search of Silvo, who used to sit out past third base at field level, but there was nobody in his seat, only vast stretches of unoccupied metal pigeonholes, roomy, chilly, in their thousands. He couldn't find his way back upstairs; the arrows and signs confused him, and he watched the rest of the game from a vacant seat downstairs, not having paid the full price. He felt nervous and guilty but no cheerful attendant asked to see his stub; nobody banished him from the third base line. Mario never got away with anything because he never tried to. Nobody came around selling peanuts; the vendors seemed lost in the empty reaches. Parched at the seventh-inning stretch he quit his usurped bench and found a nearby kiosk where nobody stood in line. He was served immediately, then had to find a lavatory, luckily next door. Mario blessed the *Régie des Installations Olympiques* for wise care of their *concitoyens*, but found the lavatory a maze of reverse-swinging doors. He had a hard time escaping, a belated rally in progress along the basepaths. Cash scored, the home forces appeared ready to carry the day. Mario fought his way to freedom in time to see the *Devinez l'assistance* figures flashed on the big board: 21,063, 19,750, 18,322, 20,004.

He thought: those are mistaken. There can't be twenty thousand people here, or eighteen thousand. I would guess maybe seven, he thought, maybe eight thousand. There is nobody buying beer, nobody helped me when I called. I might have perished in there. The board flashed the official figure: *Assistance d'aujourd'hui, 19,750.* He peered around incredulously. Had they counted sold empty seats perhaps? At Jarry such a throng would have stretched services beyond capacity. He'd never have been able to walk straight to the counter and demand a beer, not even after the game was over. Here there was infinite space, and it unsettled him. The long eighth inning continued; extra innings impended; afternoon stretched into early evening; people began to leave; the big O emptied; Mario got frightened.

He wondered if he would come back. It was so close to home, that was the thing. For his whole life, he and Ti-cul and Silvo and Kurt had been hoping for something in the east-end besides the Angus shops. Now here it was, five minutes from Rosemont, and it gave him vertigo. He looked out, squinting through the late shadows, at what-the-hell-was-it, sward? Turf? He wasn't sure of the word. *Gazon? Domtarturf?* It wasn't anything like grass, being a bright emerald, a colour never seen in the natural world, out of a laboratory, bottled. Such green as might be seen in a film about the distant future. He could see where the individual rolls had been zippered together and laughed when a tenth-inning ground ball, out past Parrish, suddenly bounded into the air as it hit one of the zippered seams in the gleaming surface and assumed a long incredible arc, hurtling past the amazed left-fielder towards the warning track. Two runs scored. Expos failed to even the count in their half of the tenth, and the game ended that way, towards six o'clock.

The players vanished like wraiths; never had Mario seen them disappear so fast. He used to stand close to the field after the final out, to watch the inept homesters make their exposed way out to the foul pole in left and into the clubhouse, exchanging discontented repartee with certain regular fans. Once that disgusting, off-speed-pitch-specialist, Howie Reed, had flipped a baseball into *les estrades populaires* as he sauntered, cursing freely and indecently in words Mario failed to recognise, into the sheltering clubhouse. There had been a scramble. Children had injured themselves. Such a thing would be impossible under the new dispensation, contact irretrievably lost. Mario felt specks and points tickling the curling hairs on his neck and looked up. Unbelievably a warm spring rain was finding its way to him from on high, hardly a rain, more a mist, spitting. Nobody was visible but a non-lingual youth who scuttled past turning seats up, mute arguably from birth; nobody could have decided on the evidence. He would have to look for Kurt and the others at the tavern; he was sure to find them there. He moved up the steps and in out of the rain; spring night enveloped him. In the dark, strange patterns defined themselves on the concrete walls as wetness slid down pocked textures.

Roofless, open, the giant structure admitted natural flow of water, perhaps its most grateful feature. He pondered this matter as he made for the main gates, wondering whether he should go home or go downtown to eat. What would the stadium be like in heavy rain, in snow, roofless or roofed? He had heard from a friend in the air-conditioning business that huge conduits, giant circulating pumps, were being installed in the building, which would in time be completed as an all-weather sports palace. But here imagination failed. How heat it in winter? Who would sit in caverns of ice to watch what? Should Expos ever make it into *la série mondiale* they would have to play night games in mid-October; his Mediterranean blood roiled and thickened at the thought. A roof would inhibit free circulation of air. How dank, how chilled it would be, pressed up against that cold stone in late autumn! What could be done about it? And he thought, as he thought most days about the way things went on, how fix?

His feet had decided for him, leading him down the tunnel towards the Métro station. Nobody on the first flight. Nobody on the second flight. Silence along the terraces, solitude beside the newsagents' stands. Inside a sandwich again, he thought, eaten by a giant. One solitary man in a glass booth opening a vacuum bottle. Steam escaped from its top, making him think of the roofless big O. In this rain, in these temperatures, there would be puffs of steam from the hole in the top, possibly even rings of vapour as if expelled from the cancered lungs of a colossal cigarette-smoker. He passed onto an almost silent train; a solitary passenger wasn't anybody he knew.

When he rose up out of the Métro at the Berri-De Montigny station, he found the same spring rain falling into the lights of evening. He thought of the plastic emerald rug; this rain would not promote its growth, false surface. He had heard that the players preferred true grass which grew long, sometimes giving them a break on a hot grounder. Long growth might then be cut to surprise visiting teams with porous infields, a bit of baseball larceny less and less available to canny groundskeepers. Too bright. Too green.

And then there was the look and feeling of the oddly-shaped hole in the roof, a shape that made him peculiarly uncomfortable, something wrong about it. He wasn't a poet; he wasn't an architect; he had a labouring job and didn't want to know about art, but he knew that the hole in the sky was quietly askew, wrong. It shouldn't curve that way because there was nothing in the curve to remind him of women's bodies. If something curved, thought Mario, it ought to curve in a useful or encouraging way.

He wouldn't go back in there; it wasn't like the old park, which had been like a village, close, warming, with the usual run of village characters. There had been a man who brought his goat to twenty games a season, and the club management connived at the smelly invasion, to court press photographers. At the opening game of the 1971 season, Mario's children had carried a huge homemade sign into the bleachers: BIENVENUE A NOS AMOURS LES EXPOS. At two in the afternoon a pressman took a picture, which appeared in the final edition of the *Star* that same afternoon; neighbours phoned excitedly during dinner to tell the family about it. The children had remembered it ever since and there was a copy of the picture still pinned to his bedroom door.

There had been that man who sprang up in the middle of rallies and danced like a dervish up and down the steps of the grandstand, executing unheard-of jigs and reels to an accompaniment of handclapping from thousands of enthusiasts around him, a lean man, crazy-looking, known around the National League as "the Dancer." His steps could not have been danced at the *Stade Olympique*. The pitch of the seats was too gradual, the stairs insufficiently raked. Some sort of classical pavanne would suit them, not the gyrations of the native Québecker.

In the twentieth row of the bleachers, right behind the third-base foul pole, had sat night after night an unspeaking man in a short-sleeved shirt, grey-headed, immobile, stumpy cigar always in place, not a word to say for himself but always there. No cheer escaped this man, no violation of the careful probabilities of baseball by fledgling expansion team could make him wince. Mario missed him terribly, searched for him during intense moments at the big O, realising finally that the man had gone forever. He might just possibly be seated somewhere in the new building in his perpetual Buddhist posture but this seemed against all odds, the betting prohibitive. What is to be done, Mario wondered, how can this be restored?

Ballplayers – on the whole an ungenerous group of men – had hated Jarry Park for sound professional reasons as well as from personal pique. Not really great and good ballplayers, most early Expos wished to avoid the inspection of nearby fans, disliked the trudge along the track to the clubhouse, finally prevailed upon management to erect a cement-block tunnel from dugout to clubhouse, rendering themselves unobservable, incorrigible. A very few who for reasons of their own wished to court public favour continued to take the outside walk; but these were popular players apt to be fringe performers, a Ronnie Brand, a Marv Staehle, José Herrera.

The old park had the world's crappiest outfield, frost-humped, deceptively grassy, stippled with rabbit holes, hell to run on. It had no foul area; the bullpens were in the laps of the fans. Visiting relief pitchers endured coarse taunts during rare Expos rallies. Expos firemen grew accustomed to the stagey resignation of the home supporters.

"Attention, Attention. Le numéro vingt-cinq, Dan McGinn, lance maintenant pour les Expos."

At this ominous declaration, Ti-cul, Kurt, Silvo, and Mario would groan, make retching noises. The Buddha of the bleachers might shift one buttock's width to right or left, or he might not.

I will go back and look at Jarry Park, Mario decided. He had clipped a panoramic view of the old place from some special issue of *Le Dimanche*, park packed beyond capacity for some extraordinary occasion. Taken from an altitude of seven hundred and fifty feet, probably from a helicopter hovering above the parking lot to the northeast of the playing field, the photo emphasised the ramshackle, spurious, ad hoc, temporary, incredible cheapness of the silly building. It had cost three million dollars. But no public facility of the contemporary scene could possibly cost three million dollars, the thing was unheard-of. It was eight hundred million or zilch – there is no other way. When Jarry had been built, not all that long ago, Mario recollected, hardly a decade, there had been no cranes sitting idle on the site over weekends, at overtime rates approaching sixty thousand an hour. Overtime for idling cranes alone had cost more at the Olympic site than the entire cost of Jarry Park, three million. How fix?

The players hated it, and it made sense: two strikes. He thought he'd go and have a final look before they started to tear it down; there was no conceivable use for the facility. All it did was work. It looked horrible. The metal flooring of the stands had leaked copiously. If you stood under it during a rain-delay, the precipitation poured down your neck and into the dank bun of your hotdog. Those hotdogs had always been dung-like, inert, without form and void. Soggy, they constituted an offence against nature. No. There was nothing to be said for the former home of the Montréal National League Baseball Club Limited.

Somewhere around the house there was a portable radio, useable on house current or batteries, a discarded Christmas gift with exhausted power pack. Mario located it, dusted it off, supplied the requisite D batteries, and took it with him across town on an indifferent, coolish, Sunday afternoon with the Cards in town.

At fifteen hundred feet a familiar Cessna 150 banked, trailing a long streamer which delivered the Gospel according to Parkside. ALWAYS A BETTER DEAL AT PARKSIDE MOTORS. The plane hastened away as Mario squinted aloft. Perhaps the pilot had forgotten himself, returned to his old flyway mistaking the open space below for the true ballgame, then found it empty. The drone of the engine faded. Jarry was really desert.

He sidled towards the exiguous metal structure. One thing about it, though lonely, deserted, vacant, boarded over, it hadn't corroded. The metal facade shone dully, white in the uncertain atmosphere. It was an afternoon of ill-defined light, little sun, light overcast, a genuine Montréal uncertainty of observation. There was nobody in the park. He passed along the chain-link fencing looking for entry. Surely some boy or dog or vandal had effected the necessary hole – and there it was, back along the third base side near the rickety ticket booths and the press gate, a gaping tear, edges bent backwards, big enough to drive a Jeep through. Somebody had been at work with a pair of wire-cutters. The edges of the severed strands were shiny-fresh and could hurt you. He passed inside.

What is quieter than an abandoned ballpark, unless the tomb? He shuddered to think where all the voices had gone. Once this place had shaken and resounded with the shrieks of fifteen thousand maddened kiddies on Bat Day, fifteen thousand miniature Louisville Sluggers pounding in unison on the metal flooring; it had been a hellish event. Householders for blocks around had complained to the authorities but the promotion had become a recurrent event. Bat Day at Jarry Park was like the Last Judgement, sounding, deeply impressive.

But unlike the judgement in this, that it was not still impending. He stole across the flat paved open area between the fence and the refreshment counters. A blue souvenir stand leaned ready to collapse, doors locked. From between the doors a feather protruded electric blue. Mario tugged at the feather end, and the whole article slid noiselessly from between the locked doors, a celebratory feather dyed red, white, and blue. The other end stuck in the door, perhaps attached to a hat inside, too big to fit through the crack. He could do nothing to release it and left it floating solemnly in the faint breeze, passed up a ramp and into the deserted third-base seats, once the best place in the city to see a game. He idled along towards the foul pole, clutching his radio. The day around him grew imperceptibly warmer, the grey lightened. Vacancy. The seats were all before him and he was at the extreme outfield end of the park, immediately over the gateway to the abandoned clubhouse. He sprawled in one seat, then stood up, chose another, put his legs out in front of him, and switched on the radio.

"...and after the pre-game show we'll have all the action for you right here at Radio 600, the voice of Montréal Expos baseball. I'm Dave Van Horne and I'll be right here with Duke Snider to keep you up-to-date on the out-of-town scores and the other developments around the majors, right after this message..."

The sun came out. Mario drowsed and listened. He saw that this was life as it ought to be lived. The game came to him with perfect clarity and form over the radio. With his eyes shut he could fancy the whole place alive around him. Nothing was gone. The Gautama of the bleachers would be right over there twenty rows up, if he happened to glance in that direction. If the Expos happened to get something going – as they did almost immediately that afternoon – the dancer would get his legs going too. The air would be filled with flying bags of peanuts. People would be passing hotdogs along the rows in a fine comradeship. All he had to do was listen, and keep his eyes shut tight.

"...opened the inning with a single, went to second on Cromartie's roller to the right side. Valentine homered, his sixth home run of the season and his nineteenth and twentieth RBIs. Perez reached on an error..."

Expos won that first game in Mario's resurrected Jarry, a shutout victory for Rogers, and after that there could be no question of viewing the games in the flesh. He started to come to the old park all the time, nights and Saturdays as well as on the Sabbath. He felt in control, as though the whole happening was invented by him. The conviction grew on him that he could influence the course of the games by wishing, commanding in imagination. He knew that this was not strictly so, but all the same the home club seemed to rally more often when he really willed them to – balls found holes in infields, defensive replacements offered models of anticipation. Rookies blossomed – three of them, almost a miracle – all through closed eyes. He now began to think about bringing his portable SANYO along. If the atmospherics were right and the power pack strong, he might be able to watch the games on TV, listen to the expert radio commentary, have his eyes opened. Would the TV picture be an adequate surrogate for all he could imagine?

Night games would tell; they were the best of all because the tall poles no longer supported myriads of hot arcs. All was still, but not dark. Those night games in May and June at Jarry, the longest evenings of the year, had always been vexed by the slow disappearance of the sun behind the bleachers to the northwest. He remembered Ron Fairly refusing to scamper onto the playing area when the umpire called "Play Ball!" because of the late sun, dead in the eyes of the first baseman. Fairly, always an intransigeant ballplayer, had been able to persuade Dick Stello to delay the game until the sun disappeared, an unlikely twenty minutes. At Midsummer Day it didn't get dark in the park until the sixth inning or even later, while across town the actual play would be shadowed in shrouding concrete, no illumination relieving the cavernous gloom. Night games were best.

Just about Midsummer Day, with a long brilliant evening light promised, he brought the SANYO along and sneaked into his usual spot. For a while he contented himself with the radio and the fading summer sun on his tight eyelids, but as the light waned he grew curious, and when darkness descended very late, past nine-thirty, he turned on the TV and focussed his gaze on the small picture, like some mystic concentrating on his mandala:

CARTER. 11 HR. 29 RBI. .268

The emission of light from the small screen was the only sparkle in the park, thought Mario. He leaned forward, the sounds of the city in the night drifting almost inaudibly overhead. He watched the final three innings, willing them to win, and they did. And as he switched to the post-game show on the radio, just as he turned his TV off, he caught a gleam of light almost the mirror image of his own at the extreme other end of the stands, over by the first-base foul pole. A line drawn from where he was sitting through centre-field to the distant glimmer would form the base of an isoceles triangle whose equal sides would extend through first and third to home. He had no intention of launching himself into the deep well of darkness in centre. But he felt drawn along the shining metal gangway which ran the length of the grandstand.

The main bank of seats in Jarry was formed in the shape of an enormous letter L, the two equal sides of an isoceles triangle with its apex behind home plate. A fan sitting in Mario's position sensed this shape as a long line extending away towards home, with the other leg of the L running out of the corner of his eye in the direction of the visitors' dressing room under the first-base stands. The whole mass had something the look of an opened penknife, as used in the boy's game of "baseball" early in the century.

The distant figure on the other side of the park now followed Mario's lead and extinguished whatever light had been showing. The whole park lay under the night sky empty, glowing with night-shine off the aluminum seatbacks. A breeze moved quietly in the grass. Mario inched his way silently towards home in the darkness, and peering through the dark he had the sense that somebody else was coming in from right-field. A faint metallic sound drifted above the pitcher's mound, shoes on metal plating. Small shoes, by the sound.

He eased forward along the runway, which stretched out in front of him like a white dusty road in the country under starlight. The towers of extinct arc-lights stood up around the park like sentinels. There was the billboard advertising cigarettes, unreadable in the dark. Out to his left the old scoreboard, which had never worked properly, loomed with comforting familiarity. Clink of shoes on metal. He strained his eyes to see across the narrowing infield. Somebody was there. He caught a glimpse of a pale face in dim reflection. Then he heard swift footsteps and saw a slender form move in the dark like the ghost of a batboy. He ran along the third-base line, reaching home at the same moment as the ghostly figure. A girl in a dark blue halter and a pair of jeans threw herself unresistingly into his arms. This terrified him. Mario had held no girl but his wife in his arms at any time these twenty years. He drew back and tried to see her. Like himself, she carried a small portable TV and a radio.

"I thought you were a ghost," exclaimed this stranger. "Heavens, how you scared me."

"I thought so too," said Mario.

"That you were a ghost? How could you think that?"

"No. That *you* were."

"That's silly," said the girl scornfully. "Anybody can see that I'm not a ghost. I'm a very popular girl."

"I'm sure you are, Miss, but I can't see you very well in the dark."

"Why are you here?"

"I like it better here."

"Oh, so do I, so do I. I hate that other place with a passion."

"And so you started to come back here, just like me, to listen to the games and watch them on your TV. How long have you been coming?"

"This is my first time."

"I hope it won't be your last," said Mario with a gallantry which astounded himself. It would have astonished his wife too.

"But we're...all alone in here?"

"There's certainly nobody here now, not even a security guard."

"Would I be safe with you?"

"Would one Expos fan insult another? And besides, now that there are two of us, others will come. I'm certain of it."

"Oh, I hope you're right," said the girl in a beseeching tone.

"I know I'm right," said Mario. "This is exactly how a house gets to be haunted." Afterwards, when he recognised the supreme justice of this observation he wondered how he'd hit on it. He considered himself habitually, by a kind of unthinking reflex, to be a stupid unfeeling person, but in this adventure he had shown, he saw, powerful imagination.

Many came after that first encounter; they came by ones and twos, then in troops, finally in hundreds. The abandoned park sprang back to a loony bootleg life all the sunny summer. People would bring their own hotdogs and beer, their radios. Somehow a cap and souvenir vendor found out about the secret congregation, and he came too one July evening with a trayful of hats and dolls and pennants. Nobody bought anything from him; they were afraid he'd disappear. Obviously the Montréal National League Baseball Club Limited knew nothing about him, a phantom souvenir salesman with phantom goods.

None of them revisited the big O. Not ever. And in the earliest hints of autumn they would laugh, and people in neighbourhood apartment blocks would wonder where the laughing was coming from, as the plangent tones of the Duke of Fallbrook oozed from the radios collected at Jarry.

"...now we know, Dave and I know, that the club is playing a bit off the pace, but really you know folks that doesn't explain the dropoff in attendance. There has to be a big audience for Expos baseball out there somewhere, and I'm appealing to you – it's the old Duker talking..."

"That's right, Duke," said the voice of Dave Van Horne, "we've got a great home stand going here, so come on out to the

Olympic Stadium and watch the Expos try to play the role of spoilers in this season's tight race in the National League East. Hope to see you real soon, right, Duke?"

"Right, Dave!"

But the ghosts of Jarry merely guffawed, an immense throng they were by now. And the first of them looked again at the wide heavens. No, he would never go back. He would spend no second afternoon in mental trouble excited by that crater in the air, gazing through the gaping enormous ellipse – was it an ellipse? – in the sky.

JOHN CRAIG

* * * * * * *

Peterborough native John Craig (1921-1982) was the author of more than twenty books, including two baseball novels, All G.O.D.'s Children *(1975) and* Chappie and Me *(1979). The latter work, which was later adapted for the stage under the title* Ain't Lookin', *was based on Craig's own experiences during the 1940s as a white player on a black barnstorming team, Chappie Johnson's Colored All Stars. The following excerpt comprises most of the tenth chapter of the novel (deletions are indicated by an ellipsis). In a 1980 interview with the* Peterborough Examiner *(March 31), Craig said that playing with Johnson's team "was an enormous experience. It was like playing with the Yankees."*

* * * * * * *

from **Chappie and Me**

Looking back, it's hard to separate what you actually felt and understood during a particular time in your life from what you perhaps should have been able to see then, but which really only became clear through hindsight. I think I realized, that summer of 1939, that the likelihood of war was growing, day by day; in retrospect, there was a terrible inevitability in the succession of events reported by the newspapers and more personally dramatized by such radio commentators as Walter Winchell and H.V. Kaltenborn.

But, although there was a nagging, occasional awareness that the world, and everything familiar to me in it, might be running downhill, it all seemed very distant, like an earthquake in Paraguay; you could see the newsreels, and read about the thousands who were dead, and the many more who were homeless and disease-ridden and starving, and you knew it was all true, and you could be very sympathetic, but it was all happening in a place you had never seen, and it wasn't happening to you.

King George and Queen Elizabeth had come to Canada earlier that summer on some kind of centennial visit. There had been huge crowds and parades and pomp and circumstance and military reviews and unveilings and speeches about the British Empire and the might of the Royal Navy; and it had all seemed phony and boring and pretty silly. [...]

And so, as the international situation went rapidly from bad to worse that summer of 1939, my thoughts were focused on other things – specifically, seeing Mary Lou Everett again, and my performance as a member of Chappie Johnson's Colored All Stars. I was counting the days until we returned to Hobblin, Minnesota. And I was trying to make it as a first baseman with one of the best ball clubs in all baseball.

I was reasonably satisfied with my play, both at the plate and in the field. I wasn't having too much trouble with the pitchers we faced, and only had one error in the first three or four weeks I was with the team. Anyway, they were plenty good enough to carry me, as to some extent they carried Pete Simpson and Sweetcorn. But, unlike our one-armed outfielder and our clown short-stop, I wasn't contributing much in the way of entertainment or comedy – just playing my position more or less adequately, and that was about all. I took part in the shadow ball, of course, which anybody could do, and Chappie had shown me a simple trick that I used a few times.

On a quick one- or two-hopper back to the mound, or to Cotton at second, the kind where the batter is going to be out by a country mile, I would take the throw and stand near the base, but not touching it. Until I finished the play, the runner had no choice but to keep coming. I would wait and wait, and then just before his foot came down on the bag, I would flick out my toe and brush the corner of it.

The guy on the base path wasn't likely to be too amused, and the ream came dangerously close to the fine line between having fun with our opponents and making fun of them; but if the crowd was in a good mood, it was usually good for a laugh, and at least it got me into the act once in a while.

For the most part I was strictly a straightman, and it bothered me some, even if it didn't seem to bother the others, that I wasn't pulling my full share of the weight.

No matter how many times I saw them, I still laughed without fail at some of the things they did, and continued to marvel at others.

Apart from his regular reams, Sweetcorn had a great natural instinct for seeing the humor in a particular situation, and milking it for all it was worth. One night in Mansfield, Ohio, the local shortstop booted two routine ground balls in a row, much to the chagrin of the hometown crowd.

Suddenly Sweetcorn was running out onto the field, carrying his glove, and hollering in his shrill voice.

"Now, don't you worry none! Sweetcorn is comin'!"

He positioned himself beside and just behind the unfortunate shortstop.

"You be all right now. We gonna do it *together*."

Playing his part, the next All Star hitter chopped the first pitch toward them on the ground.

Sweetcorn started jumping around, moving in and moving out, and the shortstop ran this way and that totally confused.

"I got it," Sweetcorn yelled. "No, no, you take it. My ball. You the shortstop. Look out! We got it."

The ball dribbled through their four legs and out into left center. Immediately, Sweetcorn ran over and confronted the second baseman.

"Why didn't you take it, man? You *seen* we was in trouble, me and him!"

And, as they argued, the runner took second, which was uncovered at the time.

The crowd, of course, ate it up.

Another time, in another town, it had rained all day and continued to drizzle as the game got underway, by which time the field was like a swamp. About the third inning Sweetcorn hit a single into shallow right, which he tried to stretch into a double by sliding headfirst into second. But there was a big pool of water on the base path, and it turned out to be more of a dive than a slide. Finding his forward motion stopped about eight feet short of the bag, Sweetcorn began to swim for it with exaggerated dog-paddle motions.

The umpire, not impressed, called him out as Sweetcorn got to his feet, dripping wet.

"Maybe I out," he shrieked, "but I ain't drowned."

We used a lot of firecrackers to spice things up. You could still buy torpedoes then, which went off on impact, and B.G. would sometimes slip one into his catcher's mitt when Luke Redding was really throwing smoke. The loud bang was guaranteed to scare hell out of any local hotshot who already knew he wasn't going to hit Luke if he lived to be five hundred. Or somebody would sneak out and drop a string of ladyfingers at the plate umpire's feet; the fans always loved to see the man in blue dance.

To open proceedings each night, maybe a half-hour before game time, B.G., Buck and Woodrow Wilson Jones would walk out to home plate, each carrying a fungo bat and a ball. In unison, they would toss the balls up in the air and hit all three of them out of the park. They'd do it casually, as if they were just testing out the place; but, no matter how big the ball park, those balls would go out of there like so many skyrockets – one over the left field fence, one in deep center, and one in right.

That was enough to intimidate any hometown ball club, right there.

One routine I always liked was used when we had men on first and second, and the batter singled to left or left center field. As soon as the ball was safely out of the infield, while all eyes were on the base hit, whoever was coaching at first would take off for second ahead of the legitimate runner – thus giving us four guys on the base paths instead of three. The man on second would score easily, so that the only possible play would be at third base. The first base coach would time it so that he would be thrown out there. Then he would jump up, shouting and pointing to second base.

"No, no, it ain't me you want. That's him, back there!"

The umpires would scratch their heads until they finally noticed that the first base coaching box was empty. Then they would have a long conference and consult their rule books, and usually came to the conclusion that there wasn't much they could do about it. In the confusion, the runners generally managed to steal third and second.

Apart from me, everybody on the club had at least one pet ream or specialty. Cotton often threw behind his back to me, and a few times he and Sweetcorn even teamed up for double plays that way. B.G. might catch an inning with his bare hands. Pete Simpson caught fly balls between his legs. Buck would hit a half-dozen line drives in a row over the left field fence, just foul, and then rifle the second one out fair.

One night I mentioned to Chappie that I'd like to work out something I could do. We were sitting in some dugout, waiting for the local team to finish infield practice.

"Forget it, Joe," he said. "You gettin' along just fine."

"Maybe, but I'd like to try."

"So you want a ream."

"Yeah."

He glanced along the bench. "Malachi, you come over here a minute?"

The third baseman joined us, sitting on the other side of Chappie.

"What I done now?" he asked.

"Nothin' I know 'bout," Chappie said. "You think you might play a little 'ain't lookin" with Joe, here?"

Malachi shrugged, but looked faintly pleased. "Sure," he said, "long as he's willin'."

"You think he can handle it?" Chappie asked. There was a kind of seriousness about the way he put the question.

Malachi thought it over. "He ain't got no wife or kids, has he?" he asked.

"No," Chappie told him.

"Oughta be all right, then," Malachi said.

"How does it work?" I asked.

"Just gotta stand there, is all," Malachi said.

"Thank you, Mr. Brown," Chappie said.

"That's okay." Malachi went back to where he'd been sitting.

"What's 'ain't lookin"?" I asked Chappie.

"Easier to show than tell," Chappie told me. "We'll try it out, first chance comes along."

Grateful for Chappie's approval, but still curious, I asked Buck about it later that night on the bus.

"'Ain't lookin"?" he answered. "Oh, that's a real good ream."

"Yeah?"

"When it comes off," he added.

"It's hard, eh?"

"Well, you know," he said, "it takes time to work out a ream."

"I guess so," I said.

"'Course, the trouble with 'ain't lookin"," he said, "is that you don't usually get a second chance."

"Why not?"

"Forget it," Buck said. "I shouldn't have said anything. No sense in getting all worked up before the time comes."

"Tell me," I said. "I want to know."

He hesitated for a few moments, as though searching his mind for just the right words.

"You ever been kicked by a horse?" he asked finally. "Where the kidneys are?"

"Of course not," I told him.

"Well, don't worry," he said, "it'll probably be all right."

"What the hell do you mean, 'don't worry'?" I demanded.

But he had switched off his light, and was already asleep – or pretending to be. I sat for another hour or so in the darkness, wondering why I hadn't been content to leave well enough alone.

The following day, about four or five in the afternoon, we were driving along the edge of a town, on our way to wherever we were scheduled to play that night, when Chappie told B.G., who was at the wheel of the bus, to pull over and stop. There was a ball diamond just off the road, deserted in the hot sun, with weeds encroaching on the bumpy infield path and a sagging, chicken-wire backstop behind home plate.

"Malachi, Joe – you ready?" Chappie asked.

Malachi was already moving up the aisle, his glove tucked under his arm.

"What for?" I asked.

"'Ain't lookin'', what else?" Chappie said.

"Oh, sure."

The three of us went across the road, through some tall grass, and around the end of the screen onto the ball field. I knew that the others who had stayed on the bus were watching.

"Come over here, Joe," Chappie said, and led the way to the first base area. It was as rough around there as ice on a pond in late March. He peeled off his windbreaker, and dropped it on the dusty, bare earth.

"That'll be the bag," he said. "Now, I want you to stand like this." He took a position facing away from the diamond, looking 180 degrees in the other direction.

I did as he said. It seemed strange, having my back to the diamond.

"How's that?" I asked.

"Fine, just fine," he said, coming around in front of me. "I'm goin' in, and hit one down to Malachi. Start countin' when you hear the bat meet the ball."

"Okay."

"Get to seven, put your glove 'round behind, like this." He held his hand, the pinkish-black palm outwards, in the small of his back, about waist high.

"Then what?" I asked.

"Just wait, is all," Chappie said, "and don't move."

Suddenly, it became clear; I was supposed to trust Malachi to hit a target, maybe eight inches round, from the far corner of the diamond, a hundred or so feet away. If he missed, I could wind up pissing blood or in a wheelchair.

"You ready?" Chappie asked.

"Oh, sure," I said, wishing I had been born with some brains.

He went away, and I stood there, staring out across fields of maturing corn. It seemed to take him a hell of a long time to reach the plate. I waited...and waited. Maybe the ream was that he and Malachi had got back on the bus, leaving me to dangle there like some kind of ass-backward scarecrow.

Finally I heard the sound of bat on ball, and I started counting – one...two...three.... When I got to seven I slipped my right hand, cocooned by the big first base mitt, around behind and held it hard against my belt. Another year or so of my life ticked away. Trickles of sweat ran down my forehead. I strained to spread my thumb and fingers, making the pocket as wide as possible. In the kidneys, Buck had said. Jesus! I winced, anticipating the pain.

Suddenly a bomb exploded in my right hand, the shock of it travelling up my arm, through my shoulder and neck, and into my head. Instinctively, the nerve hinge in my glove snapped shut, and I somehow held onto the throw. A few seconds later I turned around slowly, trying to keep my knees from shaking.

Chappie was coming out along the first base line, holding up his empty hand for the ball as if what had just happened was a routine thing.

"Let's do it another time," was all he said.

We did it again, and after that another four or five times. I dropped the ball once out of nervousness, but it was unfailingly on target, somewhere in the long trough-shaped pocket between the end of my thumb and the heel of the glove. After the first two or three tries I was able to judge pretty well when the ball would arrive, and that made it easier. Physically, any half-decent first baseman should have been able to catch a thousand in a row. The challenge was psychological; it was hard standing there with your back turned, not knowing what was going on behind you – and hard too to have enough confidence in Malachi, to believe that anybody could be that good. If just one of those throws sailed so much as six inches on a vagrant current of air, or was just a shade off-line.... Ordinarily, of course, you could adjust to any changes in the flight of the ball, compensating, shifting your glove, your stance, your whole body; but in 'ain't lookin'' there was no margin for error.

"You figure you can do it in a game now?" Chappie asked after we got back on the bus. My teammates, having watched the workout with such sadistic interest, had given no indication that they were impressed by it; even Buck, damn him, pretended he was asleep.

"Sure," I said, "how do we set it up?"

"Fifth innin'," he said. "I'll get our guy to let up a little and throw inside to righties. That oughta get us a grounder down third. Ain't the fifth, maybe the sixth."

"Okay," I told him. "One thing, though."

"Uh-huh."

"What am I supposed to be looking at out there away from the field?"

Chappie shrugged. "Don't matter," he said. "Bird flyin', maybe an airoplane, little kids playin', whatever you see."

"Won't I look pretty stupid?" I asked.

"You is *supposed* to look stupid," Chappie said, his voice a little impatient. "You wanted a ream, and lookin' stupid is part of this one."

"All right," I said.

"Don't forget you is a dumb nigger now," he told me. "Be ready when they come up in the fifth."

We played that night in Bloomington, Indiana. A college town, it seemed almost deserted in mid-summer.

"You could shoot a machine gun 'round this town, 'n not hit nothin' but a couple of dogs," Latimore Lee said as we drove through the near empty streets.

Still, eight or nine hundred showed up for the game that night, a lot of them farmers from the surrounding countryside.

"Be ready," Chappie told me as we ran out for the home team's half of the fifth.

As soon as I had taken the warm-up throws from the other infielders, I turned my back on the diamond and stared out past the corner of the left field grandstand, doing my best to look as if I was fascinated by something that had caught my eye. To tell the truth, there was nothing out there except a couple of houses, a few trees and a hell of a lot of corn. I kept peering and staring, though, like I was expecting King Kong to come into view at any second.

Every now and then I'd sneak a quick look out of the corner of my eye to see what was happening in the ball game behind me. Unfortunately, that wasn't much; the first two batters popped up to Sweetcorn, and the third struck out, even though Luke Redding was laying the ball in there as soft and gentle as a wooly lamb.

By the end of the inning some of the fans on the first base side were laughing, and a few were beginning to get on me.

"Hey, Sambo, you're missin' a good ball game!"

"Look behind you – yoo-hoo, turn around!"

"You there on first, they went thataway!"

I kept it up when they came up in the sixth. The fans were looking for it by then, and the heckling started right away. The first pitch was a called strike, and then I heard the bat make contact with the ball. I glanced around just enough to see the batter looking down the third base line as he dropped his bat and dug in for first.

This is it, I thought, as I started counting. Three...four... five...six...seven. The runner was about ten feet away, and coming hard. Close play. A lot of the fans were screaming at me to turn around. The throw must be almost there.

At the last moment I put my glove behind my back, spreading the pocket over my belt. The count might have gone to eight, perhaps nine...and then, wham, the ball was there. Perfect, right on the money! My fingers snapped over it, and at the same instant I flicked out my toe and touched the corner of the bag. The umpire jerked his arm up, and the guy was out by a step or so. Close all right.

Then, suddenly, I was aware of the crowd. Some of the fans were laughing, others clapping, a few whistling. They loved it! The applause was for me, and I loved that – although it should have been for Malachi.

Eating it up, I swung my glove toward the stands in a kind of informal salute, then threw to Cotton to start the ball on its way around the horn.

Free to go into high gear again, Luke Redding struck out the next batter on three pitches to retire the side.

Approaching the dugout I caught up to Malachi, who was never known to run when he could walk, or walk when he could sit down.

"Thanks," I told him, "I really appreciate it."

"Should, too," he said, "and remember to be good to old Malachi from here on. He just might get careless one time."

The days and nights of that July passed one by one, and the bus and truck rolled on, criss-crossing state lines – North Dakota, Minnesota, Wisconsin, Illinois, Indiana, Michigan, Ohio, then swinging back north and west again.

Each day a new town, every night a different ball park. And, if the All Stars did not really look the least bit alike, the towns were carbon copies of one another. I remember some of the ball parks, however – one where right field climbed a hill, another where the base paths were red (because of iron in the soil, someone said) – but the towns were just so many dots on a series of folded road maps.

The same thing with time. Dates didn't mean much, and it came as surprise when I discovered that we had somehow turned the corner and moved into August. On Saturdays the main streets of the towns would be crowded with farmers in for market, weekly shopping and haircuts, and sometimes there would be the sound of church bells on a Sunday morning; otherwise, I seldom gave a thought to the day of the week.

We travelled hundreds and hundreds of miles, but never really saw much; and I'd already had my fill of staring across meaningless countryside, other people's countryside, from the open doors of empty freight cars. Nobody was ever broadened much by that kind of travel. Toughened, maybe, but not broadened. The endless hours we spent in the confined, crowded, smelly prison that was the bus could only be endured by putting your mind into a state of suspension between sleep and wakefulness, or by finding a way of escape. Some played poker. Buck read. Latimore Lee sang songs under his breath that only he understood. Chappie kept his accounts.

We ate a lot of greasy food, meat that was under-cooked, vegetables that had had the life boiled out of them, stale bread, watery soup, pieces of pie that had been walked over by a hundred flies.

We hardly ever got a decent night's sleep, as most of the time we had to cramp our too long bodies into the too narrow seats of the bus. Though once in a while we lay down in the open, contoured to the grass and bare earth, under the stars and drifting clouds and sudden, cold rain.

It was a little better in states like Illinois, Ohio and Michigan, where there were a lot of blacks, because even though the prejudice was stronger, and you had to keep looking over your shoulder, the rules were more clear-cut. There were places you didn't go, things you didn't do; but Chappie knew a Negro cafe here or lunch counter there where we could get a decent meal; and three or four times we even got to sleep between clean sheets in hotels run by colored people.

I soon grew to hate the lighting equipment. The others hated it too, and some of them had for years. It wasn't hard work, but the monotony grated on your nerves; the same thing every night – put it up, take it down, put it up, take it down. The fact that it was such a practiced, almost orchestrated routine just made it worse, even if it was efficient and never failed to impress the fans who arrived early enough to see us go through it. Each player had a specific role to play in the scenario; mine was to erect the light standard back of first base, and plug in the leading and outgoing cables. I went through those steps so often that the first thing I used to think about some mornings was that damn, flimsy tower and how I would have to put it together again that night. The record for stringing the whole lighting system, and throwing the generator switch that would bring the rows of 100-watt bulbs to life, was fourteen minutes and thirty seconds; we never even came close to that while I was with the All Stars.

A lot of things were difficult. Laundry, for one. There never was a washing machine available; nor any hot water; we scrubbed our socks, shirts, shorts and uniforms in rivers and roadside ponds, and often hung them out the bus windows to dry. We shaved in water so hard that you couldn't get a lather, and had to scrape off the whiskers with a bare razor blade. There was no mail, because we had no address. The only privacy came when it was your turn to drive the bus.

In many ways we were like prisoners in a touring jail, cooped up for countless hours, cut off from the rest of the world, freed once a day to put on our show, then herded back into our communal cell.

Yet it wasn't bad. There were the shared experiences, and there was a camaraderie and a kind of unspoken, common loyalty.

Most of all, I liked playing ball every night – liked it better than anything I had ever done or known. I liked the sights and sounds of the game. I liked the more or less crowded stands. I liked the looseness. I liked the slap of the ball when it nestled into the pocket of my glove, and the solid tingle in my hands and wrists when I got good wood on a fast ball. I never tired of watching Cotton Nash go to his right, backhand the ball and flip it in one fluid motion to Sweetcorn to start a zip-zip double play. I liked the geometric perfection of the diamond, even when the chalk lines were wobbly, the outfield was riddled with gopher holes, and the base paths were chewed away by encroaching weeds. The laughs. The chatter. B.G. setting his target. Latimore Lee coming in with his high, hard one. Buck Yancey, drifting away under a well-hit fly ball, and turning at the last moment to make the catch over his shoulder at the base of the centerfield fence. The umpires, maybe not always right, but never wrong. The excitement. The action. The perfection. The errors.

The game.

I was well aware that I was no better than a Class 'C' first baseman, lucky enough to be playing with a bunch of guys who, by every right, should have been in the majors. Under the circumstances, though, I didn't think I was hurting the ball club. My new ream had given me more confidence, and I added a few other little gimmicks that contributed to the comedy part of the show.

Chappie seemed satisfied. Otherwise, I told myself, he would have sent for a replacement; the All Stars meant too much to him to put up with an inadequate performance. He was a proud man. To make sure, though, I put it to him directly one noon when he and I were waiting for a garage mechanic to put new brake linings in the truck. The others were camped a couple of miles out of the town. Chappie and I were sitting in the shade of a chestnut tree, from where we could see the truck up on the hoist with its rear wheels off. As usual by then, I was wearing the lampblack under my ball cap.

"Mr. Johnson," I asked, "you think things are going all right?"

He thought about it for a moment, then nodded. "Sure," he said, "good as anybody could expect. Just get them new linings in, we be laughin'."

"I meant me," I told him.

He looked surprised. "You itchin' to move on?" he asked.

"No."

"You gettin' along, ain't you?"

"With the others?"

"Uh-huh."

"I think so," I said.

"I ain't hearin' no complaints," he said.

"That's good."

"Stay a spell then, if you want," he said.

"I'd like to," I told him.

He leaned back on his elbows, and looked up at the white chestnut blossoms.

"You fieldin' as good as anybody I could bring in," he said.

"Thanks."

He laughed. "'Course you should be," he said, "on account of I taught you all I knows."

I laughed too. "How about hitting?" I asked him.

"Shit," he said, "Chappie'd hit .400 down here, and I is fifty-four years old."

"You would, at that," I said.

He glanced over toward the garage.

"Looks like we got wheels again," he said. "Let's get goin'."

"Thanks, Chappie," I said.

"Mr. Johnson," he reminded me.

The next night after that we played a town called Appleton in Wisconsin. We had a good feeling about the place as we turned in off the highway. Clean streets. Recently mowed lawns and flower beds around substantial looking, freshly painted houses. A nice park in front of the court house. Progressive. Pleasant. Friendly. A nice town.

It was the same at the ball park, two or three hours later. The infield path had been raked, our dugout had been swept clean of popcorn boxes, chocolate bar and chewing gum wrappers, crumpled cigarette packages. The fans started to file in well before game time, and they kept coming. You could sense that they were in a good mood, and had come to be entertained. The kind of crowd that makes you want to do your best.

Everything went fine for five innings. We trotted out all of our top reams. The crowd oohed and aahed, laughed and applauded. The local players were easygoing and didn't take losing too hard; maybe they had had a lot of practice.

Then, in their half of the fifth, disaster showed its ugly face in Appleton. There was no warning that all hell was about to break loose. I set up "ain't lookin'" to start the inning, and was staring off toward the south, watching a big, lumbering crow being chased by a posse of smaller birds, probably swallows. The first batter obligingly hit a soft three-hopper down to Malachi. I started the count and, when I got to seven, put the glove around behind at my belt. The ball was there, as always. Smack! The umpire started his 'out' motion. The fans began to rumble their appreciation.

Then the breath was knocked out of me, and I was turning ass over tea kettle on the grass. The batter had plowed into me but, even as I rolled, I knew it wasn't his fault. Hell, I'd been standing right on the bag. Careless. He'd just been trying to beat it out, like any decent ballplayer would do. I hurt some, but the ball was still in my glove and I came up laughing. No problem.

Well, there was one; my ball cap had been knocked off in the collision. Suddenly I was the world's first and only brown-haired, blue-eyed Negro first baseman. I heard a buzz running through the crowd, a hum of surprise and shock.

"Look, they got a white guy playin' first!"

"Well, by damn..."

"Never seen the like of it!"

It wasn't an angry sound, though. The fans seemed more intrigued than annoyed, and ready to see the humor in the situation.

"What's the matter, Chappie – you run outa niggers?"

"How many more whites you got out there?"

Typically, Sweetcorn picked that up right away. He ran in to a spot about half-way between the pitcher's mound and home plate. There he stopped, doffed his cap, and did a kind of pirouette as he swept it gracefully in front of him. As he did this he bent down to give everybody a full view of his head of kinky and very black hair.

"Ain't no white on Sweetcorn," he hollered. "Ain't no white on me."

The fans laughed, liking it, and the other All Stars took it from there. One by one, starting with Malachi, they spun around, pointing to their hair.

"I black all over."

While this was going on, I retrieved my cap and pulled it down over my brown hair. By then the laughter was solid all around me. When play finally resumed, Latimore got the inning over with as quickly as possible, striking out the next two hitters on six pitches. B.G. put a torpedo in his mitt to punctuate the last one. The fans gave us a big hand as we came in off the field. When we got to the dugout I looked over to where Chappie almost always sat, in the corner closest to home plate. He was laughing too.

I went over to him.

"You want me to come out?" I asked.

The laughter drained out of his face as if I had pulled the plug.

"Come out?" he asked.

"I don't mind," I told him. "It was my fault."

"What in the world you want to do that for?" He started laughing again. "Hell, that's maybe the best ream I ever did see. Oh, my!"

The laughter was contagious.

"It was pretty good at that, wasn't it?"

"I think –" he said, tears coming into his eyes, "I think we gonna do it every night!"

That wouldn't have been possible, of course, because the fans in a lot of towns would have felt cheated by a white guy masquerading as a colored ball player. But nobody in Appleton seemed upset over it.

Or hardly anybody.

We gave the crowd a good show for the remaining innings, and got a lot of applause when the game was over. The fans were filtering out through the exits and we were gathering up the gear, when we heard a voice from the dugout steps.

"You there, boy, what's your name?"

I glanced up and saw the figure of a big man, silhouetted against the lights. He was wearing a sheriff's uniform, and I caught the glint of a star on the left front of his short-sleeved shirt. There was a gun in a holster on his belt. And he was looking right at me.

"Who?"

"You know who."

The months on the road had taught me that you never got anywhere by antagonizing a police officer, but this one's overbearing manner and sneering voice made that hard to remember. He came down the rest of the way into the dugout, and he was big. Young – early thirties, I guessed. Handsome in a hard way. Slim hipped, but with the upper body of a football guard or tackle.

"My name's Joe Giffen," I told him.

The others had stopped what they were doing, and were watching intently.

He nodded, smiled – but not with his eyes.

"That's a good boy, Joe," he said. "Now, I want you to just come along with me, nice and easy."

"What?"

"Nothin' complicated about it," he said. "I'm takin' you in, is all."

Chappie pushed his way past B.G. and Malachi to stand beside me.

"You mind tellin' me what the charge is, officer?" he asked.

"Who the hell are you?" the sheriff asked.

"This here's one of my ballplayers," Chappie told him.

"Uh-huh," the sheriff said, "well, we got a choice on him."

"Like what?" Chappie asked.

"Oh, take fraud, for instance. Cheatin' the public. Then there's impersonatin' a nigger – unlawfully."

"Impersonating a nigger!" Buck said, behind me. "Holy Jesus!"

"What do you want me to do, Mr. Johnson?" I asked.

"Don't seem like there's too much choice," Chappie said. "Best go along with it. I'll be down soon as I can." He looked up at the sheriff, who was a head taller than he was, and maybe a hundred pounds heavier. "Where's he gonna be at?" he asked.

"County jail," the big man said. "Real nice. Hearin' is set for tomorrow mo'nin'."

"All right."

"Then let's haul ass," the sheriff said.

I walked beside him along in front of the stands, across a parking area and out through the main gate. He kept blowing bubbles with the big wad of gum he was chewing. The last few fans were still on their way out, and some of them looked over, curiosity in their eyes.

There was a yellow and blue squad car parked at the curb. The sheriff opened the back door and got in after me. His deputy turned around from the steering wheel.

"Where to, Roy?" he asked.

"Oh, shit," the sheriff said, "where do you think? You wanta buy him some ribs out at Porky's?"

"I was just askin'," the deputy said.

"Well, don't ask," the sheriff told him.

It took us about fifteen minutes to get there. The county jail was a square, limestone-block appendage behind a graceful, red-brick courthouse that looked as if it had been there forever.

The sheriff picked up a ring of big keys from a nail in his office and led the way through a heavy oak door and along a short corridor. There were bars on either side, and it was like a dungeon under the high ceiling. He stopped in front of the second cell on the right and unlocked the door. It squeaked as he opened it, then clanged solidly shut behind me.

"You'll be just fine here," the sheriff said as he turned away. "Have a good night now, y' hear?"

Oh, sure.

The place reeked of strong disinfectant, which was trying, with only limited success, to overcome the smells of urine, sweat, vomit and mildew. A bare, fly-specked light bulb burned overhead. There was a stool at one end, a bucket and a steel bunk with a straw mattress at either side, in one of which was sprawled the body of a man. He didn't move once while I was there, and I never did know whether he was dead drunk or just dead.

It's hard to describe how I felt. Not scared, actually. Not apprehensive, particularly. Mostly, the whole thing seemed unreal. And kind of funny. I stood by the cell door, my hands grasping the bars, and wondered what the hell was going to happen.

An hour went by, maybe two. Then I heard footsteps, and saw the deputy approaching. He was carrying a paper bag in one hand, the ring of keys in the other. It took a minute or so of fumbling to get the cell door open, after which he held out the paper bag to me.

"Here."

"What's this?" I asked.

"Ribs," he said. "Your nigger friend figured you might be hungry."

"From Porky's?"

"How'd you know?" he said.

The ribs were good – tender, meaty, smothered in a tangy, sweet sauce. I stripped the bones clean, along with a carton of potato salad, a toasted roll and a paper cup of coffee. Thank you, Chappie. Then, feeling pretty good considering my predicament, I went over and curled up on the other mattress.

I woke up feeling like a skinny old bear in March. I was stiff, a lot of muscles ached, and my mouth tasted like second base. Sunlight was coming through the only window, high up in one wall. The sheriff himself was rattling the bars with a spoon.

"You want your breakfast, you better come and get it," he said.

I stretched, rolled off the mattress, and went over to the cell door. He handed me a mug of lukewarm coffee, and a tin plate, on which some watery, greyish-green scrambled eggs had drowned a piece of toast sometime during the night.

"Thanks a lot," I told him.

"Don't be too long," he said. "Court sits in forty minutes."

"You suppose I could wash up before that?" I asked.

He took a step backwards, as if I had called his sister a whore, but quickly recovered.

"Oh no, smart ass," he said, "there won't be no destroyin' evidence. I want you in there just the way you was."

He went away, and I sat on the edge of the bunk and drank some of the coffee. I put the scrambled eggs on the floor by the other bunk, in case my cell-mate should revive, which seemed increasingly unlikely.

The sheriff came back in about half an hour and took me out of the jail, across a small yard under some big old oak trees, and through a side door into the courtroom. Outside, the sun was bright, and everything – trees, lawn, flowers, courthouse – looked freshly washed.

By contrast, it was cool and hushed in the courtroom. Only a dozen or so people, including the sheriff and me, were on hand to witness the case of *The State of Wisconsin v. Joseph Giffen.* The court reporter was a nice looking, middle-aged woman in a floral housedress. The Assistant District Attorney, a pudgy young man in his early thirties, had a lingering case of acne. Chappie, wearing his All Star windbreak, was sitting in the front row. Six or seven spectators, there for God knows what reasons, were scattered around in the polished-wood, churchlike pews.

Circuit Court Judge Wilbur Clay Calhoun couldn't have been a day under eighty, nor a fraction of an inch over five foot two. His face was thin and deeply lined under a fringe of close-cropped, grey hair, and he looked so frail that it was hard to believe there was a body beneath the folds of his shiny blue serge suit. When he glanced down at me through his rimless glasses, I got the impression that he had given up smiling some years before.

The sheriff indicated that I was to sit at a small oak table below the bench, and as soon as I had taken my place the trial got under way. The Assistant D.A. led off. He stuttered pretty badly from time to time, but I got the idea that I was being charged with fraud and false pretenses for pretending to be a black ballplayer when I was really white.

The sheriff took the stand and testified that he had arrested me the previous night after my ball cap had been accidentally knocked off. The Assistant D.A. introduced into evidence one of the posters that had been put up around Appleton, announcing that the 'Colored All Stars' were coming to town.

"I su–su–submit, Your Honor, that the clear im–im–imp–implication of this placard is that all of the players are of the nig–Negro race. And I ask that it be marked as Ex–Ex–Exhibit 'A'."

"No need to get fancy, Henry," the judge told him. "Just put it there on the table. Let me have a look at it first, though, will you?"

He studied it at arms length for a minute or so, then just kind of pushed it off the front of the bench. The court reporter in the floral dress went over, picked it up, and put it on the table.

"Thank you, Martha," the judge said.

At that point Chappie stood up.

"Your Honor, may I say somethin'?" he asked.

"Who are you?" Judge Calhoun wanted to know.

"I runs the All Stars," Chappie said.

"Oh, you do, eh?"

"Yessir, and I just wanted to say that we didn't mean no harm. We try to play good and make people laugh, that's all. Joe, here, he part of the team, like everybody else."

"I object!" the Assistant D.A. said, leaping to his feet.

"To what?" the judge asked him.

"This – this man has no o–o–official ca–ca–cap–capacity, and I ..."

"Now, Henry," the judge said, grimacing as he interrupted, "this is not exactly the Lindbergh kidnapping trial we have here. I think we can afford to be a little informal."

"But, but ..."

"Sit down, Henry," the judge said, turning back to look toward Chappie.

"Mr. Johnson," he said, "you've been around baseball for quite a spell, is that right?"

"Oh, I didn't come by just yesterday," Chappie told him.

"Neither did I," His Honor said. "Now, tell me how you came to hire this player for your team."

Chappie explained how it had happened.

"Uh-huh," the judge said when he was finished. "So you could say that it was a matter of being in the right place at the right time?"

"Yessir," Chappie agreed, "you could say that."

"And it saved you money."

"You could say that, too," Chappie told him.

"All right," the judge said. He looked over at me. "I'd like to ask the defendant a question or two."

The sheriff leaned across the table. "On your feet, boy," he said. I got up.

"Tell me," His Honor said, peering down through his glasses, "are you a good ballplayer?"

"I'm all right," I said, "but not as good as some of the others."

"Not as good as Mickey Cochrane, for instance?"

"No, sir, not as good as Malachi or Buck either."

"I always appreciate modesty," the judge said. "There's so little of it. Can you play the bag?"

"Yes, sir."

"Hit?"

"As long as I don't see too many good curve balls."

"Do you see too many?"

"No, sir, not against the teams we play."

"Did you help to entertain the fans?"

"Well, I think so, now that I got my own ream...."

"Your own what?"

I told him about "ain't lookin'."

"I see, the judge said. "What's that stuff on your face?"

"It's called lampblack," I told him.

"Oh, yes, of course. Well, that will be all, I think. You can sit down now."

He looked over at the Assistant D.A.

"Henry," he said, "I hope you won't consider this out of order ..."

Henry jumped up.

"Anything you s–s–say, Your Honor."

"Thank you. Would you be good enough to name some colors for me?"

"S–s–some what?"

"Some colors, Henry – you know, like we all learn in grade school."

"Oh, sure," Henry said. "Well, there's green and blue and o–o–orange and brown and pink ..."

"You're doing just fine, Henry," the judge said. "Keep going."

"... and white and purple and red and black ..."

"Ah, yes, black," the judge interrupted. "Now, Henry, take a good look at the defendant's face. How would you describe it, as far as the hue is concerned?"

"W–we–well, it's kind of black, but he just rubbed it on...."

"And black is a color? You said so yourself."

"Oh, d–d–damn!"

Judge Calhoun turned to face me and Chappie and the almost empty benches of his courtroom.

"The advertisement used by the All Stars doesn't say anything about how they got to be 'Colored,'" he said, "but only specifies that they are. The sun is shining and it's a nice day outside. I think we have all wasted enough time."

He picked up his gavel and banged it down three or four times on the bench.

"The defendant is found not guilty," he said. "Court stands adjourned."

LESLEY CHOYCE

* * * * * * *

Lesley Choyce has lived in Lawrencetown, Nova Scotia since 1978. A professor of English at Dalhousie University, he is also active as a writer, editor, publisher, and TV host. Among his many books are the poetry collection The End of Ice *(1985), the story collection* The Dream Auditor *(1986), and the novel* The Ecstasy Conspiracy *(1992). "Report from Right Field," which Choyce describes as his "Vietnam / baseball poem," is taken from his first volume of poetry,* Fast Living *(1982).*

* * * * * * *

Report from Right Field

Upon discovery of complete isolation
he realizes the exactness of the perimeters
of loneliness:
the topmost layer of skin.

Alone in Right Field
without even a history of flyballs
ever reaching this quadrant
he turns skyward absently forgetting
the value of holding down useless territory
for symbolic reasons
home plate only a rumour from this far out
the pitcher a wobbling wraith
and off in another country the coaches yelling
screaming for blood
tearing off hats
gnashing teeth
begging for a home run.

As if on cue
the inning ends
he defects over the fence
that helped to define the limits of the game.

He sees the woods, the roads:
the diamond trip home.

W.P. KINSELLA

* * * * * * *

A native of Edmonton, William Patrick Kinsella was educated at the University of Victoria and the University of Iowa. He now lives in White Rock, British Columbia. Since the appearance of his first book in 1977, he has published numerous story collections and several novels. His first novel, Shoeless Joe *(1982), which is regarded as a classic work of baseball fiction, was filmed in 1989 as* Field of Dreams. *Among his other baseball-related works are* The Thrill of the Grass *(1984),* The Iowa Baseball Confederacy *(1986),* The Further Adventures of Slugger McBatt *(1988),* Box Socials *(1991) and* The Dixon Cornbelt League and Other Baseball Stories *(1993). Recently, he contributed to a book on the 1992 World Series,* A Series for the World *(1992). "The Baseball Spur" was first published in* Descant *(Fall 1983) and was then reprinted in the short-story collection* The Thrill of the Grass. *Later, the story was revised for inclusion in* The Iowa Baseball Confederacy.

* * * * * * *

The Baseball Spur

For Tony

1.

"Walt (No Neck) Williams, do you remember him?" Stan asks suddenly, in the way he has of jumping from subject to subject.

"Um-hmm," I say noncommittally, after racking my brain for a few seconds. "I know the name but the details are fuzzy."

"He played for the Sox. The White Sox. They called him No Neck because he didn't have one," and Stan laughs his long, stuttering laugh, sounding as though he has peanut shells lodged in his throat. There is a car following us closely and the headlights bury themselves in the rear-view mirror, which paints a moonlight-like bar across Stan's face. As I glance sideways it looks as though he is wearing a golden mask.

"Last summer I met No Neck on the street in Chicago," Stan goes on. "I just about went crazy. 'Hey, No Neck,' I called to him, and I set down my suitcase and went running after him. You remember that, Gloria?" he directs the last words to his wife, turning toward the back seat to acknowledge her, the mask slipping around over his ear as he does. Gloria is a big, blowzy, Polish girl, cheerful and resilient. She has fouled off all the curves life has thrown at her, although over the years her brows have squeezed together in a mini-scowl as if she had been staring too long at the horizon.

"He actually edged away from me. You remember that, Gloria? I guess you must meet a lot of nuts when you're in the Bigs. I mean I kept saying to him, 'Man, I used to watch you when you played for the Sox. You were great, man. You were great.' And I hauled out my wallet and looked for something he could sign, and I didn't have any paper, not even a Master Charge slip or anything, so I got him to sign the back of Gloria's picture. It's one I've carried around for ten years, with Gloria in jeans and her hair up in a bee-hive standing beside her old man's '69 Buick. No Neck looked at me like I was crazy, leaving my wife with our suitcases and chasing after him for a block like that. Don't you remember him, Jackie?"

"I know the name, but I don't get involved with modern-day players the way you do, Stan," I say. My own wife, Sunny, is squashed into the corner of the back seat behind me. She hasn't said a word since we left the ballpark in Cedar Rapids. I catch a glimpse of the red glow of her cigarette. She is tiny as a child sitting back there. I wonder how someone so small and insignificant-looking can tear me apart the way she does.

"No Neck's only a couple of years older than us, Jackie," Stan says. "Played his last game in '75. God, you know how that makes me feel. A guy just two years older than me retired. And me still strugglin' to make the Bigs."

"You'll make it, Stan," I say automatically, just as I have been saying it every year for over half my life.

Stan and Gloria have come to visit Gloria's mother in Onamata; she's the only family either of them have here anymore. Stan's father is dead and his mother has gone to Florida to live with a married sister.

Since spring Stan has been playing Triple A ball in San Antonio, but he sprained his right hand pretty badly a couple of weeks ago and the club put him on the disabled list and brought up a kid from a Class C team in Burlington to replace him.

"I wanted to ask No Neck about how much he practised. I bet he practised like crazy or he never would have got to the Bigs. God, but I used to practise. Remember how I used to practise, Jackie, Gloria? Hey, Sunny, you're being awful quiet. I ever told you how I practised?"

Sunny draws deeply on her cigarette, but does not answer. Stan is tall and muscular, his head square, his hair cut short, but his face as wide and innocent as a husky child's. His eyes are pale blue and wide-set, his hair, though it's darker now, was a lemony colour when we were kids, and Stan was forever watering it as if it were grass that would grow stronger if wet.

"My old man never liked baseball, but I used to make him come outside and he'd stand in front of the barn and I'd make him hit fly balls to me. I spent all my pay on baseballs, all the money I earned working for old Piska the cement contractor. Saturdays I used to carry a bucket of cement in each hand from the mortar box to the sidewalk we were laying, or the garage floor. I took the money and I bought a box of baseballs, a whole dozen. I laid them out on my bed like a bagful of white oranges, and I smelled them, and touched them, and handled them like a miser fondling his money. The old man wasn't very good and every once in a while he'd foul one into the goddamn pig pen. I'd have to wash the pigshit off it, and sometimes when I went in the pen one of those big red buggers would have the ball in his teeth, and I'd have to whack his snout to make him let go and the ball would have teeth marks on it forever." Stan stops for a second or two. The highway is dark. There is an orangy flash behind me as Sunny lights a new cigarette. I see her left eye is closed, squinted up against the smoke. There is an inch-long scar, pink as a worm on her dusky skin, running vertically from the corner of her eye onto her cheekbone. There are fine age lines spreading out from the corners of her eyes. Sunny aged a good deal the last time she was away.

"I love the game. I've always loved the game, right Jackie? I used to dream about a career in baseball. It wasn't just vague hopes like a lot of kids have. I knew what I was doing. I've made a living from the game for almost fifteen years. And I'm gonna make the Bigs yet, you wait and see."

"You'll make it, Stan. We all know that," I say.

"I mean I've seen guys with twice as much talent as me throw it all away. They party all night and stagger in ten minutes before a game wearing their hangovers like badges. It's not fair that my reflexes are a hundredth of a second slower than theirs. I mean I work out three hours every afternoon. I've always hustled, haven't I Jackie?"

"You've always hustled," says Gloria from the darkness. Her voice is lifeless. She answers by rote. We've both learned to agree with Stan without even listening to him.

"I put a washtub on its side, used it for homeplate, and I'd make the catch and rear back, and I got so I could hit that tub on the first or second bounce about nine times out of ten. You know what the difference is between the Bigs and the minors?" Stan waits only one beat, not expecting an answer. "Consistency. The whole thing is consistency. There are players in the minors who make spectacular plays and hit the ball just as hard as in the majors, but the guys in the Bigs are more consistent. They make the plays not just nine out of ten times but ninety-nine times out of a hundred." He pauses thoughtfully for a moment. "You know, I'd hit nine out of ten, but that other one might end up thirty feet down the line, or hit the barn door fifteen feet in the air, making a sound like a gun going off. Hey, Jackie, how about you come out and hit me some flies in the morning?"

2.

When we got home after the game I kissed Sunny gently and pulled her against me. Her lips were dry and she made them thin and did not return my kiss. I did everything I could think of to please her. I touched her with my fingertips, gently undressed her, massaged her, fondled her, loved her with my hands, my tongue, held back my own passion, waited for a response from her, received none.

I remember once, at a time like this, when Sunny was in one of her moods, she said something bitter, something designed to make me hate her.

"Can't you tell by the way I touch you that I love you?" I said.

"No," said Sunny, precipitating a long silence.

Eventually I made love with her. Actually I made love to her, not with her. Her body was unpliant, mannequin-like. I wanted so desperately to arouse her, I controlled myself carefully, rocked her so gently for a long time until our bodies were slick and delicious.

"Can't you finish up," Sunny said, not even in a whisper. "I'm tired."

If she knew how close I came to killing her it would have made her happy.

I threw myself off her without a word and lay like a rock in the darkness, my body taut, nerve ends twitching. Late in the night I heard her leave. I woke to the tinkling of hangers in our closet, knew she was packing a few blouses, a couple of pairs of jeans in the same battered black suitcase she arrived with twelve years ago. I lay, tense as piano wire, afraid to speak, afraid not to. She closed the front door quietly; I listened to her tiny footsteps descend the stairs, fade away as she moved down the sidewalk. Where does she go? How does she get there? There are no buses, no traffic. I suppose she walks to the interstate, stands at the side of the road...I can hear the sinister hiss of air-brakes as a truck pulls over.

I recall a night many years ago, when I ran out of a restaurant after her, frantic that I might never see her again. I recall the face of a man in a Tennessee pick-up truck. I don't suppose he was over thirty-five, although he looked old to me. I'll never forget the uncomprehending look of loss and pain on his face. I've seen that look many times since. My reflection wears it like a tragic mask.

3.

I met Sunny twelve years ago, at the restaurant in Iowa City where I worked part-time. She came in accompanied by a large rumpled-looking man who was dressed in a blue pin-stripe suit. He was tall and cadaverous and it was impossible to guess their relationship. He might have been father, husband, lover, brother. As they crossed the dining room she trailed after him, a waif covered in a feathery-grey calf-length dress of some material that seemed to attach itself to her, as if both she and the cloth were charged with static electricity.

Her chest was flat, her dark hair hacked in a boyish cut; her lips were thin and when she did open her mouth there were spaces between each of her teeth. She took a crumpled pack of Winston's from a very used-looking handbag that had once been black leather. The man ignored her as she searched the tiny purse until she found a book of matches. She squinted her left eye to keep the smoke at bay, drew deeply on the cigarette, licked her lower lip with a cat-pink tongue.

By the time I approached their table to ask if I could get them anything from the bar, I was in love. Sunny was hunched over the table smoking as if she expected to be arrested for it. Her eyes were brilliant, the irises an orchid-violet, floating in whites pure as snow. I tried to imagine my tongue bringing her tiny nipples erect. I wanted to taste her mouth, feel her tongue exploring my teeth. She might have been fifteen; she might have been thirty. It didn't matter.

All through the meal I circled their table like a hawk, replenishing their water, coffee, lighting Sunny's cigarettes, asking again and again if the meal was satisfactory. The man had a deep voice with a strong southern accent; Sunny's voice was breathy in a peculiar sort of way, as if she were acting, speaking in a voice not entirely her own. They talked very little. I eavesdropped on every word, ignoring my other tables. In spite of my attentiveness I was unable to learn her name, their business, or their relationship.

In desperation I followed them to the parking lot as they left the restaurant, tearing off my apron, grabbing my jacket from the pronged chrome hanger next to the bar. They got in a faded red pick-up truck with Tennessee licence plates. I memorized the number – in fact I still remember it, PNT-791 – and I stood helplessly as they pulled away, envisioning myself writing to Motor Vehicle Registration in Nashville to obtain a name and an address. To my immense relief the truck simply pulled across the street and stopped in the parking lot of the Evangelical Christian Church. The man got out, lumbered toward a side door, and disappeared inside.

As I walked up to the passenger side of the truck Sunny glanced at me. I motioned for her to roll down the window, which she did.

"You're very beautiful," I said.

She looked at me, really looked at me for the first time; I prayed she'd like what she saw. She smiled then and I could tell it was involuntary. I bet I'm the first person who's ever told her she's beautiful, I thought. And she was, to me, in that magic way no one can explain. Her nose was too flat, and her hair looked like she cut it herself to spite someone. She was covered in freckles, even her fingers were freckled. And I smiled at her as if I were witnessing a miracle, and recalled how, when she brushed past me as she entered the restaurant, I got the first whiff of her, a tangy sweetness, not of perfume but of her. And I could feel my tongue rearranging the freckles on her neck, her breasts, her belly. And the feeling has never left me, will never leave me; the breathlessness, the tightness in my chest when Sunny enters a room. The desire that makes my knees weak. The love that makes me able to endure the way she tortures me.

Sunny is one of those women who comes and goes. Whatever demons she wrestles with require that she be on the move a good part of her life. She vanishes for days, weeks, months, then returns as mysteriously as she leaves. It is like she is alternately plucked from my life, and parachuted back into it.

4.

She eventually climbed down out of the truck. Reaching over the tail-gate she heaved out a small, black, overnight bag. We stood talking for a while. I babbled nervously about my job, about the big old house, ten miles away in Onamata, where I lived alone, about my interest in baseball history. I told her of my plan to do a master's thesis on the history of the Iowa Baseball Confederacy, a semi-pro league that existed in Eastern Iowa shortly after the turn of the century. I didn't realize at the time that she told me nothing.

"Can I buy you a drink?" I finally said, waving vaguely toward the restaurant, toward the rest of the town. "That is if you're old enough to..."

"I'm old enough to do anything," said Sunny. And I think, under her breath, she added, "And I have." But I was never sure.

Just as we were leaving the truck, the side door of the church opened and the truck-owner stepped outside. I didn't know what was expected of me. Sunny seemed willing to continue right on. I stopped, turned my head in the direction of the man, who held-up suddenly, making a skidding sound on the gravel.

Sunny turned and waved, a cheery, impersonal gesture. "Thanks for the ride," she said, "maybe I'll see you around."

The man raised a hand, not waving but a gesture as if he were reaching out for her. Then he joined his two large, helpless hands together at the belt-level. He didn't speak but his gesture and his stricken face said more than he intended. We continued across the street and toward downtown. Sunny never looked back; I glanced over my shoulder once, the man was standing in the same position.

"There's an old bar called Donnelly's," I said. "Dark wood and dark mirrors, you'll like it."

"First thing I want is to hit the john and get rid of this," Sunny said, running her hands down the slippery, clinging material of her dress. "This was his idea, said it makes me look Amish or something."

5.

I shouldn't allow her to come back each time as if nothing has happened. I should be angry. I should curse and scream and punish. Each time I am alone I promise myself I won't take her back. If I do there will be conditions, perhaps even written down, a contract.

But then a car stops on the gravel deep in the night. A door slams. There is a long silence. I picture her standing, small as a child in the darkness, psyching herself up for what she is about to do. Then comes the crunch of her small steps on the gravel; the door opens. Silence while her eyes get used to the dark.

At the bedroom door: "Jack?" She is smoking a cigarette.

"Over here." She bumps a table, finds the ashtray on it. I always keep one there, although I have never smoked. There is a tiny crackling as she puts out her cigarette. She takes off her jacket and tosses it on the floor. Her arms go up in a supple motion and her tee-shirt skids over her head. She kicks one boot off with the help of the other, bends and dispatches the second one. My desire for her is so wild I feel as if I'm all liquid. I can smell her; the tart, sweet scent of her sweat. The odour of a car interior. I grab the waist of her jeans, pull her toward me until she stands at the edge of the bed. Her nipples are like hard candy. The musky, smokey taste of her fills my senses. Her mouth finds mine. Her tongue is like a bird set free. She tastes faintly of whiskey.

"Fantasy Land," I say, tossing back the covers, pulling her down on top of me.

6.

There was never any question about her coming home with me that first night. We sat in Donnelly's for a while. I talked, Sunny studied me, eyeing me as if she were figuring some kind of odds, trying to guess how I would react to her secrets. She pursed her lips each time she laughed, making laughter seem a gesture of self-control.

At the bar, Sunny fished her clothes from her small bag, disappeared to the washroom, emerged in jeans, a white blouse, a tattered denim jacket faded to the colour of skim milk. She returned from the washroom empty-handed, the dress nowhere to be seen, "I have more lives than a cat," she said in reply to my questioning look. "I just used one of them up."

"You'll need a dress to get married in," I said.

"You mean that, don't you?" she said, crinkling her nose, her violet eyes measuring me again.

"I mean it," I said.

"Then you'll have to buy me another one."

Later, as I stopped the car in front of my home, I turned to Sunny where she sat, her thigh touching mine. "You wear your clothes as though you want to be helped out of them," I whispered, my fingers unbuttoning a button on her blouse. Suddenly, Sunny grabbed onto me fiercely, her mouth melting into mine. She held me as if her life depended on getting closer to me than anyone had ever been.

My passion was so complete it was more than enough for both of us. She loved the house; my tall, square, white-painted house. Sixty years old, its green shutters the colour of spring leaves, solid, permanent, an anchor, a rock, a root. Sunny explored it the next morning, tentatively, poking her head into each room before allowing her body to follow. The floors of the bedrooms and living room were a sunshine yellow; the rooms smelled subtly of wax, of dust, of old upholstery.

"Do you like it?" I asked.

"It's like a fairy tale. You're sure it's yours?"

"It can be yours too. I need to share this with someone." I put my arm tightly around her waist.

"This is really yours? I mean, I've dreamed of a big, solid home like this. If I drew a picture of the house I've dreamed about this would be it. And it's really yours? You're so young. Your parents aren't coming home next week from somewhere?"

"My father's dead. I have a mother in Chicago, who's married to a very rich man. And a sister who blows up buildings."

"Really?"

"Everyone should have an outlaw for a sister," I said.

7.

I've always felt that Sunny's biggest quarrel with me is that I haven't treated her as badly as she thinks I should.

"I'm trouble," she said in the sweet darkness of my bedroom. "Don't say I didn't warn you."

"I'm warned," I said.

"I'm a little like smoke," Sunny said. "There isn't a door I can't get under, or over, or through, or around."

"I'll take my chances," I said.

8.

For two years, while Sunny was gone, I even tried dating. I hung around the University of Iowa Bookstore, a bar called the Airliner that was frequented by students, a restaurant known as Bushnell's Turtle. But the girls I met, just as they were ten years before, were either too young, too silly, or too serious. I hate dewy-eyed girls talking about meaningful relationships; I hate perfumes, deodorants, hair-sprays, sweaters and bras and knitted dresses, manicured nails, cosmetics, loud music, football pennants, stuffed animals, and vegetarian dishes. Each one I met was so eager and so inexperienced. I talked a lot about Sunny.

9.

"I've done things that would curl your hair," Sunny said to me once in the warmth of our bed. She had just returned from a two-month absence.

"Don't tantalize me," I said fiercely. "If you want to tell me, tell me. If you don't, shut up. There's nothing you can tell me that will change how I feel about you."

"Maybe I should try?"

"Sunny, whatever it is you want, I won't do it. I won't punish you. I won't abandon you. I won't send you away. I refuse to cage you. You have to stay with me because you love me."

10.

I didn't fully realize it, until I stood staring into the half-empty closet the morning after Sunny left me for the first time, but my mother was another one of those women who come and go. I suddenly remembered my father rambling through empty rooms of this same house, stopping to stare into the same half-empty closet, shaking his head in disbelief, then going into his study and staying there for days. It is the same study where I have spent half my life pursuing the same elusive dream my father was never able to capture. The dream of the Iowa Baseball Confederacy. My father was not an easy man to live with. I always felt that my mother had some justification for her extended absences. Perhaps I have not been so easy to live with. Living with someone who is chasing a dream, like running after a butterfly across an endless meadow, a dream no one else sees or understands must be difficult.

Well, my father and I shared not only the dream, but he must have passed me something else through his genes: a fatal fascination for transient women.

11.

I remember a conversation I had with Gloria last week in Iowa City; I bumped into her on Dubuque Street and we walked over to Pearson's Drug Store for malts. Tall chocolate malts, thick as cement, served in perspiring glasses.

"Geez, Jack, you understand Stan better than anybody, maybe even me," Gloria said. "He looks up to you. If you could hear him talk about you all the time; he wishes he had your intellectual ability. He'd like to be able to read and understand things the way you do, you know. I bet Stan's never told you, but two summers ago, the year he turned thirty-four, I talked him into retiring."

"No, he didn't," I said.

"We'd wintered in South Carolina. He got a job in a warehouse; we had a nice apartment; I started thinking about getting pregnant. It was really nice, Stan home every night, me being able to cook supper for him, you know. And Stan was adjusting. He really was. He was nervous as a coyote in a pen but he was getting by. Then him and a couple of guys from work hooked up with a softball team. The league started in late April and at first I figured it wasn't such a bad idea. He could still play, you know, and I figured he wouldn't miss the game so much. The team was sponsored by Red Ryder's Pizza Parlor. The uniform-jerseys were cardinal-red, made of slippery material, with the silhouette of a square-jawed cowboy on the back where the numbers should have been.

"Oh God, Jack, it was sad to watch him. I mean he was the star of the team; he hit about .500 and they hardly ever lost. But it wasn't baseball and it didn't mean anything to him. The guys would all go back to Red Ryder's after a game and the owner would give them all the pizza they could eat and all the beer they could drink. After six weeks Stan was starting to develop a paunch on him.

"About the first of June he came home from work one evening and he was sitting on the edge of the bed putting his jersey on. I couldn't stand watching him no more; I reached over and I stopped him from pulling that slippery cloth down over his head. I grabbed hold of it, peeled it off him, tossed it into a corner, and leaned down and kissed him. I never seen Stan smile so hard, except when I said I'd marry him. I thought his face was gonna bust. 'Glory,' he said, 'I hear there's a Class B team down around Tidewater in a bad way for players. I think they might be glad to see a veteran outfielder...'

"And I says, 'I'm with you,' and next morning we were packed and heading south."

"He'll always get by, Gloria, as long as he's got you," and I reached down the counter and squeezed her hand.

"But I don't know what I'm gonna do, Jack. He was batting .220 and playing hurt, and his legs are gone. He was never fast but now he's like a big bear in the outfield. The fans boo him when he can't get to a long ball or a Texas leaguer."

"I'll do what I can," I told her. "But take care of him. He needs you."

"How are you and Sunny doing?" Gloria asked.

"Not very well, I'm afraid."

"She's been awful quiet; she looks down."

"She'll be gone again soon."

"I'm sorry, Jack."

"There's nothing anybody can do. She'll go and she'll come back. She'll be changed ever so subtly, like a piece of furniture that's been shipped across the country one more time. And I'll get a little more eccentric while she's gone. I'll haunt the University Library, do some more research on the Iowa Baseball Confederacy; the more my ideas are ridiculed the more stubborn I get, Gloria. Did I tell you I'm thinking of building an addition onto the front of the house – sort of a geodesic dome in the shape of a baseball?"

Gloria takes her lips away from the straw in her malt; she lifts her eyebrows; there is genuine concern in her eyes.

"When you have the name you might as well have the game. The university people, the baseball people, they all think I'm crazy to keep on pursuing the confederacy. The people in Onamata are worse; they don't know about the confederacy. They say, 'Jack Clarke's spent most of his life on some crazy research project. Something to do with baseball. Jack Clarke lives all alone in that big old house. Plays the piano at night and takes odd jobs when I hear he's got more money in the bank than he could spend in two lifetimes.' That's what they say, Gloria. That and, 'Jack Clarke had a wife and couldn't keep her.'"

12.

I got up early, left my empty house, spent all day in the University of Iowa library doing little research, sitting silent, dreaming of Sunny.

As I open the door to my house, smells of abandonment rush past me like bats. Though it is nearly July the air that meets my face is cold as a meat locker. Without Sunny, I don't think I will ever be able to live in these drafty rooms again. I close the door. The screen door makes a sharp snap. I need at least two doors between me and Sunny's memories and odours. In the fresh, moist warmth of the Iowa night I bed down on the cushions of the wide, white-painted porch swing.

Footfalls on the sidewalk and front steps awaken me. A dark silhouette stands before the front door, hand poised to knock.

"I'm over here, Stan," I whisper.

Stan starts as if someone has walked over his grave, throws his head back in a gesture of surprise.

"My god, you scared me, Jack. I was trying to decide how hard to knock."

I ease myself to a sitting position. The swing slices back and forth, cutting air. "Is it late?"

"Very," says Stan. "I can't sleep. Why are you out..."

"Sunny's gone again," I say.

"I'm sorry, Jack. I know how much you care."

I nod. The porch and yard are silvered by moonlight.

"Makes my problem seen pretty small, I guess." Stan goes on. "A telegram arrived at the house last night. I told the club there was no phone there – I couldn't stand the thought of some secretary phoning to tell me I'd been cut."

"Is that what the telegr..."

"I haven't opened it. Gloria went to bed mad. I wouldn't let her open it either. Gloria's old lady looks at me with her lips all sewn shut...like I was something in a zoo."

"Do you want me to be there when you open it?"

"I don't know what I want. It was just laying there like a death sentence on that walnut-wood table in the front hall. Geez, but that's a depressing place, that hall. You seen that table, it's covered with a linen runner, with coloured tatting all around the edges. The baseboards are enamelled black and about a foot tall, and the newel post is black and shiny as a skull. I wanted to turn and run. I don't run from many things, Jackie, you know that. The telegram just lay there on the linen runner like a yellow stain, evil, liquid, changing shape. Gloria's old lady was standing there, her hands clasped in front of her, her hair pulled back until her eyes bugged out.

"'For goodness sakes open it,' Gloria said. But I wouldn't touch it or let her touch it. I mean I *know* what's in it, Jackie. I'm not dumb. There was something rotten in the air when they put me on the disabled list. The manager had a crafty look about him. I'm thirty-six years old, and I been playing hurt. I've been released. I know it."

"Maybe it's not..."

"I *know*," Stan says emphatically. "You understand better than anybody, Jack. I need to go for a walk, or a drive. I want you to come with me."

"Okay," I say.

"Man, you should have come to our place when you found Sunny was gone. You shouldn't be alone."

"Let's go," I say, standing up. The arc of the swing lessens until it is barely trembling.

"It's not fair," Stan says, as we make our way down the silent, leafy streets, the air slightly sweet from the last lilacs of the season.

"What isn't?" I reply.

"I want to go into Iowa City," Stan says. "My car's just around the corner. I parked there a while ago and tried to walk it off, the way I do when I take a foul-tip on the shin. But it didn't work."

We try to close the doors quietly. We are probably the only people awake in the whole town of Onamata.

"This cast is supposed to stay on for ten more days," he says, banging the white plaster against the steering wheel as he turns the car out onto the silent, bluey highway. "But I bet I could get it off in seven if I concentrated. You heal faster if you concentrate all your energy on the sore part of your body, did you know that?"

"No."

"Well, you can. A week and I'll be good as new. It was unfair as hell for them to let me go instead of letting me work my way back from the disabled list. I've still got a few good years left in me. I might still make it to the majors. I know I'll never be a starter, but I could still be a utility man, fill in a game here and a game there, pinch hit once in a while, play defence in the late innings. I've still got a few years left in me, haven't I, Jackie? Thirty-six ain't too old, is it?"

"It's not too old," I say. I look in the rear-view mirror expecting to see Gloria's form in the back seat, the glow of Sunny's cigarette.

"You know, yesterday, when I went into Iowa City, I went to see Gloria's brother, Dmetro, went down to the railroad yard and he showed me around. I only did it to please Gloria and her old lady. Dmetro's a checker there in the yards. I'm not sure what he really does – they don't let him touch the switches or nothing like that – he has a chart and a clipboard and I think he makes sure the right cars are on the right trains. He started that job the day after he turned fifteen. His old man made him quit school and got him that job. Made Gloria quit on her fifteenth birthday too, but she went back after she got out on her own. Her old man worked for forty-nine years for the flour mill; he died six months after they retired him. Dmetro's my age; he's got a job for life. He'll never get laid off or bumped or anything. I guess he's happy. 'I can do my job in my sleep,' he says. 'I don't have to think or nothing.'"

I want to say something to comfort Stan, but the right words are elusive. Instead, I gesture helplessly with my hands.

"Dmetro offered to get me a job there. Did I tell you that? Gloria wants me to take it. I mean the three of them set it up. They think I'm so dumb I don't know. I'd be a kind of gofer to start with, working the midnight shift, not very steady at all." Stan pauses, looks over at me.

"You know, Jack," he goes on, "last week I drove up to the stadium in Iowa City, I was running in the outfield, doing stretching exercises on the grass, stuff like that, when I happened to look up at the sky. There were little white puffs of cloud all across it, like a cat stepped in milk and then walked across the blue. I thought it was so beautiful I told Dmetro about it. He just stared at me. 'I ain't looked at the sky in ten years,' he said. I believed him." Stan guides the car with the tips of the fingers that peek from the white cast and slaps his other meaty hand on the dashboard.

"There was something else too, something that really bothered me, Jackie. Dmetro was telling me the names of the spur lines, the dead-end tracks where they store boxcars or move them in and out of the yards. There was the Exxon Spur, the Texaco Spur, and the Miller Spur that runs right down to the brewery. There was the Ice House Spur from when they used to cut ice from the Iowa River and store it in sawdust. Then there was a spur out at the edge of the yard that had ties piled across it. Dmetro told me they use that one to store broken boxcars. He didn't name it at all, but later he spotted a boxcar with a cracked wheel and said it would have to be moved to the Baseball Spur."

"Where's that?" I asked, pricking up my ears.

"Back in the old days, according to Dmetro, the Baseball Spur used to run out of town for a mile or more to a ballpark. On

Saturday and Sunday afternoons whole families used to get dressed up and pack picnic lunches and catch the train out to the baseball game. His old man said there used to be two trips both ways. He remembered it, though he never went himself. But they tore down the grandstand back in the twenties, and the railroad figured it was cheaper to let the roadbed rot than to tear up the tracks. Some junk dealer eventually made off with most of the steel, but the track still runs a few hundred yards, and you could still follow the roadbed if you really tried. All that's used of the Baseball Spur now is the hundred yards or so inside the railroad yard."

Stan eases the car to a stop on a dark side street not far from the railroad yard. Again, we are both careful as we close the doors.

"Hey, Jackie," Stan says in a voice too loud for the night. "Remember how in high school I spotted that the West Branch pitcher stood a certain way on the rubber when he was gonna throw a curve?"

"I remember," I say.

"And I wouldn't tell anybody else what I knew – just you and me?"

"I remember."

"'If I stand with a bat on my right shoulder, it's gonna be a curve,' I told you. You whacked a triple to deep centre."

"The only triple I ever hit," I say.

"Yeah, you were never much with the bat, were you? Well, he got two quick strikes on me before I saw him set his foot in a certain position. I took a deep breath and waited. The ball was still rising when it cleared the fence, and those two runs put the game right out of reach."

The railroad yards loom in front of us as we top a rise: acres of boxcars, and bluey ribbons of track criss-crossing like tangles of wool.

"Is this where we're going?" I ask.

"Yeah, I want you to see this place, Jackie."

In the yard, outdoor lights sway slightly, casting long, eerie shadows. The roundhouse hulks in front of us, high as a grain elevator. There are men in coveralls scurrying about, the air is steely-smelling, full of grease and hot metal. Bright blue stars from welding torches bloom in the yellowish light. The door of the roundhouse gapes wide. Inside there are figures in white tee-shirts climbing like ants over a tall black engine. No one pays any attention to us.

"We fit right in," Stan says.

He's right. We are both wearing white cotton tee-shirts and jeans. A row of picks and sledge-hammers lean haphazardly against the corrugated metal wall of a shed. Stan stoops, picks up a sledge-hammer, hoists it on his shoulder like a bat. I bend and pick one up. It is heavier than I imagined.

"The Baseball Spur is way back here," Stan says, pointing between two dark rows of boxcars.

There are two cars on the spur, each with a wheel partially broken away, the fractured surface of each bright as a new coin. We amble past the damaged boxcars, walk between the rails where ankle-high grass heavy with dew wets our shoes and cuffs.

"This feels good," Stan says, hefting the sledge and moving into a batting crouch. "Rogalski in the on-deck circle," he announces. "Rogalski beat out Dave Winfield for the centrefield spot on the Yankees. 'It's a shame to have a player of Winfield's calibre sitting on the bench,' the Yankee manager said, 'but Rogalski's just too good.'"

We come to the edge of the railroad yards and the end of the Baseball Spur. There is a barricade across the tracks, consisting of a sturdy six-by-eight driven spike-like into the roadbed on each side of the track, then five ties stacked across the tracks and bolted at each end to the six-by-eights. I walk behind the barricade where the spur passes into a tangle of raspberry canes, willows, and saplings. In the distance I see a tiny scratch of silver where wind and snow have scrubbed the rust away. A moonbeam touches down on it like a wand and it shimmers bright as a needle in the creamy warmth of the Iowa night.

"See, what did I tell you. It's here just like I said it was. Think about all the history here, Jackie. Doesn't it just make you tingle. Like the first time I knew a girl was gonna let me put my hand down her blouse," and Stan grins wildly, his face turned up toward the moonlight.

"Hey, Jackie, do you remember how when we were kids there used to be ads on the backs of comic books and sports magazines. I don't remember who sponsored them, but they were for groups – you know, churches and boy scouts and things like that. They wanted to see who could sell the most salve, or Christmas cards, or wrapping paper. And the grand prize for the group that sold the most was a baseball field. They claimed they'd come out to your town and build you a baseball field, you know, level it, sod it, put up a backstop, I don't know if they built an outfield fence or not. But they always showed a picture on the back of the magazine with new bases sitting out there white as Leghorn hens and the grass an unreal green, a heavenly green, and the whole field covered in kids wearing red-and-white uniforms. You know what I always dreamed, Jackie? That I was a charity, or a church group, and I sold the most stuff, and they came and built me a baseball field."

I'd like to step around the barricade and hug Stan, if men did that sort of thing, and tell him I understand his fears, and how trapped he feels, and that I appreciate his dreams, and have had a few of my own. But it's better not to be aware of too many of the workings of the world. My curse is that I understand too much, at least about Sunny. It's better to be like Stan, to be continually amazed. Stan is always amazed by what happens to him, but not surprised. I'm still surprised by life, and I know that isn't good.

The barricade across the Baseball Spur has been put there to stop any boxcar that might manage to coast that far. Stan and I grin at each other as if we've just completed a double steal. The moon is so bright that the yards look almost beautiful in the distance. The tracks are blue and silver and gold, while only feet away they are coated in rust and disappear into weeds and wild grass. There is just a hint of ground mist in the ditches and there are mosquitoes purring about my face.

Stan squares his shoulders, takes the sledge and swings it back sideways as if he were ringing a gong, and brings it forward landing a mighty blow to one of the ties. The barricade barely budges. But Stan swings again and again, chipping the ties, splintering them, breaking them away from the blue-headed bolts. He sets down the hammer and lifts the broken ties one by one and tosses them into the ditch. Each time a little puff of coolness, sweet with the odours of grass, rises and envelops us.

GARY HYLAND

* * * * * * *

Saskatchewan poet and editor Gary Hyland lives in Moose Jaw, where he teaches high-school English. A former publisher and founding member of Thunder Creek Publishing Co-operative, he is the author of a number of poetry books, including Just off Main *(1982) and* After Atlantis *(1991). He has also co-edited four anthologies for Coteau Books. "Casey and Me" originally appeared in* 100% Cracked Wheat *(1983) edited by Robert Currie, Gary Hyland, and James S. McLean. The poem was later reprinted in Hyland's 1984 collection* Street of Dreams.

Asked about his baseball experiences, Hyland writes, "Although I played catcher and second base in four local leagues, I was never all-star material, batting somewhere around .240 and throwing somewhere around the intended target. I later coached Little League and played two glorious games on Eli Mandel's 1977 Fort San Poet-Kings fastball team [see Robert Currie's story about the team elsewhere in the anthology]. My love of baseball began with bubblegum cards, sports magazines and World Series broadcasts in the early fifties. I have never forgiven the Powers-That-Be for moving the Dodgers out of Brooklyn, root for the White Sox and Expos, and dream of making a comeback."

* * * * * * *

Me And Casey

In one of my dreams Casey Stengel has a dream
the night before the seventh game
of another Yankee-Dodger series
when he is sleeping more off than on
yet dreaming of the bottom of the ninth
with the Bums one run ahead
but Rizzuto safe on second
two out and Lopat the chucker
set to bat.
                    Ol' Case spits in the dirt
and scans the bench for a saviour-slugger:
Bauer's been used, Henrich looks tired
Woodling's got a swollen wrist
(Oh God for just halfa DiMaggio)
then he spots the Canadian kid
the rawest of rookies up from K.C.
reading Steinbeck at the end of the bench
and a flash of scientific instinct
tells him the kid is ready to go,
"Hyland," he snaps, "get in there and hit."
That's all.
                    I've been waiting for this.
I grab my special bat, disdain warm-ups,
and wriggle into my stance in the box.
HYLAND BATTING FOR LOPAT says the P.A.
The stadium graveyards into silence
the reporters rifle roster sheets.
On the mound ol' Preacher Roe grins.
I see him lifting his right leg,
suddenly his long left arm uncoils
something slaps behind me. "Stee-rike unh,"
roars the umpire. Caught winking.

I concentrate on the left hand
tucked in the glove over his head
and this time follow the blur all the way
a smoking waist-high plate-splitter
but just below my home-run plane
so I pass and the umpire booms,
"Stee-rike tew." Then Berra saves my life
grabbing Case as he steams towards me
with the leaded warm-up bat.
"Hit them strikes, you one-eyed frog," he yells
as they bump him down the dugout steps.

Preacher he just grins like he's found
the partridge patch of his dreams
and I know I have him lulled,
then he cranks up and lets fly
a fat chest-high change-of-pace
right where I can skin it bald.
I gather my weight at the very edge
of my balance point, the crowd cranes,
Casey stops chewing, the ball floats in.
I step out releasing easy power
and miss it by the width of the bat.

Casey convulses on the dugout floor
then wakes in a sweaty twist of sheets
and there I sit cheshired on his bedpost
in my Jackie Robinson T-shirt.

When he shoots I climb down from my dream
like the beanstalk boy still grinning, still grinning.

WILLIAM KLEBECK

* * * * * * *

William Klebeck lives in Wynyard, Saskatchewan. He has contributed fiction to a variety of periodicals, including Prism, Grain, *and* Canadian Fiction Magazine. *His first book of short fiction,* Where the Rain Ends, *was published in 1990. He has just completed work on a second collection,* Run Toward the Horizon. *"Picnic" is a revised version of the story "Playing Ball," which originally appeared in the anthology* More Saskatchewan Gold *(1984) edited by Geoffrey Ursell.*

"Having grown up in rural Saskatchewan," writes Klebeck, "most of my baseball experience was gained playing scrub at school, playing some organized minor ball for short spring seasons before school let out and, later, playing some senior fastball, usually at small town tournaments on sun-baked Sundays. Now I'm content just to watch the pros on TV, always looking forward to the play at home plate."

* * * * * * *

PICNIC

Clutch

Yuktum Boogie's cruising up Main when I stop him in front of the Post Office. It's a muggy Friday evening in July, a beer-drinking night if ever we needed one. "Hey Yuktum," I say, leaning out the window of my Charger. Cathy Cathcart is with him. I tug my Expo cap and press my left arm – which is hanging out the window – hard against the side of my car to make my bicep look bigger.

"Hey Clutch," Yuktum yells above his perking Merc. "What's up?"

"Wanna play some ball?"

Yuktum knows me, that I'm not nicknamed Clutch because of my abilities on a ball diamond, so I quickly tell him my father, being the entry man, just got notified Naicam was withdrawing from the two-day Co-op Picnic set to go tomorrow at the lake, leaving only fifteen teams in the fastball tournament. There are enough of us High School boys around this summer who aren't playing senior ball, and there won't be any entry fee, Naicam having already forfeited. I figure we should field a team.

Jerry Hoevig and Michael Povey drive up behind Yuktum in Jerry's old Valiant.

"I dunno," Yuktum says. "We'll get blown away."

"I talked to Rudy and Eugene already. They're over at the Liquor Store right now, waiting to see how many guys we can get."

The Myksymytz boys' Bronco is parked in the paved lot of the new government Liquor Store at the end of Main Street. "I dunno," he says, turning to Cathy beside him.

"Party time," I say. We all know how Yuktum Boogie got his name.

"If Eugene's arm holds up," he says, "maybe we'd even win a game or two."

"Meet you at the Liquor Store." I let the clutch out and my new Charger, the car my old man bought me two months ago for graduation, idles forward easy as a boat on calm water. "Hey Jerry," I say, pulling up next to his Valiant. "What you boys up to this weekend?"

Our infield would be pretty solid up the middle with Mike and Jerry. Povey played second base on both our baseball and softball teams this spring, has a sure glove, hot and cold with the bat. Jerry Hoevig plays short or third – when he plays. He isn't as good a ball player as he thinks but, if he took the game seriously, probably could be. He's too busy trying to show the gearshift of his Valiant to as many girls as he can.

Jerry and Michael have nothing better to do this weekend.

I've rounded up seven players, including myself as a fielder, when I coast into the lot of the Liquor Store. Rudy and Eugene Myksymytz, our pitchers, are strong Ukrainian boys from south of town. Eugene, a year younger, has better stuff but they're both good athletes, play all sports intensely. They're leaning against their Bronco, talking with Yuktum, Cathy and Boris Kluzak whose '59 finned Chevy is parked next.

"Clutch Kemp," says Rudy.

"Chucker buddy," I say, sauntering over.

"I can get my old man's camper-trailer," Boris says, his blue eyes bulgy through lenses the thickness of magnifying glasses. He's our catcher, can't see far enough to play field.

"Great." That means we're looking at an over-nighter.

"In case we have to play Sunday."

"We'll have to win a game if you want to play Sunday," Eugene says.

"We got to get enough players first," his brother Rudy says, "before we do anything."

"Jerry and Mike are going to play," I tell them. "We only need two more."

Walter Neugebauer and Wayne Hunter drive by on their way to the poolhall. I wave and Wayne cranks his old man's Ford pick-up across the double line into the lot. Wayne Hunter is a farmer's son who, every time he does something physical, pushes his muscular body to the limit. Our clean-up man. Noagie's a long-haired druggie who wears tie-dyed T-shirts.

You know whoever's with him is usually in the same shape he's in. With enough smoke, Noagie could probably be persuaded to take right field.

We're all trying to decide where to go drinking when Jerry and Mike cruise in. "Looks like we got a team." Michael jerks his thumb towards a twenty-four pack of Pilsner in the back seat.

"We should buy as much beer as we can tonight," I say. "We play Hudson Bay at ten-thirty and we don't want to have to come back to town for beer tomorrow."

We pool our money, pick up thirteen more cases of Pil, one of OV, and meet out at Pumphouse Hill four miles southeast of town. We sit on the hoods of our vehicles, tipping back beer. Michael Povey, always thinking, wonders out loud who has a cooler so we can keep the beer cold. Jerry says his father will probably let him take the six-man tent they have down in their basement. With that and Kluzak's camper-trailer, we'll have lots of room to crash. Boris says we can all go in his car. It'll be a little crowded but what the hey, we're a team, right, got to travel together.

When Yuktum arrives, after dropping Cathy off at her sister's, we get around to weighing our chances. "If we win a couple games," Mike says, "could be in the money."

"Don't count your chickens, Povey," Rudy says. "They offer a thousand dollar first prize, they get some good teams."

"Yeah," I say. "Swan River's coming down. Hudson Bay, Perigord, a couple teams from Yorkton, one from Regina."

"If you can go a game, Rudy," Jerry says, "and Eugene's arm holds up a game, game and a half, never know."

"My arm's strong," says Eugene, flexing. "We got a good chance."

"If we're going to be playing ball tomorrow..." Rudy drains his beer, then slaps a mosquito on his wrist and looks at his brother.

"Have another beer," Yuktum says.

"Bugs are coming out," Eugene says, sliding down off the hood of the Bronco. They drive away, Rudy waving and shouting, "Ball tomorrow, boys!" We raise our beers and watch their dust trail away.

Rudy Myksymytz

"Povey's right, you know," Eugene says, sitting at the kitchen table, mopping up runny eggs with toast, "two wins are all we need to get in the money. Win the first two, or lose one and win the next two."

My little brother is always so goddamn optimistic. The Co-op Picnic and Gymkhana draws in some good hungry teams.

"We got the makings of a good team," he says.

I've been thinking about that. Whether we do anything or not will depend on our arms, mine and Eugene's. If we can keep our stuff for a few innings, we can be tough, though once we've both lost it, there's no back-up.

As for the rest of them, Kluzak's steady behind the plate; Yuktum's got a snag glove on first; Povey and Hoevig are tight up the middle. The two liabilities are Clutch and Noagie. We'll have to put Hunter in centre field between them; he can roam out there and try to cover up.

Hitting-wise, who knows? Hunter and I should be good for a couple hits a game but the others, it's hard to say.

I'm standing at the kitchen counter, eating peanut-butter and toast, when I see through the window over the sink Kluzak's Chevy drive into our farmyard, the Scamper camper-trailer snaking behind. Looks like he's already picked up the rest of the team, judging by all the hands waving out from the car's open windows.

"C'mon," I grab my glove off the counter. "They're here."

I crawl into the front seat overtop Povey and Hoevig and Eugene somehow crowds into the back. From the sounds and smells filling up Kluzak's car as we head down the highway to the lake, there's no doubt some of the boys gave 'er last night. But there's a lot of enthusiasm in their burnt-out bodies, and we're all hooting and hollering, shouting out the chorus to The Kid is Hot Tonight when it comes on the radio. Then I smell the pot. Noagie's lit a joint and I get the feeling our time on the ball-field today is going to be short and ugly.

When we get to the campsite at Milligan Beach, Noagie spends fifteen minutes running around looking for a hammer while Hunter and I pound the plastic tent pegs into the ground with a bat. After we're set up Yuktum cracks everyone a beer, for good luck.

We walk over to the ball diamonds shortly before ten-thirty. Hudson Bay look like what I expected: large beerbelly loggers on small spiked feet, wearing white uniforms with pin-stripes that make them look even bigger. They all wear their caps low so the peaks shade their eyes, but not low enough to hide their contempt when they see us take to the field for warm-up in blue-jeans and T-shirts.

Their pitcher doesn't look like much, a tall lanky guy with a peachfuzz moustache and the top of his trousers bunched together around his waist with a narrow belt, its long black tongue snapping like a whip with every pitch. But he steps off the rubber with a windmill wind-up and shoots from the hip. We can't hit him, all of us swinging in a swish of air underneath his rising fastball. The first time up I strike out in four pitches. The second time I dig in right at the front of the batter's box, hoping to chop the fastball before it takes off, but it doesn't matter. A couple foul tips and a panic third swipe at a ball low and outside and I'm dust again. I don't get another trip to the plate, and Hunter's the only guy on our team to get a hit, a blooper over the short-stop's head.

They get one in the third on a sharp double to left centre which Clutch fields cleanly. The runner goes to third on a pitch Kluzak bobbles behind the plate and scores on a sacrifice fly. It's respectable, one-nothing, when they break it open in the fourth, their sluggers finally catching onto Eugene's inside curve and connecting so much wood they must have thought they were back out in the bush. Hudson Bay scores eight runs before we scramble for three outs. "That's it," says the ump. "Game's over." In the six-inning tournament games, if you're behind by more than seven runs after four innings, you're done.

Clutch runs off to see what time we play again while the rest of us straggle back to the campsite.

I'm walking next to Eugene. "How's the arm?"

"Okay."

Hunter, jogging by, slaps Eugene on the shoulder with his glove. "'S okay buddy," he says. "One bad inning."

Eugene nods to him. "I can start the next game," he says to me.

We sit on logs around the empty firepit, sucking back cold beers. Clutch comes back to tell us not to drink too much. "We play again at two. The loser of Perigord and Pittsburgh Glass from Regina."

Some of the boys, giving way to heat and dedication, are into their third beers when I see Noagie digging in his shirt pocket for another twister. I put my empty bottle in the cardboard case and stretch. "Anybody wanna see what we're coming up against?"

Hunter and I walk over to Diamond #4 and, sitting on the hood of somebody's half-ton, watch the orange-clad, black capped farmers from Perigord take on big city labourers in green and yellow. It's a good game until the Perigord pitcher throws his arm out in the fifth inning. I can tell right away it's out by the wince on the guy's face just after he releases the ball. Perigord brings in their relief, a pitcher who's pushing forty and still uses the old-style wind up. The first batter for Pittsburgh Glass pounds the old man's second pitch over the right fielder's head and gets an easy four-bagger. Pittsburgh Glass get a couple more runs in the sixth and that's all she wrote.

"If that's the pitcher we'll be facing," I say to Hunter as we're walking for hotdogs, "we got a chance."

The old-style pitcher is the only guy warming up for Perigord when Noagie, Yuktum and Clutch show up at the diamond a little before two. They're all giggly as hell. "C'mon Kemp." I rifle a softball at Clutch who flinches but manages to get his glove in front of it.

We have a two-run lead when I take over from Eugene in the third. He's lost his control and walked three in a row. Right away my arm falls comfortably into that familiar groove-snap rhythm and I give up only one run on a flyball to left, a strike-out and a grounder to third.

My confidence builds with the innings. The bottom is falling out of my slider, Perigord gets only two on base through to the sixth, and we take a three-run lead into the last inning when Povey knocks Hunter home from second with a sharp single to right.

I get their lead-off man on a line-drive to Hoevig, walk their second batter on a close hanging curve. The old-style pitcher comes up next and waits out one of my best change-ups of the day, pulling it over the third base bag past Eugene for a double. Runners on second and third, one out. No sweat. I fire a slider down and away to the next batter but, with a good eye, he slaps a high fly ball to right, to Noagie, who's underneath it. The ball lands in his glove, bubbles out, and falls to the ground.

Stupid dope shit. They score two and the tying run glides easily into third. I kick at the rubber.

"That's okay, big shooter," Hoevig shouts from short.

"We got 'em, Rudy chucker buddy," Povey yells behind me.

Forcing my next fastball, trying for something extra, my wrist brushes too hard against my pantleg. The ball's in the dirt, way inside, past Kluzak. I break to the plate but it's too late. The runner from third crosses home even before blind Boris can find the ball back at the screen.

The chatter is more quiet now, then gone completely when I walk the next two. I'm shook, no doubt about it. I'm forcing the ball, trying to do it all myself, and hang a curve-ball that's singled to right. Noagie fields the ball cleanly this time but our game is finished.

Walking off the field, I throw my glove down at the foot of our bench. "Hey Rudy," Yuktum says. "It's all right. Now we can get down to some serious partying."

Christ, how I hate playing with losers.

Hunter

Yuktum, the crazy shit, suggests a dip in the lake. We're three beer past Perigord and I'm the only one willing to join him. Three beer are about my limit at any one sitting.

We change into our bathing suits in the tent and, subject to catcalls, a two-fingered whistle from Jerry, make our way across the wide hot natural sand beach to the water, which, at first, is cold, shocking, then, as I crawl to the buoy with crisp strong strokes, refreshing as hell. I make four laps to the buoy and back, sucking wind on the last, while Yuktum paddles around waist-deep.

"How can you do that?" Yuktum asks when I come in. "After playing ball all day?"

"Feels good." I shake my head, flinging water out of my hair. "Just splashing, laying around, feels good."

We saunter down the main beach towards the developed cabin area, the dwindling afternoon sun still hot, drying up the waterdrops on our bare shoulders.

"Just like California," Yuktum says.

"I wish."

We drag our feet through the water and both of us see her at the same time. We can't help it. A girl with the most monstrous breasts I've ever seen is leaning over, digging for something in a motorboat, when one of her boobs just slips out over her bikini top. She knows it's happened, but doesn't know we're watching, and tries to shrug it back into the top nonchalantly.

"Look at that there!" Yuktum shouts loudly enough for her to hear. She becomes embarrassed, tries to tuck it in quickly, and in her motion, the other boob pops out.

"Look at that!"

Now the girl's really embarrassed, crossing her arms in front of herself to cover up, and here come those big boobs again, out either side. Yuktum's going crazy on the beach, jumping up and down, pointing, yelling. "Look, look!" I grab his arm to settle him down.

Her last resort, the girl jumps into thc water, which is deeper than she thought, and in a few seconds, she's struggling, gasping. She can't swim. I look at Yuktum.

"Don't look at me," he says.

I take a couple steps closer to see if she's faking it, trying to make us look like fools. But she's not. I stride up the dock, pick a styrofoam floatboard out of the boat and throw it to her, almost hitting her on the head. She grabs onto it and gradually begins treading water.

"You okay?"

The girl flicks a strand of wet hair off her face. "Yeah," she says hoarsely. She's holding onto the float with one hand and trying with the other to pull her bikini top overtop what look like to me, in the deep water at the end of the pier, more than sufficient life-saving devices.

"Sorry about my friend."

With the bikini properly in place, she frog-kicks towards the pier, pushing the board in front of her. "That's okay." The slight twitches at the corners of her mouth I take for a smile. "It must have been kind of funny."

I bend over, grab her wrists and pull her up onto the dock. A big girl, water running off her tanned skin, she stands tall and straight, a posture unusual for most girls with that carriage. "Thanks," she says, offering her hand. "I'm Claire."

"Wayne Hunter," I say. "I don't think I've seen you around here before."

"I'm Debbie Setterlee's cousin, from Kenora."

"Oh." Thinking Canora. "Just down for the day?"

"Kenora, Ontario," she says.

"Oh, yeah. Right." What a fool. I look at Yuktum who's casually gazing across the lake and scraping a half-circle in the sand on the beach with his big toe. "Look," I say, "I have to go, but if you and Debbie aren't doing anything later on, why not drop by the campground? A few of us have been playing ball all day and we'll probably be celebrating most of the night."

"I'll see." Claire throws the floatboard back into the boat.

"Tell Debbie that Cathy and Karen are coming out." I try not to swagger down the dock. "It'll be a good time."

"I'll mention it."

"Hey man," Yuktum says excitedly, falling in step beside me as we walk back to the campsite.

"She's from down east, staying with Debbie Setterlee out at her cabin. Sounds like they might come by later on."

"Oh yeah," Yuktum says suggestively.

"She seems like a nice girl."

"I think," Yuktum says, shaking his head, "her top's just too small."

I slap him on his bare back.

At the campsite Rudy and Eugene are in the bush, hatcheting wiener sticks. Boris and Noagie are coming up the road with armloads of firewood from the park attendant's bin. Clutch Kemp opens us a beer.

It's dark when Debbie Setterlee and her Kenora cousin finally arrive. Michael is hopping around the blazing firepit like a wild man, trying to shake out of his pantlegs the handful of ice-cubes Jerry dropped down the back of his jeans when he was bending over, searching the cooler full of Pil for one of his OV's.

I've been watching for the girls, notice them when they're still dark shapes down the beach. Probably the least drunk of the bunch, having drunk only four beer since our supper of hot dogs and potato salad that Boris's mother sent along, I stand up, greet them as they enter our circle.

"Hi Wayne," Debbie says. Debbie Setterlee has green eyes and long dark honey-colored hair. In my opinion, she's one of the best-looking girls in Milligan High. Unfortunately, she's never seemed to have much use for farm boys. "Not much has changed with you guys, I see." She's nodding towards Michael.

"Drowning our sorrows," I say, looking past her to Claire, who's wearing a thick Icelandic sweater.

"Oh yeah," says Debbie, stepping back. "Wayne Hunter, this is my cousin, Claire Bernier. I believe you met this afternoon.

Noagie

My running shoe is just fried.

One of the last things I remember, I'm sitting next to Debbie Setterlee on a log by the campfire. Debbie's good-looking for a Milligan chick, but stuck-up, out of touch. She asked Clutch, who was sitting on her other side, whether he's burnt any clutches out in his Charger lately. Old hat, dumb.

Anyway, I'm just sitting there, watching the smoke trail off into the dark sky, when Debbie says, "So you guys lost out, huh?" It takes a while before I realize she's talking to me.

"That's why we're celebrating," I say, guzzling half my beer.

She stands up. "Your Adidas is melting to that rock."

When I wake up this morning, struggling to free myself from the damp sleeping bag, I notice my running shoes in a corner of the tent. The spongy sole of one of them is a melted black blob. I look at Clutch lying next to me. "Don't breathe on me," he says.

Leaving my sneakers, I unzip the door flap and crawl outside. It's drizzling and Wayne is picking up empty beer bottles, putting them into cases. "Morning, Noagie," he says.

I stumble into the bush behind the camper-trailer and, with a sigh of relief, send a patter of piss to the already wet ground. I come back and sit out of the rain on the step of the camper-trailer, watching Wayne, always energetic, gather up dead soldiers.

"So Hunterman, get lucky last night?" I remember Wayne and Debbie Setterlee's well-endowed cousin going off for a private stroll down the beach. Later, they huddled together in the front seat of Kluzak's classic.

There's a rattle of bottles as Wayne plops another case in the stack of twelve-packs he's accumulated against the back fender of the Chevy. "She's a nice girl," he says, looking at me.

"Big kajungas." I gesture balloons on my chest.

Wayne doesn't say anything, just smiles. Little drops of water drip off his trimmed blond moustache.

Suddenly I hear someone skinning coyotes in the bush. From inside the camper-trailer, Rudy shouts, "No wonder you're sick, Eugene. You got puke in your stomach."

I feel movement behind me and turn around to see Boris's face pressed against the mesh window, his thick glasses smudged and dirty like he just crawled through a pile of sawdust. "Morning, Noagie," he says.

I get up and help Wayne collect bottles. We dive into the tent when the drizzle becomes a shower and wait until there's a let-up. Then the whole team is scrambling around the campsite, packing up.

I gather as many empties as I can find. We killed most of the beer. Five lone brownies anchor the cooler as Clutch pours the dirty ice water into the firepit. It doesn't even hiss.

"Anyone want a beer?"

Usually someone goes for it, but not today. It's cold, and wet, and we're out of the tournament, and hungover. Michael and Jerry keep rolling up the tent. I want to go home, lay on the couch under one of Mom's warm afghans. Boris and Wayne are latching down the top of the camper-trailer.

"Hey, wait," I say, walking over. "Since there's nine of us have to crowd into Boris's car again–"

"Eight. Yuktum went home with Cathy last night."

"Seven and a half, counting Eugene."

"–maybe a couple of us could ride in there." Pointing to the camper-trailer.

Boris and Wayne shoulder the top up and water runs down the aluminum rim, falling in our faces as we peer in. There's room enough for two people if they hunch over.

"Naw," says Wayne. "It'll be too uncomfortable."

"Yeah, right."

"You go if you want to, dope shit," Rudy says. He's still pissed off at me for dropping that fly ball against Perigord. I'm tempted to go for it, to show asshole Rudy, but Wayne and Boris slam the top down again.

"C'mon," says Eugene. "I'm cold."

We all pile into Boris's Chevy.

"Lucky thing we lost those two games yesterday."

"Yeah, nobody'll be playing ball today anyway."

"Jesus Christ," says Clutch, when Wayne opens the tupperware bowl of leftover potato salad.

Boris steers his car straight into the only curve in the highway from the lake. The gray sky blends into the dark pavement and Boris doesn't realize he's into the curve until it's too late. He jerks the steering wheel to keep the Chevy on the road but the camper-trailer slides across the wet pavement. The narrow outside tire grabs the sharp edge of the shoulder of the highway and the camper-trailer twists off the ball-and-chain hitch, cartwheels into the ditch, rolls over twice.

As Boris slows down, we all look back at the camper-trailer upside down in the ditch, one battered wheel still spinning.

KEN NORRIS

* * * * * * *

Ken Norris teaches at the University of Maine in Orono and spends his summers in Montreal, where he remains an active member of the literary community. Since the mid-1970s he has published over a dozen volumes of poetry, including In the House of No *(1991) and* Alphabet of Desire *(1991). He has also edited five anthologies and is the author of* The Little Magazine in Canada 1925-1980 *(1984). "The Agony of Being an Expos Fan" is one of several poems that Norris contributed to the baseball section of a special issue of* Descant *(Spring-Summer 1987) devoted to "Comedy and the Sporting Life." Norris notes that during the past decade his heart "has been broken about equally by the Montreal Expos and the Boston Red Sox."*

* * * * * * *

The Agony of Being an Expos Fan

It's like having your finest innocent hopes shattered, your heart ground to dust. Your pancreas has been removed and now you must eat pure sugar.

You have many questions that will always remain unanswered. What was the cosmic attraction between Ron Leflore, Tim Raines, Terry Francona and the left field wall? Who stole Steve Rogers' fastball? Was Rodney Scott the finger in the dyke? Did Bill Lee put a macrobiotic curse on the team? Was John McHale in league with the devil? Whatever happened to the team of the eighties? (you suspect it was traded or sold down the river)

You watch the current team play, and sigh. You miss Al Oliver, Gary Carter, Scott Sanderson, the Spaceman; you miss what never will be. In your worst nightmares Rick Monday's homer just clears the fence. You wish Charles Bronfman would sell the team, or put it out of its misery

It's like watching John Keats *not* die, and then he goes on to become a second-rate hack somehow.

PAUL QUARRINGTON

* * * * * * *

Paul Quarrington lives in Toronto, where he is active as a novelist and playwright. Since 1978 he has published eight books, including the baseball novel Home Game *(1983) and two hockey-related novels,* King Leary *(1987) and* Logan in Overtime *(1990). His non-fiction work* Hometown Heroes: On the Road with Canada's National Hockey Team *appeared in 1988. "Home Opener, 1908," which is from a work-in-progress, was first published in the baseball section of a special sports issue of the literary magazine* Descant *(Spring-Summer 1987).*

* * * * * * *

Home Opener, 1908 (from a novel in progress)
for Yoshiko

> 'There is one thing in connection with the subject of youthful sports which merits special attention, and that is the tendency of boys to forego such pastimes and to replace them with habits of their leisure hours, which are at war alike with health and morality.' *Sports & Pastimes of American Boys*, H. Chadwick.

HOME OPENER, 1908

In 1908 I became the junior baseball reporter for the *New York Clipper*, I was twenty-two years of age, and fairly young for that. My uncle got the job for me, pulling strings and calling gambling debts, but I must say in my own defense that I had worked on newspapers for six months previous and knew a little about baseball.

My home was Boston, and as a child I had dreamt of becoming a member of the Red Sox. An unhappy love affair drove me away from that city. I arrived in New York with painful memories and an accent so pronounced that I soon became known as 'Harvard Harry'. The irony is that no less than four of my fellow sportswriters had attended that establishment (I had not) but with their coarse ways and manners no one ever suspected.

Joe Vila, for example, graduated from Harvard, but looked for all the world like a pirate. He had smooth dark skin and black eyes. When Mr. Vila got angry, which was regularly, his eyes would light with cruelty and his nostrils would flare. Joe worked for *The Sporting News* and was supposed to be unbiased, but for a reason we could never figure he despised the New York Giants. He hated them all, from John J. McGraw to the rookies. Joe Vila even hated Christy Mathewson. The only player Vila could tolerate was Turkey Donlin.

Donlin was called 'Turkey' because of his strut (his name being Mike). Donlin's strut was neither haughty nor boastful. It was the eager and joyful gait of a man anxious to get about the business of living a life. When Donlin came on to the field the fans would cheer ecstatically, even the coloured.

I am remembering Turkey Donlin now, and the first time I saw him. It was the home opener for the New York Giants, the year of our Lord 1908. I was at the Polo Grounds in my capacity as junior baseball reporter for the *Clipper*. I arrived about an hour early. I went to the Press Loge and found it all but deserted.

The sole occupant was a shrivelled old man who sat near the back wall, surrounded by books and charts. The old man wore a beard that tumbled halfway down and as he worked – consulting pages and scribbling figures – spittle fell from his mouth to lace with the gray-white hair. The old man was totally oblivious of my arrival. He picked his nose vigorously, flicking the findings away after a brief sidelong glance.

'Hello,' I said.

'When were you born?' the old man demanded.

I responded, 'Eighteen eighty-six.'

'When, when, *when*?'

'The time of day, do you mean?'

'The time of day, the time of day!'

'I understand it was about three o'clock in the morning.'

The old man gave me an angry look and wrote something, I suppose this trivial information concerning my birth. He picked up a leatherbound volume and began turning the pages. The old man lost all interest in me.

I moved forward so that I stood behind the row of desks lining the balcony. Below me the groundskeeper and his man were still working on the diamond. The ground was a burnished gold, the grass a rare green.

Though the stadium seemed uncommonly quiet, the stands were nearly full. The few spaces remaining would be taken within minutes, and those supporters who couldn't get admission would stand contentedly outside the Polo Grounds and share whatever information they could muster through the walls. Many would crowd Coogan's Bluff, where they could only barely see the action.

Sam Crane entered the Press Area. I recognized him at once, even though he was rather a plain-looking fellow. Crane was the writer from the *New York Journal* and had, in 1890, played second base for the Giants. He was as vehement in his support as Joe Vila was in his denigration. According to Sam Crane, the Giants were incapable of losing a game. Fates, gods and other forces could conspire against them...umpires could be blind, stupid and out-right lunatic...but McGraw and his battlers were never less than champions. Crane wore a perpetually startled expression. He possessed enormous hands, one of which he offered to me. We shook and exchanged names.

Sam Crane took out a cigarette. He performed a little ritual with it, twirling it around his right forefinger, as if the cigarette were a miniature baton, and bringing an end down hard upon the nail of his right thumb, tamping the tobacco. Crane could make the cigarette twirl three and even four times in one go, and it was always the same end that hit. He did this without seeming to notice. Sam Crane pursed his lips, thinking. After a good many twirls, Crane put the cigarette in his mouth and lit. 'I think,' Crane observed, 'that this Giant team is one of the finest ever assembled. It shall certainly claim the flag.'

'Whither there be prophecies, they shall fail,' came a new voice. 'For we know in part, and we prophesy in part. But when that which is perfect is come, then that which is in part shall be done away.'

'Hullo, Sid,' said Crane, a little sullenly.

The newcomer (I knew instantly it was Sid Mercer of the *Globe*) was an uncommonly handsome man. His hair was long, which gave him a slightly bohemian look. He was dressed casually, a sweater with a high collar, light cotton slacks, but managed to look much more elegant than either Crane or I, both in suits. Mercer eyed me and then offered his hand. 'Call me Sid,' he instructed. 'And when the zezanas of this great metropolis have robbed you of your spirit, come to me for guidance and enlightenment.'

'I will, thanks,' I told him.

'But, Sid,' Sam Crane persisted, 'you have to agree with me. Look how well we've done so far. We swept these Superbas and took two from three out of Philly. Fourteen to two last Saturday.' Crane chuckled and prodded me in the side. 'Were you there, Harry?'

I shook my head. My superior had elected to cover these first few away games, and the *Clipper* could not afford to send us both.

Crane laughed harder. 'Philly sent in this fellow Moren, who invented that trick pitch.'

'The knuckle ball,' Mercer supplied, although he seemed distracted, staring down at the playing field intently.

'We knocked it to pieces,' Crane told me. 'A slugfest.'

Charlie Dreyfuss joined us. He was my superior, but he looked young and boyish, perhaps more so than myself. Charlie was small and elfin, as slender as a rail. His hair was violent red colour, and his face matched. Charlie appeared to be always blushing, his cheeks flushed and rosey.

'How do, how do,' Charlie addressed us all. 'And how fare the literati this day?' Charlie Dreyfuss put his arm around me in a fatherly manner. 'Have you all met the boy from Bahstin?' Charlie didn't wait for answers. 'Lookee yonder, fellers!' Charlie pointed down to the diamond. 'The mighty Superbas is took the field!'

The Brooklyn Superbas were warming up. I watched them for a long time. It was thrilling, and made me think of my boyhood without reminding me of the unhappiness.

Charlie Dreyfuss nudged me in the side and offered me a pewter flask.

'What is it?' I asked.

'What do you think it is, lad? What do all self-respecting newspapermen drink? Apple juice, of course!'

'Apple juice?'

'Mr. Crane,' asked Charlie, 'would you care for a sip of this apple juice?'

'Sure would,' said Crane. He took the flask, had a long sip, then passed it to Sid Mercer. Mercer didn't drink right away. He asked Dreyfuss, 'Is this high quality apple juice?'

'Apple juice,' stated Charlie, 'is apple juice.'

Mercer had a very small tug and scowled. 'Very bad apples.'

The flask was given to me. I took a long pull and swallowed hard. It left me short of breath and dizzy, as if I'd just done work. I contained the various coughing and gagging sounds that my body implored me to make.

'I see you are no stranger to apple juice,' noted Charlie Dreyfuss.

I suppose I assumed a very young, proud and sickly smile. 'I was the beer drinking champion of the North Point Tavern,' I told them.

'Good for you,' said Mr. Mercer. Then he laughed lightly about, I guessed, something else.

'Oh, now, say now,' said Dreyfuss. He had assumed a sort of hoity-toity tone. 'Mr. Walter Trumbull, Esquire, is gracing us with his imperial presence.'

Walter Trumbull of the *Press* sauntered over, his black manservant trailing him. Trumbull was peeling off his driving gloves, tossing them over his shoulder to the valet. 'Hello, hello, hello!' he called. 'The traffic is awfully awful!'

Mercer asked, 'Is it awfully *awfully* awful?'

'It is, Sidney. It is.' Trumbull grinned and thrust his hand at me. 'Neophyte, I grant you greet.'

I took his hand.

'You should sit with me and watch and learn. The reason that I am the best baseball writer in the city is that I am so very much above it. I have no personal stake in these childish displays. I merely record what happens, dispassionately and sensibly.'

Sportswriters were now arriving all the time. I was introduced to Bill Kirk from the *American*, John Foster of the *Telegram*, Wally Aulick from the *Times*, Charlie Dreyfuss would whisper in my ear, giving me the lowdown on all of them. 'Kirk,' Dreyfuss told me, 'likes to see how much he can sneak by the copy editor. Last year there was a pitcher named Eugene Krapp – K-R-A-P-P – who let a couple of men on base and then struck out three in a row. Kirk wrote "Krapp squeezed out of a tight hole."'

I laughed, probably much more loudly than the story warranted.

'Foster there,' Charlie Dreyfuss went on, likes fruity words. Everything is *peachy* and infielders are always "picking berries" and so on.'

Then I saw Joe Vila for the first time. His arrival in the Press Loge quieted everyone, the laughter dying quickly away. No one said hello to Vila, he said nothing to us. Vila went to one of the seats, tossing a pad and many pencils on to the desk. Joe Vila wrote 'HOME OPENER, 1908' in huge block letters at the top of one of the pages. The air became electric.

The Giants had taken the field. Like everyone else in the crowd I watched Christy Mathewson walk toward the pitcher's mound.

Christy stared intently at his own feet, as if the act of walking was mysterious to him. He held a baseball in his right hand, gripped tightly between his thumb and first two fingers. Every so often he would rotate the ball, feeling the seams, pressing the horsehide. As he neared the mound, lost in his own thoughts, Mathewson flipped the ball behind his back. The bean shot into the air, suspended itself, and then dropped softly into Christy's waiting mitt.

The stands went wild. Mathewson, startled, looked up for the first time. It seemed to take a while to register that the applause was meant for him. When it did, a vague grin crept across his face. Suddenly Christy began adjusting his uniform, hitching up his trousers, cinching his belt, adjusting the collar of his jersey, beating dust from the tiny dark cap. Mathewson looked at Roger Bresnahan, his battery-mate, and snaked his gloved hand briefly through the air. Christy reared back and threw.

The smack of the ball into Bresnahan's glove was plainly audible. Mathewson received the ball and threw once more. This pitch seemed to travel even faster. It danced on the air wilfully. Mathewson nodded, watching the flight of the ball. He seemed deeply satisfied.

Christy wasn't handsome in the same way Sid Mercer was. No one looking at a photograph of Mathewson's face would ever suspect the extraordinary beauty that life granted those simple features. Christy seemed somehow to be perfectly made, huge without being monstrous, and he combined a colossal energy with a saintlike serenity. I remember sometime back watching a nature show on television with my grandson. The narrator spent quite a while explaining why the Great White Shark was perfectly adapted to its environment, the ocean. I turned to my grandson and told him, 'And Christy Mathewson was perfectly adapted to his environment, the earth.' The child looked at me as if I was crazy. At any rate, I was wrong and knew it. Christy Mathewson was gassed while in training for the Great War, and he died of tuberculosis, a very young man.

But at the moment which I am remembering the Big Six was so full of life that it's a wonder he didn't burst.

'Christy Mathewson is exemplary.'

I turned around and saw that Mr. Chadwick had entered the Press Area to make this pronouncement. Mr. Chadwick was eighty-four years old, and his voice was barely audible. There was still a strong English accent, although Mr. Chadwick left his homeland while still a young boy of thirteen. Mr. Chadwick was enfeebled. He supported his weight (which looked to be not more than seventy pounds) with two oaken canes. His face appeared to be nothing more than a dense webbing of wrinkles, but looking closely one could see the vestiges of civility – a small trim moustache, a tiny pointed goatee. Mr. Chadwick pitched himself forward, alarming me. He steadied and I saw that his intention was merely to get closer to the playing field below. 'Exemplary,' he repeated, 'not like most we know, eh, lads?'

My fellow sportswriters laughed. Mr. Chadwick silenced them with a quick glance. 'You don't understand,' he accused us collectively. Mr. Chadwick looked at me. 'I was with the *Clipper*, of course,' he said. I was startled by this recognition. 'It is a very fine newspaper. Or, at least, like everything else in this world, it was once very fine. What is the world coming to? It is coming to retrogression. Ain't it, Sidney?'

Sid Mercer nodded.

Mr. Chadwick swung his hips and managed to move an inch or two closer to the railing. 'They made him captain of the team,' he said, 'and he is a drunken scoundrel.'

'He's taken the pledge,' said Sam Crane. 'He's hopped on the waterwagon.'

'And he will hop off,' Chadwick said with certainty. 'He's married to that woman, ain't he?'

Many of the men nodded slightly.

'Donlin wouldn't do as a cricketeer. He wouldn't do at all.'

The old man near the back now spoke up. I had forgotten he was there. 'Do you want to hear his hits to at-bats quotient, Chadwick?' The old man took no pains to be polite.

Chadwick ignored him. 'This is further retrogression, this numbers nonsense. And to think that the league encourages crack-minded dwarves like this. And what's more, you lads pay them cash money! For what? For numbers. Meaningless numbers.'

'Meaningless numbers?' The old bearded man leapt to his feet, spilling pages, upsetting his ink bottle. I saw that Chadwick's use of the word dwarf was accurate, if cruel. 'What do you think the world is?'

'Marlin,' said Chadwick, 'you and I are both too old to argue about it.'

'But I must say, Father Chadwick,' Walter Trumbull piped up (a number of the men chuckled at the address), 'that Michael Donlin is a bully chap and a grand baseball player.'

'When I was twenty-three years of age,' Mr. Chadwick said – whether in answer to Trumbull's statement or in ignorance of it we could not tell – 'I ferried across to the Elysian Fields. I cannot convey to you the brilliance of that summer day, the feeling in the air that life had been created not many minutes before. The

Knickerbockers Baseball Club was playing – against whom I've either forgotten or never knew – and I watched. All my life was like a minuet, or a painting, or a very lovely poem. Baseball was exactly that beautiful. Then.' Chadwick nodded at the playing field. 'Now it is a game played by hooligans and drunkards for the entertainment of gamblers and the press; the press, incidentally, being composed mainly of hooligans and drunkards.'

Crane shrugged his shoulders. 'What's a few drinks?'

Chadwick deigned not to answer. He sucked in his breath sharply, an act that made his small chest shudder. He died of pneumonia five days later.

The next morning – I get ahead of myself in the telling now, but only briefly – I awoke with a hangover. To my mind, it was the worst hangover I've ever had, although there were probably some more severe, some more crippling. This one owed of its severity to its being my first experience with true alcohol sickness. It took many minutes for life and the consciousness of it to penetrate. When it did, I found to my surprise that I was clutching a copy of *Sports and Pastimes of American Boys*, by Henry Chadwick. The book was one of twenty I'd brought with me from Boston. I'd owned it since the age of seven. The cover of the book was a collage of coloured drawings. It pictured boys bicycling, fishing, sculling and playing football. In the centre – the biggest drawing of them all – boys were playing baseball.

Turkey Donlin put on a little gag for everyone.

It was around that time in history that they first lowered the players' benches some inches into the ground, roofing them with clapboard so that the boys wouldn't have to sit in the sun. Just to the left of this 'dug-out', two or three rows back, stood a young woman. She was smoothing out the dress around her behind, gathering in the material before she sat down, trying to be very prim and proper. This gal was extremely busty, a fact that most of the crowd had noticed. Turkey, running toward the dug-out after catching popflies in the outfield, saw the woman and momentarily stopped dead in his tracks. The stands buzzed lightly at this, snickering. Then Donlin put on his best Turkey strut, his limbs pumping happily up and down, dancing from side to side. The woman had just finished seating herself when she saw Mike staring at her. She smiled hesitantly and blushed. Donlin acted like a real swell. He grinned cockily, then reached up and tipped his cap to the woman. The crowd laughed, because everyone saw what was coming. Turkey Donlin flipped headfirst into the dug-out.

We went wild.

There was a second act to this little show, and everyone in the crowd seemed to expect it. In a box just behind home plate, a young woman in a Merry Widow hat stood up, threw her hands on to her hips angrily and stared daggers at Turkey Donlin. This got the biggest laugh of all. The woman turned to the crowd, shaking her head with exasperation.

Turkey climbed to his feet and started massaging his rump in an exaggerated way, his face lined with mock pain. He saw the young woman in the Merry Widow hat (who was brandishing a tiny, perfect fist) and grinned sheepishly. Donlin took his seat on the players' bench.

The young woman crossed her arms and sat down heavily, full of petulance, unforgiving.

That was Mabel Hite, Turkey's wife.

In those days I knew nothing of the workings of my own heart, and I discounted the few heavy beats that sounded in my chest, putting them down to the excitement that filled the Polo Grounds. I think now that the heart is often wiser than the thoughts that try to tame it.

Mabel Hite was not a beautiful woman in any classical sense. Her jaw was a touch too square, even manly, her eyes oversized and spaced widely. She was most often referred to as 'pretty' in our columns, and we used the same word to describe the mayor's wife. Clothes in those days did not make it easy to appraise a woman's figure, but Mabel Hite would never be taken for a full-bodied woman, and seemed to possess a leggy, almost boyish physique.

If Mabel Hite had been born fifty or sixty years later, I think she might have been very famous, for I've noticed on television more and more actresses with her look. There's one in particular that is very much like her – I can't recall the gal's name, and the programme she appears on, being violent and silly, is confused in my mind with all the other violent, silly programmes. I watch this show only out of happenstance. The young woman often appears in a bikini bathing suit so small she might as well be nude. When this happens I get up and change the channel, although I usually have to wait several moments for the pain to ease out of my stomach.

THE CLIPPER

Mighty Matty mowed them down mercilessly yesterday but when the final frame came the Giants had only tallied one run to Brooklyn's two. John J. McGraw, pacing like a little Napoleon, sent in young Freddy Merkle to bat for Christy to start our half of the ninth. Merkle, a gangly greenhorn but a good one, watched two strikes sizzle over the dish. Then young Fred saw one that looked tasty and sent it for a ride into the right-hand crowd. It was called for a ground-rule double. Shannon sacrificed, moving the tenderfoot on to the hot corner. Then it was Tenney's turn, who chose to ignore the advice of the record crowd, and instead of hitting a circuit clout merely drove the bean hard into the infield. Young Merkle was forced to scamper back to the third bag when the ball was fielded easily. With two out a cloud of gloom began to materialize over the Polo Grounds. It was not noticed by Captain Mike Donlin, who assumed his position in the box apparently under the impression that the Giants led by a considerable margin. Donlin assessed McIntre's first offering as being unworthy of anything other than a disdainful glance. Unfortunately, Umpire Emslie thought otherwise, tagging it as strike number one. Mike also merely gandered at the next pitch – he and the umpire Emslie agreed that it was a ball. The next pitch? Again there was disunity, Donlin assaying it as well outside, Emslie insisting that it came over the plate. Emslie's opinion held. Donlin must have decided that Emslie was a disputatious and cantankerous fellow. He pushed his cap back, the better to see McIntre's next bean, and he cocked his rear leg in a manner that suggested that Turkey meant to clobber this one, if only so that he and Emslie might live together in accord. Donlin hit it. He hit it so hard that, as one old-timer had it, when it came down in the right-field bleachers, Donlin was still hitting it. Pandemonium erupted in fandom. Hats and seat cushions flew skyward as young Fred Merkle crossed the line to tie, and as Turkey Donlin passed the threshold he was raised up by the crowd and carried into the clubhouse. No one clapped harder than Mabel Hite, Mrs. Turkey Donlin, who wore out three new pairs of gloves with delighted flapping. A look of concern did cloud her pretty face as she watched her husband being borne hero-style. 'I hope they don't hurt him,' she said, and then she dropped back into her seat with a gurgle of delight.

JUDITH FITZGERALD

* * * * * * *

Toronto native and resident Judith Fitzgerald is the author of more than a dozen volumes of poetry, including Given Names *(1985), which won the Writers' Choice Award, and* Rapturous Chronicles *(1991), which earned a Governor General's Award nomination. A frequent contributor to anthologies and periodicals, she has also edited a number of anthologies. Her "Country Side" column is currently syndicated by the* Toronto Star. *From 1985 to 1987, she was a columnist for the magazine* Innings. *"How Do You Spell Relief" is taken from "August," a sequence of baseball poems that Fitzgerald published in* This Magazine *(July 1987).*

* * * * * * *

How Do You Spell Relief?
for Hugh Hood

Midnight and the clips manage a manic arrangement
on the screen; somewhere the reenactment of the seventh
inning occurs and occurs and winces in full colour;
the reminder, the replay, the lack of.

And, how do you spell relief? Bring in the terminator
from another channel/league, a different wavelength? Bring in
    the ace
stopper (in the hole), watch the left hand's precision unfold slo-
mo terrific? Imagine Willie rising on the right side of a star?

Concentrate. Each wild pitch out of your control as the kite
red sun sets infinitely blue in the moonlight window, hangs
disconsolate while eyes gnaw the heart of a dilemma —
to go beyond and get out of the inning, this game.

Think over plays in fields memorized without originals backing
accurate imagining; the way only Roger Angell can call a season
    dulcet;
the way George Bowering can call a muscle move, a pitch, a
    game before
the action knows its inspiration, cause, effect.

Relief. Heart-hazed soft sun/moon evenings; the stands forgotten
as the bases fill up and grand slams glaze intaglio the superimposed
fields. The go-ahead in the batter's box and here comes the pitch
and it's a swing and a miss. And it doesn't matter. And it does.

ALISON GORDON

* * * * * * *

The first woman assigned to the American League beat, journalist Alison Gordon covered the Toronto Blue Jays for the Toronto Star *from 1979 to 1983. She later described the experience in* Foul Balls: Five Years in the American League *(1984). Since then, she has published three accomplished baseball mysteries*—The Dead Pull Hitter *(1988),* Safe at Home *(1990), and* Night Game *(1992)—featuring the Toronto* Planet's *senior baseball writer, Kate Henry. The following selection is from the opening section of Gordon's first Kate Henry novel.*

* * * * * * *

from **The Dead Pull Hitter**

The reading light over my seat didn't work. It had been burned out the last time I was on the plane, so I shouldn't have been surprised. I moved to the aisle seat, the one with the non-reclining chair back, strapped myself in, and opened my book.

I was already in a bad mood. We had been sitting on the ground at LaGuardia Airport for half an hour. The equipment truck had a flat tire, and we couldn't leave until it got there. The passengers in the rows behind me were socking back drinks and getting more unruly by the minute. I wanted a cigarette badly.

Claire, the purser, leaned across me and lowered the tray table on the window seat. She set down a couple of baby bottles of vodka, a can of tonic, and a glass of ice.

"You look as though you could use this."

"You are an angel. How much longer?"

"The truck just got here," she said. "The way the guys are going, I hope they load fast. It's getting pretty drunk out."

"Tell me about it," I said.

The guys she referred to were the Toronto Titans baseball team, currently in first place in the American League East. They had just swept the Yankees in New York and our charter flight was headed to Toronto for the last home stand of the season. They were more cocky and arrogant than usual. And that's going some.

"Yo, Hank! What kind of shit did you write tonight?"

Stinger Swain, the third baseman, yelled at me from his seat five rows back, a mean little smirk on his sallow face. He had just folded his poker hand and was looking for other sport. I tried to ignore him.

"Yo, Lady Writer! I'm talking to you," he said, tossing his empty beer can at me. "Did you write about your hero Preacher's catch in the eighth inning? If my white ass looked as good as his black one in uniform, would you write about me all the time, too?"

And kids lined up for this guy's autograph? I turned in my seat.

"I wrote about you today, Stinger."

"The lady's finally learning to appreciate the finer points of the game."

"I wrote about the way you looked sliding into third: like a pregnant seal trying to climb an ice floe."

That earned me a few appreciative hoots. Alejandro Jones, the second baseman, barked and slapped his palms together like flippers.

"Shut up, Taco-breath," Swain said, then turned to Goober Grabowski, his seatmate. "Deal the cards."

We finally took off, to the accompaniment of sarcastic cheers and vulgar noises. As the no-smoking sign clicked off, Moose Greer, the team public relations director, dropped his seat back in the row in front of me and peered at me through the gap.

"Glad to be going home?"

"It's been a long road trip."

And a long season. I had spent just about enough time on the Flying Fart, which was what the clever fellows behind me call this elderly bird, for reasons I won't go into. Trust me, the name is appropriate.

Because of the one a.m. jet curfew at Pearson International, and, I suspect, the high pockets of Titan owner Ted Ferguson, we fly a propeller-driven plane after night games. It's the airborne equivalent of the spring-shot buses that at one time or another transported most of this same gang through the minor leagues – reliable, but not luxurious. The seats are covered in faded orange and green, clashing horribly with the sky-blue-and-red pop art patterns on the bulkheads. But we ride in relative comfort, with a friendly crew and plenty of food and booze.

It's a funny little world on the airplane, a society in which each member knows his, or her, own place. Literally. The seating never varies.

Red O'Brien, the manager, sits alone in the right front row of seats. The travelling secretary has the left side. Coaches take the next two rows and the trainer, his assistant, the equipment manager, and Moose Greer are just behind.

The writers and broadcasters sit in the next couple of rows and the players have the rest of the plane: the Bible readers and sleepers towards the front; the cardplayers and drinkers next; and the rookies in the very back. I am the only woman on board who doesn't serve drinks.

I'm Katherine Henry. My friends call me Kate. I am a baseball writer by trade, and for the past five years I've spent the best months of Toronto's calendar everywhere but at home, following the Titans all over the American League map.

I'm forty, older than most of the Titans, including the manager. I'm tallish, prettyish, and a lot more interesting than most of the people I write about, but I love baseball. On the really good days I can't believe I'm paid to do my job.

I'm also good at it, to the active disappointment of some of my male colleagues, who have been waiting for me to fall flat since the day I walked into my first spring training. By now I have earned some grudging respect.

So has the team. They have never finished higher than fourth in the tough Eastern Division in the ten years they've been a team, but this season they began winning in spring training and forgot to stop. They slipped into first place in the beginning of June and have been there ever since.

There are a number of reasons for this. Stinger Swain is one. He's having a career season, with a batting average well over .300 and 37 home runs going into the last week of the season. But he isn't the only one. Red likes to say that if they award a new car for the Most Valuable Player this year they should make it a bus. Managers always like to say that. They find it in the media phrase book they get at manager school. It's right in there with "He pitched well enough to win," "We're just taking it one game at a time," and "You can't win any ballgames if you don't score any runs."

But Stinger is this year's star, unfortunately for the writers. Swain is a singularly unpleasant person, a vulgar, racist, sexist bully who embodies everything wrong with a society that finds its heroes on playing fields. He delights in making the writers uncomfortable. In my case, he insists upon doing all interviews in the nude. And his hands are never idle.

But there are more pleasant players. The best story of the year is Mark Griffin, an engaging lefthanded rookie reliever with 20 saves. He's just twenty-one, a real pheenom, and a Canadian, born and raised in my neighbourhood. They call him "Archie," because he's got red hair, freckles, and went to Riverdale Collegiate. His best buddy on the team is another lefthander, Flakey Patterson. When he and Griffin became friends, some of the players started calling Flakey Jughead. Swain and Grabowski called him Veronica.

Griffin is relatively sane, but Patterson is a Central Casting lefthanded pitcher – loony as a tune. During the three years he has been with the Titans, he's tried meditation, EST, self-hypnotism, macrobiotics, tai chi, and Norman Vincent Peale, and he alternates periods of extreme self-denial with bouts of excess. During the All-Star break, in protest over not being chosen for the team, he dyed his hair bright orange and wore it clipped close on the sides and long on top: as close to punk as is possible in the conservative world of sport.

He is the third starter in the rotation. The first, the Titans' erstwhile ace, is righthander Steve Thorson, Stevie the K, a twelve-year veteran and winner of a couple of Cy Young awards when he pitched for the Dodgers. His handsome blue-eyed face and body that won't quit are used to sell everything from breakfast cereal to men's cologne. He's mobbed for autographs wherever he goes. Grown men and women pack giant K's in their ballpark bags to wave when he strikes a batter out. He's the biggest star the Titans have ever had. And he's an insufferable prick.

The television guys love him, because he's always glad to see them. It might have something to do with the money they slip him for interviews, but I think it's also a matter of control. They only want thirty-second clips and feed him soft questions. He can do without the print guys. It's not that he refuses to talk to us, he just talks such self-serving crap that I hate to write it down.

He's not popular with the team, either. He always finds a way to blame his failure on others. The centre fielder or second baseman should have caught the ball that fell in for a game-winning hit. The catcher called for the wrong pitch. The manager shouldn't have taken him out of the game when he did, or, sometimes, should have when he didn't.

But he's a winner, which counts for a lot. Or he was until this season. Either age or opposing hitters caught up with him, and the former 20-game winner had only 13 going into the last week of the season.

It's ironic that the season they might win it all has been his worst, but I'm secretly delighted. His role as a winner was taken over by Tony Costello, nicknamed Bony because he's not, a lefthander with his own set of idiosyncrasies. He's a lunchbucket kind of guy from New Jersey, simple and matter-of-fact, but a total neurotic, so wrapped up in his phobias he has trouble functioning. He's afraid of flying, heights, the dark, germs, snakes, insects, and, most of all, failure. This last despite the fact that he's having a dream season. With 21 wins, he's a contender for the Cy Young Award, carrying the team on his pudgy shoulders. That scares him, too.

I looked back to where he was sitting, just behind Swain. He clutched a drink in one hand and a cigarette in the other, staring straight ahead. There were eight little Scotch bottles lined up on his tray. A typical trip for Bony. He's a candidate for the detox centre after a trip to the coast.

This road trip had been rough: Chicago, Detroit, and New York, all towns in which a person could get into a lot of trouble if she were so inclined. This late in the season I was so inclined I was almost bent. I was looking forward to a long night in my own bed.

I undid my seat belt and headed back towards the john, excusing myself past the players in the aisles. A few pretended not to hear me or refused to move, then made lewd remarks as I squeezed past. Steve Thorson yelled something about the back of the plane being off limits to the press. What a bunch of jokers, eh? Some fun.

The smiling face of Tiny Washington was a beacon. Surely the sweetest man on the team, he never gave me a hard time.

"The lovely Kate Henry," he murmured as I got to his seat, his voice a rich bass. "It's always a pleasure to see you. You're always welcome in my part of the world."

"Cut the crap, Tiny," I said. He winked.

"Stop by for a visit on your way back. We'll have us a little conversation."

Washington was one of the most sophisticated players on the team, but he hid it well. If people wanted to think he was nothing but a slow, friendly, shuck-and-jive kind of guy from the ghetto in Washington, D.C., that was fine with him. It made his life a lot easier. But I was lucky enough to find out early on what was behind the facade. It had made my life a lot easier.

That first spring, Tiny came up to me by the batting cage after a few days, introduced himself, offered to answer any questions I might have, then left me alone. I took him at his word and used him as a sounding board for my early perceptions.

It wasn't characteristic of him. He usually let reporters come to him. At the end of the season he explained why, late one night in the hotel bar in Cleveland.

"I watched the other writers and the way they were treating you. I listened to the other players. I could see how scared you were, but more important, I could see that you had pride. I thought maybe someone should give you a chance."

Then he had sensed how moved I was, finished his drink, and moved on.

"Hey, I give all the rookies a hand, if they know how to take it," he said. "You knew how."

That season, Tiny was the only legitimate star the team had. He was a veteran, admired by players all over the league. He set an example for the young Titans, especially the blacks, and smoothed my way with a word here and there to players on other teams. It helped a lot, and I was grateful.

Now he was at the end of his career, and smart enough to know it. He might have a few years left as a designated hitter, but there was a young player ready to take his place at first base. Hal Cooper, a.k.a. Kid, was a big farm boy from Nebraska who had been biding his time in Triple A for the last couple of years. He was called up when the rosters increased in September and Tiny had gone out of his way to help him. I hoped the Kid knew how to take the hand, too.

* * *

I ran the water into the toy sink until it was cold, then splashed it on my face. I felt grubby and looked like hell in the dim cold neon light. I'd lost the battle for control of my curly red hair, and the dark circles under my eyes weren't wayward mascara. I did the best I could with lipstick and hairbrush and went back out.

And walked straight into a fight.

Steve Thorson was halfway out of his seat, talking angrily to Joe Kelsey, the left fielder, who was standing in the aisle.

"What are you worrying about the pitchers for, Preacher? You just concentrate on catching routine fly balls and I'll do my job."

"How do you catch a fly ball when it lands in the upper deck, Thorson? That's where yours are going lately."

"Go read your Bible. I've got better things to do than talk to some asshole with all his brains in his bat. Or read some scouting reports, for a change, if your lips aren't too tired. The Bible doesn't tell you how to play left field."

Kelsey started towards Thorson, but Tiny Washington moved between them.

"You got a big mouth, Thorson," he said, "and a short memory. Seems like you only remember games we lost. I do believe that the Preacher has won one or two for you over the years. So why don't you go back to sucking on your beer and leave the man alone."

Thorson settled back in his seat warily. Not many players stood up to Tiny Washington when he stopped kidding around. When he was angry, it was best to keep out of his way.

Looking around him, Tiny realized that he had an audience.

"Seems like there are too many people on this team thinking about themselves," he growled. "All's we got to do is win four more games, but some folks think it's time to start fighting each other. How 'bout we save it for the Red Sox."

As he walked back to his seat in the sudden silence, the others squirmed like Sunday school kids caught stealing from the poor box. He smiled at me and motioned me into the middle seat in his row, next to Eddie Carter, the right fielder.

"You don't want to go making something big out of this, now. They're just kids. The pressure is getting to them."

"Thorson's no kid, Tiny. He's been through the pressure before."

"He's no kid, but he's stupid sometimes. Preacher shouldn't have listened to him."

"Preacher was right," said Carter, Kelsey's best friend. "Thorson's always blaming everything on us."

"Yeah, but anybody that knows anything knows that Thorson is full of shit. Excuse me, Kate."

Tiny's old-fashioned courtliness always tickles me. He should hang around the newsroom sometime. The language is worse there than in any locker room I've visited.

"So what do you think, Tiny? Are you guys going to win the pennant?"

"Sweeping the Yankees in their park was big. Even if they win the next nine games, all we have to win is four. At home. Looks like a lock to me."

"But what about the fat lady? It's not over until she sings."

"I do believe I can hear her warming up."

Carter chimed in with a falsetto hum, and we all laughed.

"Seriously, Tiny. People in Toronto are used to losing. They're just waiting to see you blow it the way the Maple Leafs and the Argos do every year."

"Well, you just write in your column that Tiny says not to worry. We'll have the whole thing wrapped up by the end of the weekend."

"Yeah? You're playing the Red Sox and the Yankees are playing Cleveland. You can't count on the Indians to help you."

"Then we'll just have to help ourselves."

"Okay, fine. I'll pass on your inspirational message to my faithful readers. You just keep your guys in line and get it over with."

I went back to the front of the plane. As I strapped myself back into my seat, Bill Sanderson, the *World* reporter, looked up from the book of statistics on his food tray.

"What's happening back there?"

"Nothing," I lied, opening my book.

Terminal One was deserted when we landed at one-thirty. The whole planeload trudged, some stumbling a bit, through the long corridors to the immigration desks. I found the line with the fewest Latin American players in it. If anyone was going to get held up it would be one of them. I was behind Archie Griffin. He greeted me warmly. He hadn't been around long enough to know that he was supposed to hate reporters.

"Hi, Archie. Nice game tonight."

He looked a bit embarrassed, and maybe a tad tipsy.

"Can I ask a favour, Kate? It's personal."

"Why not?"

"Could you stop calling me Archie? I hate that name."

"We've been calling you Archie all year. Why didn't you say something?"

"I'm a rookie. What could I say?"

"The season you've had, they should call you anything you want, Mark."

He smiled, a little sheepishly.

"Thanks. It's really been getting to my mum. Mark was my dad's name."

His father had died when Griffin was nine. His mother was a professor of medieval history at the University of Toronto who didn't know what to make of the alien being she had created.

"How is your mum? Enjoying the pennant race?"

"You wouldn't believe it, but she is. She even rented a TV."

"Amazing. You're up."

Griffin turned and went to the immigration desk. It didn't take him long to be passed through. I had my citizenship card out, gave it to the inspector, told her I had nothing to declare, and was handed a card with a code scrawled across the top, describing me, I hoped, as an upstanding citizen.

I met Gloves Gardiner on the escalator to the baggage claim. Just the man I wanted to see.

"What was that all about between Preacher and Thorson?"

"Sir Stephen's got his shorts in a knot and Preacher was handy."

"What's his problem now?"

"He's in a fight with his agent."

"Sam Craven? I thought he fired him."

"So did Steve. But there's still six months to run on their contract and Craven's not going to stand aside. He's threatening to sue."

"I don't blame him. Thorson's Titan contract is up for renewal and his agent's cut will be a nice little taste."

"You got it. Craven showed up at the stadium before the game tonight. Before you got there."

I'd missed the team bus, distracted by a late lunch with an old flame during which we had challenged the Aquavit supply of a Danish restaurant near his office. The players who had noticed I missed the bus were giving me a hard time about it.

"What happened?"

"Some shouting in the clubhouse."

"Were any of the other writers around?"

"No."

"Thanks for the tip."

"You didn't hear it from me."

"Hear what?"

Gloves was my spy. A man with a strong iconoclastic bent, he had taken a liking to me as soon as he saw how much some of the other reporters and players disapproved.

He has been around for dog's years, never a star, but good enough to hang on. He's appreciated not for his hitting or, goodness knows, for his speed on the basepaths, but because he knows how to handle his pitchers: which one needs coaxing, which one needs teasing, and which one needs kicking in the ass. He's aware of how much each had to drink the night before, and after a few warmup pitches he can tell what pitches are working and which aren't, better than the pitcher himself.

He's an odd athlete. He went to college for more than sport. He majored in English and history in the last gasp of the politicized sixties, and he both protested against the Vietnam War and lost his best friend to it.

I leaned against a post by the carousel and yawned. The players were playing baggage roulette, a ritual at the end of a road trip. Flakey Patterson collected a dollar from each player, and the pool went to the guy whose bag appeared first. Preacher Kelsey won it for the second time in a row. He and Eddie Carter exchanged low fives while the others muttered darkly about a fix.

My bag was third. I grabbed it and humped it past the weary-looking customs agent, who took my card and let me go.

Even at that hour, the waiting area outside was crowded with women and small children, the players' families. The wives were carefully coiffed and made up, most of them dressed to the nines. The kids were cranky.

Until six months ago, I'd had someone waiting for me, too. Mickey used to joke about the recipes he'd exchanged with the other wives and threatened to run away with one of them every time the plane was late.

Mickey worked for the CBC, a nice, solid liberal man who had decided after living with me for three years that he wanted someone waiting for him when he got home. Our parting had been passionless. Now I use an airport limo.

There was a larger group than usual waiting. The booster club was also on hand, sitting off to one side under a crudely painted banner. They were a sweet but sorry collection of misfits wearing Titan hats and tee-shirts. Rodney Hart, the pimply teenager who published their newsletter, called my name. I waved and went the other way, in no mood for statistical analysis at that hour. Besides, he'd probably phone and let me know what he'd found. I could always count on Rodney, bless his heart.

Grumpy drivers waited by half a dozen limos, forced to wait until the last plane landed. That was us, but they wouldn't get any business from the ballplayers. What are wives for? Only those of us on expense accounts were customers.

I passed up the first one on principle. He had an anti-smoking slogan prominently displayed. He was still yelling at me when my driver pulled away from the curb. We both lit up.

He was a wonderful driver. He put on a classical tape and didn't say a word. We glided down the 427 to the QEW, towards the blinking lights on the CN tower. Home.

I was dozing when we turned down my street, floating on music. The canopy of trees, lit by the street lights, had a golden glow. Autumn was coming.

ROBERT CURRIE

* * * * * * *

Poet and fiction writer Robert Currie teaches school in Moose Jaw. An active member of the Saskatchewan literary community, he served as Chairman of the Saskatchewan Writers' Guild and was a founder of both Salt *and the Thunder Creek Publishing Co-operative. Since 1970 he has published several volumes of poetry as well as the story collection* Night Games *(1986). He has also co-edited two anthologies. "How I Became a Poet" first appeared in* Grain *(Fall 1988) and was then collected in the anthologies* Sky High *(1988) edited by Geoffrey Ursell and* 200% Cracked Wheat *(1992) edited by Gary Hyland, Barbara Sapergia, and Geoffrey Ursell.*

"When I was a kid," writes Currie, "I sent away sight unseen for what sounded like a terrific fantasy novel about a boy who was part human and part bat and who lived amongst monsters. When I received Garth Garreau's Bat Boy of the Giants *in the mail, I discovered the monsters were guys like Johnny Mize and Mel Ott. And I was hooked on baseball – playing it and reading about it. As a reader, I still love and re-read Mark Harris's glorious trilogy of novels about that marvellous left-hander, Henry Wiggen. As a player, my fondest memory is hitting two for two as the Fort San Writers, under the inspirational coaching of Eli Mandel, creamed the opposition one golden day in the summer of 1977."*

* * * * * * *

How I Became a Poet

I'm standing on a platform in James Hall, conducting the brass section, but my mind is up the hill somewhere, looking across Echo Lake, wisps of cloud drifting through the sky, their white reflections drifting on the waves. Long, cool waves, but here the air is hot and still, heavy with the smell of sweating bodies. As I swing the baton, a drop of sweat runs down my nose and falls onto the music, a small, wet stain on the "Earle of Oxford's Marche." Then I miss a beat, harmony gives way to discord, and I'm back with my young charges.

Sure, I finally get Horton blowing his trombone instead of bumping somebody in the head with the slide, and it's me that messes up. Now he's off again, bopping the kid in front of him.

"Horton! A wind instrument is not an instrument of torture. It's meant to be blown through. Now, let's try it once more – from the top."

I stab the air and the sound comes, louder this time and more constant, but only a fair approximation of the score that William Bird once wrote. I wonder when music got to be so mechanical – and why. Ten minutes later we're done. The kids jam the double doors, eager to be down the stairs and free for an afternoon at the beach.

I go out the other way, through the door that's always open in what's usually a vain attempt to divert some fresh air into the hall. I sit on the steel fire escape and light a cigarette, taking a long drag, the smoke somehow cooler in my lungs than was the air inside the hall.

In front of me is the old nurses' residence, transformed now to writers' quarters. The only nurse who lives here these days is the one who passes out aspirin to the kids who get homesick and decide they don't like coming to a summer school. It's been years since this was a tuberculosis sanatorium. Sometimes, I forget it ever was. With the hills on either side of us climbing to the sky, the bandshell out front, the boardwalk running past the pavilions with their long, shaded porches and bright green lawns flowing down to the lake, it seems as if it must always have been a school of the arts.

I stub out my butt on the fire escape and flip it towards the parking lot. There's action down there now, people trooping from the writers' residence, carrying ball gloves and a kit bag with a couple of bats sticking from it, dumping everything in the back of a Chev wagon. Voices float up to me.

"We could maybe play a woman in right field," says a tall guy with a red beard. "Lorie's a better catch than most of us anyway."

"No," says a little guy who looks just a bit like Phil Rizzuto, except he's got a pot belly and is maybe twenty years over the hill. "It's not a mixed tournament. We've got to have at least nine guys."

"Well, Rhonda's kind of flat in the chest. Maybe, we could –"

"No dice! Try Harry. Maybe he's finished his story by now."

The lucky buggers, I think, off to a baseball tournament. Just the kind of thing I'd like to do, get out in the sun, whip the ball around, no music to think about, just legs and lungs working in the clean, country air. You know, I always wanted to be a ball player. Pop used to think it was a good idea too, but I guess it wasn't meant to be.

The writers are milling around the Chev when I see Greg Tilson looking up at me. Greg's from Thomas Gray Collegiate, same as me – only he's an English teacher. A poet too, writes this modern stuff – you couldn't find a rhyme in it to save your soul. Of course, you can hardly blame a fellow for how he spends his spare time.

"I think I got our problem solved," says Greg, and he's coming up the fire escape two steps at a time. "You finished teaching for the day?"

"Might be – if it gets me playing baseball."

"Softball. There's a sports day up in Lipton. Just for hellery, we entered a team. The Fort San Writers. We're one man short."

"Everybody's a writer?"

"Sure," says Greg. "The little guy in the blue – he's our manager – famous novelist from Toronto."

"Jeez," I say. "He don't look like Pierre Berton."

"Come off it, Fred. You gonna play or not?"

"Sure thing. You got an extra glove?"

So we go down the fire escape and he introduces me to the team, only it sounds more like an introduction to advanced creative writing or something, 'cause what we've got here is four poets, two short story writers, a journalist and a playwright – not to mention the Toronto novelist. Whether there's any fielders, let alone a pitcher or a catcher, is something else again. But I don't really care. I haven't hit a baseball in four years – and then only at the staff barbecue – and I can hardly wait to get a bat in my hands.

I climb into the Chev along with Greg, three other poets, and the Toronto novelist, and we head out of the parking lot, all three cars spraying gravel just like teenagers. I'm even beginning to feel like a teenager again.

Our manager, the Toronto novelist who's sitting in the front seat, cranks his head around and stares at me as if he's trying to recognize me.

"You're not in the poetry class by any chance?"

"No, no. I'm a music teacher. Brass."

"Oh."

He turns around and sits there, squirming for maybe sixty seconds, before leaning over to Greg. "We're listed as the Fort San Writers, aren't we?"

"It's okay, Eldon," says Greg. "We paid our fee. They don't care if we're the Fort San Poufs."

"Mmm...I suppose so."

"Look," says Greg. "I drove up to the Lipton pub last night with the registration. Soon as I said who we were, the whole bunch in there damn near bust a gut."

"Yeah?"

"Yeah. Five, six years ago, somebody put in a team from Fort San. They got beat twenty-three to zip. In three innings."

Even from behind I can see that Eldon is troubled. "Three innings?" he says.

"Sure. They got a rule that if one team's up by more than seven runs, the game's over after three innings. Speeds up the tournament."

"Well, I suppose that makes sense." Eldon pauses. "I'd sure hate to get knocked out in three innings though."

"Don't sweat it," says Greg. "This is just for laughs."

Eldon nods his head, slowly, as if he doesn't mean it, and slumps back in his seat. Pretty soon, he swivels around for another look at me. "You've never done any kind of writing, eh?"

I grin at him. "Sure. Last summer. I wrote a solo for slide trombone."

"Good!" he says. "Good. Welcome aboard." His smile is so relaxed and generous, I decide not to tell him that nobody's ever seen the solo but me.

We've left the lake behind now, climbing out of the Qu'Appelle hills and onto prairie that stretches for miles into the north, so flat and wide you'd think the valley was way behind. Here the land is as smooth as a major league infield. It gets me remembering summers when I was a kid, evenings when Pop and I would lug a bat and a bag of balls over to the school grounds. There was just a softball diamond, but Pop would pace out the sixty feet and pitch to me. He had a bum leg, stiff and shorter than the other – his souvenir from the war, he said – it made his style awkward as a stickman in a wind storm, but after he reared back into this double-jointed wind-up of his and lunged forward with his clumsy kick, that ball was really flying! I'd stand against the backstop and he'd pitch twenty balls, moving them around so that I was hitting high and low, inside and outside. "Hit 'em where they're pitched," he'd say, and, being left-handed at the plate, I'd pull the inside pitches to right field, slapping the outside ones to left. When he'd thrown all the balls, I'd pick up the ones I'd missed and toss them back to him, then hit those too. When they were all gone, the tough part came. With his bad leg, Pop didn't believe in logging any extra yards, so I'd head for the outfield, trotting back and forth till I'd found all the balls. Only once did I come up short. That was one time when Pop gave me his high hard one, and I connected just right, the good feeling surging from bat to wrists and up into my shoulders, the crack of ball on wood carrying, I'll bet, all the way to Main Street. No use looking for that ball. It was just starting to level out when it hit the roof of the school. There was a good, loud whap when it struck; then it bounced out of sight. For all I know, it's up there yet. Pop looked sort of mad at first – like I shouldn't have hit his fast one – then he grinned and said, "Well, son, they ought to write that one up in the papers."

Of course, Mom didn't think much of talk like that. She figured that baseball was just foolishness, that when Pop stepped onto a ballfield he was being silly, stepping back into his childhood. "There's no future there," she used to say. "But you stick with your music, and you'll have a good job some day. It's nice clean work; you can teach and play too."

Pop always used to snort at that. "Look at the papers," he'd say. "Joe DiMaggio. Ted Williams. Stan Musial. But who ever read a headline about a trombone player?" He had her there, I guess.

By this time, ahead and to the left, I can see elevators against the sky. Lipton. And I start to get nervous.

The other two guys in the back seat must be religious or something 'cause they're talking about archetypes and epiphanies. Sure, I think, praying might help, but can anybody pitch?

I ask Eldon and he says, "We're all set. We've got a fellow pitches in a league in Saskatoon."

Greg throws him a worried look. "Who?"

"Cod."

"Cod?" For a second, I think we're going in the ditch. The car swerves to the right, shuddering and fish-tailing in the loose dirt on the shoulder of the road. "Jesus, Eldon, that's a slow-pitch league."

"Slow pitch?"

"They throw so you can hit. They have to loft it like a bloody beach ball."

"Oh," says Eldon.

There's a long pause.

"Well," he says, "I'm sure Cod has a fast one too."

I think I hear him mutter, "He better have," but maybe that's just me, wishing out loud.

Anyway, we turn left off this grid road that's been running straight north, and, just before Lipton, grab a right, bouncing over railway tracks and onto a road which is just two ruts that lead into a field and peter out.

This is it, all right. There's a big tent, with the sides rolled up and a Bingo game going full blast, the numbers almost lost in the roar whenever the loudspeakers pick up the wind. There's even a merry-go-round, faded wooden horses bolted to long poles that swing round and round over a series of belts and wheels, turning to music that must've been nice a dozen years ago, but is mostly static now. Still, there's a line of kids laughing and pushing like this is the world's greatest ride.

And there are three ball diamonds. We drive over to number three, which is just pasture grass, the base paths worn deep through years of running, but there's a screen behind home plate, and, behind that, three rows of bleachers. A big guy decked out with umpire's pad and mask lumbers towards us. "You guys the writers?" he says and laughs.

While we lug out the equipment, Eldon is staring at the other team. "My God," he says, "they're wearing uniforms. I thought this tournament was for amateurs."

The uniforms are gray, with black pin-stripes. When somebody pops a fly our way, the fellow who lopes over to catch it is an Indian. "Standing Buffalo," it says on his chest.

"They're from the reserve," says our catcher, whose name is Leon. "Probably just play in the odd tournament."

"Sure," says Eldon. "No reason why we can't beat 'em. Hell, even the Pirates beat the Cards once in a while."

I decide not to think about that.

It's almost time for our turn in the field when I see that we're going to have uniforms too. Three of the women writers pile out of a Volkswagen, its door left hanging open, and trot across the field to us. Two of them are carrying Summer School of the Arts

T-shirts, a nice bright orange that will maybe blind the opposing batters. The other one has a box under her arm.

"We whipped into Fort Qu'Appelle for ball caps," she says. And she grins. "They were a bit more than we expected. So we had to settle for these."

When she opens the box, I nearly faint, 'cause what she pulls out is a stack of engineer's caps, the kind they used to wear to drive those old steam locomotives. Casey at the bat all right, but we'll look more like Casey Jones.

I take a good look at our team. Our right fielder is a shrimp with skin so pale he must do all his work at night, and by candlelight at that. Still he seems like an athlete beside our centre fielder, who has a black Afro hairdo and a huge beard which make his head look twice as big as his chest. His eyes look like they're peeking through a thicket. With his engineer's cap perched on all that hair, he looks positively top heavy. I swear, if he tries to run, all that weight is liable to flip him hair over heels in a perfect somersault. He's one of the poets. In fact, when we take the field for warm-ups, I realize our outfield is all poets. Eldon is hoping to keep them out of harm's way, I guess. I wonder if he gave any thought to having three water-boys. The infield better play deep 'cause sure as hell they'll be out there trying to dream up a fancy metaphor for softball when one goes flying over their heads. Our pitcher is going to be worse off than Charlie Brown.

Eldon is hitting grounders to the infield. The first hit to me is a fast one. I get my glove on it, but it pops right out – like it's made of rubber or something – so I scramble for it and throw too quickly, heaving it a good ten feet over the first baseman's head.

"Some arm," says Eldon. "We better play you at third."

"Just a little rusty," I say. "I'll get the next one down." Which I do. Hitting Wally, the first baseman, in the shins on one bounce. I don't know, but I used to play this game pretty well. Still, even making errors, it feels good to play again. My next throw is better, and Wally stretches for it and has it. He's long and lean and quick. We've got a real first baseman, I see – and a catcher too. Leon behind the plate is leaping out of his crouch and, smooth as quicksilver, whipping the ball down to second. Laying it right on the bag.

I'm sort of half-watching Leon when there's another crack of the bat and Eldon knocks one between my legs. I'm slow getting down and just wave goodbye at it.

"Hey there, coach," says an Indian who's leaning against the backstop, his grin so big he could swallow home plate. "You writer fellas wouldn't wanna make a little wager on this game, would you?" And he laughs, the umpire chortling along with him.

Eldon is about to drive another ball, but he turns around real quick. Leon is even quicker. "No," he says, "we're not betting men."

"I think mebbe I see why," says the Indian.

Before Eldon can get a word in, Leon hustles him over to our side of the field. I didn't think poets had reflexes like that, but I guess Leon is the exception that proves the rule.

Eldon is furious, his jaw working away at ninety miles an hour on whatever he's chewing. Gum, probably, though it looks just like chewing tobacco. He's not happy with Leon either, but he keeps his voice down so I can barely hear him. "Look. I don't mind losing a bet, but nobody insults the team. I mean, how'll the guys feel if I won't even bet on them."

I don't hear what Leon says, and I don't care. Eldon may be a writer, but I like the guy. From now on, I decide, no grounders are going through my legs.

A minute later Eldon calls us in for a quick huddle before the game begins. While he's talking, he makes a point of slapping us all on the shoulder or the back. "We've got a good chance," he says. "The way I see it, these reserve guys are over the hill. Look at the bellies on them. Probably train on beer and pretzels."

"Sure," I say, punching my glove. "We can take 'em."

Eldon grins, but nobody says a word. The three outfielders stare at me like I'm part of a line that doesn't quite rhyme. Or, even worse, one that does.

"I almost had some money down on you," Eldon finally says, "but Leon put the kibosh on a good thing. No matter. They get first bats, then we go to work." He claps his hands together, once, good and loud. "Okay. Go get 'em."

We trot onto the field, and Cod takes his warm-up pitches. He's wearing these little, round granny glasses and they suit him perfectly, 'cause he's throwing just like my grandma would – *if* her arthritis were a lot worse. He lofts each pitch into the air almost as if he's trying to knock off the crow that's right now circling the infield, his cawing like an old geezer's laughter. Yeah, and I can see what he's laughing at too.

I nearly break a leg getting over to Cod. "Jeez, Cod," I say, "hadn't you better try your fast one?"

He turns to me with this sheepish look on his face.

"That's it," he says. "I didn't want to tell Eldon. He's taking this pretty serious. I mean, nobody else can pitch at all."

"What're we gonna do?"

"Well," he says, "I could throw my slow ball."

I'm still trying to think of a comeback when I look down at home plate and see the first batter, just itching to get at it. He's about six feet tall and built like a granary. I head back to third and get ready to protect myself.

Cod goes into this screwy little wind-up, curling his left leg over his right and his arm behind his back and then tosses the ball like he's pitching to some girl in grade three. That batter is so eager to clobber that ball, he's all the way around and flat on his ass before the pitch is half-way to the plate.

"Stee-rike one!" says the ump.

"Hey, hey, the ol'sucker ball," I yell, pretending this is how we've got it planned.

When the batter dusts off his pants, he looks mad, glaring first at me and then at Cod. This time he waits before he swings, his left foot striding down toward me at third like he wants to squash me into the dirt. Then crack! and before I can get out of the way, my hand's stinging and there's the ball – caught tight in the pocket. One out, and I don't even have to throw to first. Which may be just as well.

The next guy up is slim and agile, muscles like elastics under his dark skin. Probably got that way bulldogging cows or steers or whatever they do on the reserve. Anyway, he goes after the first three pitches, coming around too soon on each, and that's two down.

He drags his bat back to where his team's sitting on the grass. When he squats down, I hear him say, "You got to wait for it. It's even slower than it looks."

The next batter is strong-looking, but fat, his stomach wobbling as he kicks out a spot beside the plate. He takes a couple of preliminary swings, then settles into a stance that looks comfortable and dangerous. We may be in trouble.

"Time out!"

I see an Indian stand up behind the backstop.

"Time out," he says again. "There's something hanging over the plate."

There's a roar of laughter from his cronies in the bleachers, but the batter just pats his belly and says, "Gonna be hangin' over first base in a minute." Then he eases back into his stance, looking even more relaxed than before.

Relaxed enough to get his timing just right, I guess, 'cause the first pitch comes back about ten times faster than it went in. In fact, it's still picking up speed when it disappears over a bluff of poplars in deep centre field. It'll probably come down about Prince Albert. This Indian is laughing so hard, it takes him nearly three minutes to get around the bases. When he comes past third, he says, "A pitcher like that does wonders for race relations."

I hear Eldon yell, "It's only one, guys, only one."

Then Leon starts in: "Just a little luck, Cod, babee. That's all. Pitch ball, babee, pitch ball, we get 'em, we got 'em."

And the ball comes floating in like another balloon just waiting to be popped, and wham! there it goes again. Except this time somebody's after it, running hell bent for election, and when the force of gravity finally remembers how it's supposed to work and brings the ball down, he's right there to gather it in. One of those poets, if you can believe it. The fellow with the Afro.

We come in for our licks, and Eldon's feeling pretty good. "One run," he says. "We can get that back easy."

I look at their pitcher, and I'm not so sure. Like their big hitter, he's got too much pot hanging over his belt, but I notice it doesn't get in the way of his arm when he whips it around in a windmill that sends the ball slashing across the plate. One of the outfielder poets is looking at him too. He's also beginning to look a little green.

"Don't worry," says Greg. "I can hit him." And he does, blooping the second pitch over the shortstop's head for a single. Well, like I said, he's really a teacher, not a poet. Besides, I seem to remember him hitting the ball pretty good at our staff barbecue. The next batter is the Afro, all that hair balanced crazily between man and cap. I guess he's a real poet 'cause he swings and misses the first three pitches, each one faster than the other, maybe one of them in the strike zone. He trots back to our side, looking relieved that he's escaped with his life.

"I like a fellow who stands up to the plate," says the umpire, who seems to be enjoying himself. While the catcher is gloating over this, Greg steals second. Nobody even notices he's going till he pops up out of a cloud of dust, and there he is. Pretty as a picture. One of these poets could maybe improve on that simile, but I'll bet he couldn't move like Greg.

We've got another of them at the plate, I see. I don't know what it is about these fellows, but they sure like to grow a crop of hair on their faces. Why, this guy's got muttonchops, make him look like he's stumbled out of another century. He isn't taking any chances on getting hit either, 'cause he's right at the edge of the batter's box and leaning back for all he's worth. He's got his bat on his shoulder, and that's exactly where it stays. Still, six pitches and they walk him.

Leon is up next, an athlete at last. He lets the first pitch go by him, maybe wanting to see what this guy has on the ball. When he lines the next one to centre field, Greg is off and running, coming around third like a greyhound after a rabbit. In fact, he's across the plate while the fielder's still bobbling the ball. Ol' muttonchops would've made it too, but he's busy watching the juggling act in centre field and doesn't see Eldon who's waving him on so fast his arm is about ready to whirl out of its socket. Muttonchops finally scuttles down to third after he hears Leon pounding up behind. Leon stops at second and spits in the dirt. I guess he'd rather have a triple.

Next up is Wally, who takes a good cut, fouling three pitches into the backstop, which – I notice now – has more holes than mesh. Every time he fouls one, three rows of bleachers look like a peanut scramble – except everyone's ducking away from what's thrown. Wally finally walks, and we've got the bases loaded and only one out. The next batter is another poet; so right away there's two out. At least we've still got the bases loaded.

Enough poets, I think, this has got to stop. And it does. The next one up is me. When I step into the batter's box, I'm not sure this is such a good idea. I mean, the dirt's worn away beside the plate and it's like standing in a hole and trying to hit a ball coming from an arm that's working like a sling. Sheesh, I think, at least with these poets, nobody expects them to hit. The first pitch comes at my head like a tomahawk and I'm so busy protecting my scalp, I sit right back on the seat of my pants.

"Stee-rike!" says the ump. He grins down at me. "Caught the inside corner."

That must be one hell of a curve, I think as I stand up, trying not to feel as foolish as I must look. The pitcher is laughing so hard he almost misses the ball when the catcher lobs it back to him. He is so bloody confident he looks a lot like Lightning Johnson, the best pitcher there ever was in the Moose Jaw Church League. And that's okay too, 'cause back in grade eight, I suddenly remember, I was the only guy on the Trinity Tigers who could always hit Johnson. I used to stand at the plate and grin at him. I never knew whether the grin made him nervous or me brave, but something worked, 'cause against Lightning Johnson I had a batting average of .623.

So I step back into the box and give this pitcher such a grin he maybe wonders what's wrong with my face. His pitch is inside, but it can hit me before I budge even an inch.

"Ball one," says the ump, and the catcher swears once, quietly.

"No swearing," says the ump. "I run a clean game."

Which gives me even more reason to smile.

Yeah, I'm grinning wide now, damn near laughing out loud, and that pitcher is looking a bit worried. Maybe he's got reason. His next pitch is fast and chest high, and I'm a little late with the swing, but the sound and the feel are right when I connect, and the ball takes off down the third base line like Willie Mays just hit it. I've got to admit, it feels so good, I almost forget to run, but a minute later I slide into third.

I'm safe with a triple, and this is as close to heaven as I've been since grade school. The three guys who've just crossed home plate are jumping around like they're nuts, and Eldon is so excited he comes out of the coach's box and hugs me. Right there in front of all those people. "Yessir," he says. "Poetry in motion."

And it's not over yet. A minute later, I'm home, and everybody's hitting. By the time they finally get out number three, the score is seven–one for us.

We're busy laughing and clapping and pounding one another on the shoulders, almost forgetting that we've only played the one inning. Eldon somehow manages to get us all back on the field and in the same positions again, but we're still kind of floating over the grass. What brings us down to earth is the first batter who watches two balls waft by him and then slams the third into the outfield poplars.

Cod looks shaken. He takes off his granny glasses and starts rubbing them on his T-shirt. Anything to postpone his next pitch, I guess, but right away Leon starts up his chatter behind the plate.

"Nemmer mind, Cod babee. We got this one. Pitch ball, babee. Chuck her here. We get him for you, Cod, get him quick, get him slick, get him easy!"

Cod throws one wide pitch, then waves for Leon, who tosses off his mask and trots out to the rubber. They stand there, talking, gesturing with their hands. Then they start to grin.

Eldon sidles towards third and glares at them, his lower lip shoved out like maybe he's Leo Durocher or something. When he can't take it any more, he tugs at the peak on his cap and says, "What the hell is that all about? Go check."

I trot over, and I can hardly believe what I'm hearing.

"For Pete's sake, you guys," I say, "this is a *ball* game."

They just look at me.

"Listen," I say to Cod. "I know you haven't got a fast ball, but can't you put a little spin on it or something?"

"Sure," says Cod, "the old sucker ball."

Leon laughs. "Chucker chatter," he says and walks back to the plate, pounding his fist in his mitt.

Eldon's waiting right there when I get back to third. "Well?" he says.

"Poetry – for Chrissakes!" I shake my head. "Cod's telling Leon he should write a bloody poem. Fulla the things that catchers yell to pitchers." Eldon's face twists up like maybe he thinks everyone but him and me belong in a cuckoo ward. "Yeah," I add, "he's gonna call it 'Chucker Chatter'."

Well, Leon really hits the chatter now, getting fancy, working on his poem, I guess, the words pouring out like magic.

"Come on babee, come on babee, you and me, babee, shoot it to me now. Groove it, eh? Move it, babee. Blow it by his nose."

Damned if Cod doesn't have that batter swinging like a barn door too. It's just like Leon has him convinced. He gets a little spin on the ball, and a little speed. Strikes him out on four pitches. And Leon is really singing now.

"We get 'em for you, babee. Team'll do it for you. Dream team, babee. On a beam. Shoot here, Cod. Pitch smoke, fella, pitch fire. Now you hot, babee. Burn him, burn him, burn him!"

I wouldn't believe it if I didn't see it. I mean, he must have them convinced too, 'cause in the next two innings there are five towering flies to the outfield, and those poets are bounding around like gazelles, dodging gopher holes without even a glance at the ground, snaring every ball that's hit. And that Afro, why, he doesn't look strong enough to catch a ball, let alone run after one, but he chases a fly that looks like it's gone forever. Man, he's out there, dodging poplar branches when he finally makes the catch. It's like Willie Mays in the '54 series, and I'm not ashamed to say it either.

"It's a plot," says one Indian, the only one to get as far as third base. "You knew we were death on fastballs and brought in a specialist."

"Sure," I say, "we had our scouts check things out."

"Injuns send out scouts too – with war parties." He looks mean when he says it, but right away he breaks into a grin. "We musta scouted the wrong teams though. Overlooked you guys." Then he really grins. "Good thing your scouts forgot to mention you should bet on this game."

"Buddy," says I, "if we hang on to this lead, I'll buy you a beer."

"Buddy," says he, "if you do, I am gonna need a beer."

Things are going so well that somebody even drives back to Fort San for the school P.R.O. to take some pictures.

Well, I don't mind admitting that I get up to bat once more, with men on second and third this time. After my triple down the third base line, they're all playing me to that side, but I've got my timing now and knock the ball over first, and that's it. We've got an eight run cushion, and the game is over. As I'm taking off for first, I hear the umpire giving Leon the needle: "Should've took that bet, catcher."

And ain't it the truth? Still, we've won, and that's all that matters. Eldon is so worked up he runs right across the field, almost beats me to first base to shake my hand.

"Great!" he says. "Just great!"

We're all milling around now, socking each other, boasting a little, maybe, floating even higher off the ground, when I notice the look of purest joy on Eldon's face. "You know," he says, "even if we lose the next game, we'll still have a better record than the Blue Jays had against the Twins."

Well, we do lose the next game, but that's okay. I mean, nobody can expect more than one miracle a day. Besides, there's something else that happens.

By the end of the summer, half the weeklies in the province end up running the same picture. It's a photo of me slamming the last hit of the game, concentration, co-ordination like a teenage athlete, every muscle tense, a swing like Stan Musial.

Maybe the headline does say, "Poet slams triple," but – what the hell – I guess that's okay too.

PAT JASPER

* * * * * * *

Pat Jasper was born in New Jersey, but, as an army brat, travelled extensively during her early years. Educated in New Mexico, she moved to Toronto in 1974, became a Canadian citizen in 1986, and now lives in Markham. A frequent contributor to literary periodicals and anthologies, she is the author of two volumes of poetry, Recycling *(1985) and* The Outlines of Our Warm Bodies *(1990). "The Girls of Summer" is one of several baseball poems found in the latter collection. An earlier version of the poem was published in* Cross-Canada Writers' Quarterly *(Summer 1989).*

"I began playing sandlot ball," Jasper recalls, "at the age of nine, but was unable to participate in Little League (one of the great tragedies of my life) due to the misfortune of being born female. One of the coaches took pity on me and taught me to keep score so I could sit in the dugout as official scorekeeper. I've actually earned money over the years scoring and, to this day, score every Blue Jays' game I attend or watch on TV, even important games on radio.

"I once earned an A in my freshman English class for knowing Stan Musial's batting average (.529 – early in the season). My teacher was also a coach. St. Louis was my favourite team when growing up.

"In my 20's, I played women's softball in the same league as my sister. We shared a glove between us. When we played each other, she'd toss me the glove on her way in from the pitching mound as I was on my way out to second base. She now coaches high-school girls' softball in Colorado.

"In my 30's, I played for General Electric in an Industrial League in Toronto. We won our league championship two years running due largely to our pitcher, who could often strike out the

side on nine straight pitches. (She was better than most of the women in League of Their Own.*)*

"In my 40's, I played on two teams: one fast-pitch, one slow-pitch – sometimes with games the same night, one after the other! But last year, finally making concessions to Mother Time, I decided to concentrate on slow-pitch. The masters' team I was on placed fourth in our division in the Ontario championships.

"'The Girls of Summer' was written to try and capture the closeness and camaraderie among teammates that I've experienced on these teams. Each team is different and it's never the same once the season ends, but how wondrous while it lasts!

"Rabid Blue Jays fan. Being a second-baseman, Robbie Alomar is my god."

* * * * * * *

The Girls of Summer

This is our time to howl –
Come Friday night, otherwise respectable women,
decked out in stirrups and tight pants, grab
sleeping bags and hit the road. In their trunks,
a favorite bat, dusty gloves, suntan oil
and enough beer to stun an army.

Behind, we leave glum husbands and grieving children
who will subsist on Kraft Dinner until our return.
Ahead, the adventure of the unknown, in Tottenham,
Fenelon Falls, the outskirts of our lives.

The sidelines buzz with rumors of ringers:
pitchers equipped with dropballs and risers;
sluggers we plot to walk each trip to the plate.
Covering all the bases, we chat up
the ump, offer the opposing coach a beer.

Minutes till game time, we stretch hamstrings
and quads, begin to soft toss and psych
ourselves up. The shortstop swallows a valium.
Balancing a cigarette on the lip of the dugout,
the lead-off batter takes her cuts. The catcher
bellows, *Coming down!* and unloads to second.

Seven innings of screaming profanities we'd soap
our kids' mouth for uttering, butt-slapping,
jeers, bone-crunching slides. Nothing matters
but what is happening here, on this field:
one down, tying run at third. What's the sign?
Sac fly? Squeeze? We come from behind, win
two close ones; the next day are afraid
to change anything, even our underwear.

Afterwards, we drink and rehash each play:
the mile-high pop-up lost in the sun,
the bases-loaded triple down the line.
Some ice down sore arms,
wrap knees in Ace bandages.
The smell of A-535 permeates the air.

The fraternity of locker rooms, mingled
sweat. We are among the initiates, violating
male bastions, proving ourselves
to ourselves. Into the breach,
brandishing plastic trophies.

On the long drive home, empties rolling
at our feet, heads slumped on a teammate's
shoulder, we nurse hangovers and vague dreams.
Sliding into home headfirst in a cloud
of dust, the roar of the crowd. The elation
of excelling at a useless task. This taste
of life, undomesticated.

EDO VAN BELKOM

* * * * * * *

Edo van Belkom lives in Brampton, where he works as a freelance writer. During the past few years he has published numerous stories in a variety of magazines and anthologies, mostly within the science-fiction and horror genres. "Baseball Memories," which was written while van Belkom was employed as a sports writer at the Brampton Times, *originally appeared in* Aethlon: The Journal of Sport Literature *(1991) and was subsequently reprinted in* The Year's Best Horror Stories: XX *(1992) edited by Karl Edward Wagner.*

* * * * * * *

Baseball Memories

Samuel Goldman had a memory like most of us when it came to regular things. He forgot the odd birthday or anniversary now and then but no one ever thought him forgetful.

He was no more absent-minded than his neighbor, who still hadn't returned Sam's lawn-mower even though Sam's lawn was rapidly becoming a neighborhood eyesore.

Sam remembered what he wanted. His wife Bea could tell him a hundred times to take out the garbage but he never took notice of her if he was doing something important – like watching a baseball game.

Sam had a talent for the sport which relied so heavily on numbers and statistics as a measure of a player's worth. He could ramble off records for all of the Toronto Blue Jays' pitchers from opening day, 1977. He knew, by heart, the averages of the top hitters of every major league team in baseball as well as records for stolen bases, home runs, RBI's and ERA's for just about anybody who was anything in the sport.

It was a hobby of course, something he liked to do with a cup of coffee and a book late at night after his family had gone to bed.

His seemingly boundless knowledge of baseball was always good for a few laughs among his friends. All of them were baseball fanatics; the only difference being, they didn't have his talent.

He was a great conversationalist at parties too, as long as talk centered around his favorite subject. Once he got his hands on somebody who was willing to drill him or be drilled about baseball history, he never let them out of his sight. The only way to get rid of Sam was to ask him how much he knew about hockey – which was nothing at all.

Some of Sam's friends began calling him "Psychlo" because he was a walking, talking encyclopedia of baseball. They would sit around the picnic table shooting the breeze over a few beers and suddenly the discussion's decibel level would turn up a few notches. A finer point of the game would come under question and it was up to Sam to turn the volume down and restore order.

"Sammy, what did George Bell hit on the road in 1986?"

".293," Sam would say without hesitation.

"And how many homers?"

"Sixteen of his thirty-one were hit on the road."

"Thanks Sam. See I told you," one pal would say to another before the talk moved on to another trivial statistic that might ultimately change the world.

Sam considered himself gifted. He thought that what he had was a natural talent for numbers; something that might one day get him on the cover of a magazine or on some television talk show where he might finally be recognized for his achievement.

Sam's wife Bea wasn't so crazy about baseball.

She put up with it though, as most wives do with their husband's vices. She thought it was better for him and their marriage if he spent late nights with his nose buried in a baseball book instead of some bar flirting with a woman with an "x" in her first name.

"As long as he sticks to baseball it's pretty harmless," she always said – half telling someone, half telling herself.

And then one day she began to wonder.

The two were sitting at the breakfast table one Saturday morning when Sam said something that put a doubt in her mind about the mental well-being of her husband.

"Why don't we take a drive up north today and visit your cousin Ralph?" he said.

Bea was shocked. She looked at Sam for several seconds as if trying to find some visible proof that he was losing his mind.

"Ralph died last winter, don't you remember? We went to the funeral, there was six inches of snow on the ground and you bumped into my mother's car in the parking lot. She still hasn't forgiven you for it."

Sam was shocked too. He could remember how many triples Dave Winfield hit the last three seasons but the death of his wife's cousin had somehow slipped his mind.

"Oh yeah, that's right. What the hell am I thinking about?" he said and added, "I better go out and wash the car."

Things were fairly normal for the next few weeks and Sam was able to wow them with his lightning-fast answers and astounding memory. As long as baseball was in season, Sam was one of the most popular guys around.

A co-worker of Sam's even figured out a way to make some money with it and the two were making a few hundred dollars a week – tax free. After work they'd go out to some bar where nobody knew about Sam. Armed with the *Sports Encyclopedia of Baseball*, they'd bet some sucker he couldn't stump Sam with a question.

"Who led the Cleveland Indians in on-base-percentage in 1952?" the sucker would ask, placing a $10 bill on the bar.

"Larry Doby, .541, good enough to lead the American League," answered Sam and after a quick check in the encyclopedia for verification, the two had some pocket change for the week.

Sam was astonished at the financial benefit of his talent. He always thought of himself as an oddball, but if he could make some money at it – tax free to boot – then why the hell not. Money made him study the stats even harder, looking to increasingly older baseball publications to make sure he knew even the most trivial statistic.

Late at night he would thumb through the rabbit-eared encyclopedia and discover a new figure he hadn't known about.

"Well would you look at that," he said as his eyes bore down on the page and his brain went through the machine-like process of absorption, processing and filing. It took less than ten seconds for him to remember forever that a guy by the name of Noodles Hahn led the Cincinnati Reds pitching staff in 1901 with a 22-19 record. Hahn pitched 41 complete games and had 239 strikeouts, leading the league in both categories. No mean feat considering the Reds finished last with a 52–87 record.

The information was stored in a little cubby-hole in his brain and could be recalled at any time like a book shelved in a library, picked up for the first time in fifty years. The book, a little dusty, would always be there and its story would always be the same.

* * *

Bea went to see Doctor Manny Doubleday, the family physician, after Sam did another all-nighter with his books. She was concerned about him.

It was true Sam had brought her some very nice things since he'd been making money in bars but she felt the items were tainted. The fur coat had been in the hall closet since the day he bought it for her, not only because it was summer, but because she was ashamed of it. She wouldn't show it to guests, even the ones who might have thought Bea the luckiest girl in the world – and Sam the greatest husband.

She sat quietly in the office waiting for the good doctor. Dr. Doubleday had been the Goldman's family physician for what seemed like forever. He delivered both Sam and Bea into the world and always looked upon the couple as a match made by his own hands. He was also a former minor league pitcher and big baseball fan. He had gone to several ball games with Sam over the years; he liked Sam and thought it wonderful that he knew so much about the sport.

The office was decorated like a tiny corner of Cooperstown. On the walls hung various team photos and framed newspaper clippings about Manny Doubleday in his heyday. On the desk were baseballs signed by Mickey Mantle and Hank Aaron, even one signed by Babe Ruth, although no one really believed it because the "Bambino" had allegedly signed his name in crayon.

From down the hall the doctor's melodic whistle pierced through a crack in the door and into the room. Moments later the door burst open and in strode the portly doctor.

"What seems to be the problem Bea?" he asked, picking up a dormant baseball and wrapping his fingers around it as if to throw a split-fingered fastball right over the plate.

"It's Sam, I think he's – "

"How is the old dodger?" the doctor interrupted as he took a batter's stance and imagined swinging through on a tape-measure home run. "You know I've never seen anyone with a memory like his, it's uncanny the way he can tell you anything you want to know at the drop of a hat."

"Yes that's what I mean, I think he's overdoing it a bit," said Bea sitting up on the edge of her chair anxious to hear some words of support.

"Nonsense," replied the doctor. Bea slumped back in her chair.

"What your husband has is a gift. He has a photographic memory that he's chosen to use for recording baseball statistics. It's harmless."

"It used to be harmless, he used to do it in his spare time but now he lets other things slide just so he can cram his head with more numbers. He's beginning to forget things."

"Bea," the doctor said putting down his invisible bat, forgetting about baseball. "Forget for a minute that I'm your doctor and consider this a discussion between two friends.

"Most people are able to use about ten percent of the brain's full capacity. Your husband has somehow been able to tap in and exceed that ten percent. Maybe he's using twelve or thirteen percent, I don't know, but it happens. He could be making millions at the black jack tables in Atlantic City but he chose to use it for baseball. Just be happy it's occupying him instead of something more dangerous. I'll talk to him the next time he's in. How are the kids?"

Bea was brought sharply out of her lull and answered in knee-jerk fashion. "Fine and yours."

She was satisfied, but marginally. It was one thing for the doctor to talk about Sam's mind in the comfort of the office, it was another thing entirely to sit at the dinner table and watch him to try to eat his soup with a fork.

"Honey," she'd say. "Why don't you try using your spoon? You'll finish the soup before it gets cold."

"Yeah, I guess you're right *handed batters versus lefties*," Sam would reply and then sit silently for a few moments. "Did I say that? Sorry, Bea, I don't know where my head is."

Sam knew he was spending a little too much time with his baseball books. He was weary of the numbers and after a couple hours' study some nights the inside of his skull pounded incessantly and felt as if it might explode under the growing pressure. But he loved the game too much to give it up.

Anyway, the money he earned on the bar circuit was good. It was so good in fact that he could probably put the kids through college with his winnings; something he could never do working at his regular job.

Sam worked as an airplane mechanic in the machine shop at the local airport. He was good at his job and always took the time to make sure it was done right.

One day he was drilling holes in a piece of aluminum to cover a wing section they had been working on. The work was monotonous so Sam occupied his time thinking about the previous night's study.

"Pete Rose hit .273 his rookie year, .269 his second, .312 his third..."

The drill bit broke and Sam was brought back into the machine shop. He stopped the press, replaced the bit, tightening it with the key.

"Lou Gehrig hit .423 in 13 games for New York in 1923, .500 in 10 games in 1924, .312 in his first full season in 1925..."

Sam started the drill press and the key broke free of its chain, flew across the shop and hit another mechanic squarely on the back of his head.

He was once again brought back into reality, shut the drill off and rushed over to see if his fellow worker was still alive. A crowd gathered around the prone man and all eyes were on Sam as he neared the scene.

"What the hell were you thinking of?"

"You gotta be more careful."

"That was pretty stupid."

The mechanics crowed in unison and Sam felt like a baseball that had been used too long after its prime. His insides felt chopped up and unravelled as he looked at the man lying on the floor.

A groan escaped the downed man's lips, "What the hell was that?" he asked and the group around him breathed easier. Sam felt better too, but just a little. The shop foreman walked up to him, placed a comforting hand on his shoulder and told him to go home.

"Why don't you take the rest of the day off, before he gets off the floor and these guys turn into a lynch mob."

"Sure, boss. I'll go home *run leaders for the past twenty years.*"

"What?"

"Nothing, nothing. I don't know what I was thinking of."

On the way home Sam stopped by "The Last Resort," a local sports bar with a big-screen T.V. and $2 draughts. He needed a drink.

After what happened at the shop, Sam thought he was going crazy. Baseball trivia was fun but if it turned him into an accident waiting to happen, he might as well forget all about his baseball memory.

He sat on a stool in front of the bartender and eased his feet onto the brass foot-rail. Comfortable, he ordered the biggest draught they had.

As he sipped the foam off the top of the frosted glass, he overheard a conversation going on down at the other end of the bar.

"Willie Mays was the best player ever to play the game, and believe me, I know...I know everything there is to know about the greatest game ever invented."

Sam watched the man speak for a long time. He stared at him – trying to see right through his skull and into the folds of his brain. Sam wanted to know just how much this blow-hard really knew.

"Go ahead, ask me anything about baseball, anything at all. I'll tell you the answer. Heck I'll even put $10 on the bar here – if you stump me it's yours."

"How many home runs did Hank Aaron hit in his first major league season?" asked Sam as he carried his beer down the bar toward the man.

"Aw that's easy, thirteen, Milwaukee, 1954. I want some kind of challenge."

"All right then, in what year did Nolan Ryan pitch two no-hitters and who did he pitch them against?"

"Another easy one. Nolan Ryan was pitching for the California Angels and beat Kansas City 3-0, May 15, and Detroit 6-0, July 15 – 1973."

Sam was startled. No-hitters were something he studied just the night before. This guy was talking about them like they were old news.

"Okay, now it's my turn," the man said massaging his cheeks between his thumb and forefinger. "But first would you care to put a little money on the table?"

"Take your best shot," answered Sam slamming a $50 bill on the bartop.

"Well, a $50 bill," the man was impressed. "That deserves a $50 question!"

The man looked into Sam's eyes. A little sweat began to bead on Sam's forehead but he was still confident the bozo had nothing on him.

"Okay then. Who was the Toronto Blue Jays' winning pitcher in their opening game 1977 and what was the score?"

Sam smiled, he knew that one. But suddenly something about the way the other man looked into his eyes made his mind draw a blank. It was as if the man reached inside and pulled the information out of Sam's head before Sam had gotten to it. The beads of sweat on Sam's forehead grew bigger.

"I'm waiting," said the man, enjoying the tension. "Aw, c'mon, you know that one. I only asked it so you'd give me a chance to win my money back."

Sam closed his eyes and concentrated. Inside his brain, pulses of electricity scrambled through the files searching for the information, but all pulses came back with the same answer.

"I don't know," said Sam.

"Too bad. It was Bill Singer, April 7, 1977, 9–5 over Chicago. $50 riding on it too. Better luck next time, pal."

The man picked up the money and walked out of the bar. Sam stood in silence. He'd never missed a question like that – never! He finished his draught and ordered another.

Sam said nothing about the incident to Bea over dinner. He ate in silence, helped his wife with the dishes and told her to enjoy herself bowling with the girls.

When she was safely out of the driveway, Sam dove into his books. He vowed never to be made a fool of again and intensified his study. He looked up Bill Singer and put the information about him back on file in his head. He studied hundreds of pitchers and after a few hours their names became a blur.

Noodles Hahn, Cy Young, Ambrose Putman, Three Finger Brown, Brickyard Kennedy, Kaiser Wilhelm, Smokey Joe Wood, Wild Bill Donovan, Twink Twining, Mule Watson, Homer Blankenship, Chief Youngblood, Clyde Barfoot, Buckshot May, Dazzy Vance, Garland Buckeye, Bullet Joe Bush, Boom Boom Beck, Bots Nickola, Jumbo Jim Elliot, George Pipgrass, Schoolboy Rowe, Pretzels Puzzullo, General Crowder, Marshall Bridges, Van Lingle Mungo, Boots Poffenberger, Johnny Gee, Dizzy Dean, Prince Oana, Cookie Cuccurullo, Blackie Schwamb, Stubby Overmire, Webbo Clarke, Lynn Lovenguth, Hal Woodeschick, Whammy Douglas, Vinegar Bend Mizell, Riverboat Smith, Mudcat Grant, John Boozer, Tug McGraw, Blue Moon Odom, Rollie Fingers, Billy McCook, Woody Fryman, Catfish Hunter, Vida Blue, Goose Gossage, Rich Folkers, Gary Wheelock.

Sam closed the book shut. His head was spinning.

He felt like he couldn't remember another thing, not even if the survival of baseball depended on it.

But then a strange thing happened. Sam swore he heard a clicking sound inside his head. His brain felt as if it buzzed and whirred and was suddenly lighter.

He reopened the book and looked at a few more numbers. He then took them in, closed the book once more and recited what he had learned.

"We're back in business," Sam said out loud and returned, strangely refreshed, to the world of statistical baseball.

Bea came home around eleven o'clock and found Sam in the den asleep with his face resting on a stack of books.

Doesn't he ever get enough? she thought and poked a finger into his shoulder trying to wake him.

"Huh, what...*Phil Niekro, Atlanta Braves 1979, 21-20 at the age of 40. Gaylord Perry, San Diego Padres 1979, also 40, 12-11...*"

"Sam, wake up. Isn't it time you gave it a rest and went to bed?" Bea said pulling on his sleeve hoping to get him out of his chair.

"Who are you?" asked Sam looking at Bea as if they were meeting in a long narrow alleyway somewhere late at night.

"Well, I'll say one thing for you Sam, you still have your sense of humor. C'mon, time for bed."

"Which way is the bedroom?" Sam thought his surroundings familiar, but he wasn't too clear about their details.

"Into the dugout with you. Eight innings is more than we can ask from a man your age!" said Bea, caught up in the spirit of the moment.

After the two were finally under the covers, Sam lay awake for a few minutes looking the bedroom over. The pictures on the wall looked familiar to him and he thought he might be in some of them himself. Comfortable and exhausted he finally dozed off.

* * *

Sam's brain was hard at work while the rest of his body rested in sleep.

It had started with a faint click but now his brain hummed and buzzed with activity. After being bombarded with information over the past months, every available cubby-hole in Sam's brain had been filled. There wasn't room for one more ERA, one more home run, not even one more measly single.

But like an animal that has been adapted to its environment over the course of generations, Sam's brain was evolving too, and decided it was time to clean house.

The torrent of information it had been receiving must be essential to the survival of the species, the brain reasoned. Why else would so many names and numbers be needed to be filed away? So the brain began a systematic search of every piece of information previously stored, from birth to present, and if it did not resemble the bits of information the brain was receiving on a daily basis, out the window it would go.

Sam's brain decided it wasn't essential that he remember how to use the blow-torch at work so it was erased to open up new space for those supremely important numbers.

By the time Sam awoke, a billion cubby-holes had been swept clean.

Sam walked sleepily toward the kitchen where Bea already had breakfast on the table.

"What's that?" asked Sam pointing to a yellow semi-sphere sitting on a perfect white disk.

"Are you still goofing around?" Bea answered. "Hurry up and eat your grapefruit or you'll be late for work."

Sam watched Bea closely, copying her movements exactly. He decided he liked the yellow semi-sphere called grapefruit and every bite provided a brand new taste sensation on his tongue. Sam's brain couldn't be bothered to remember what grapefruit tasted like, not even for a second.

Bea helped Sam get dressed for work because he said he couldn't remember which items on the bed were the ones called pants and which were the ones called shirts.

Bea decided she'd see Dr. Doubleday the moment she got Sam out of the house and insist he come by and give Sam a check-up. She nearly threw Sam out of the door in her rush to see the doctor.

As the door of the house closed behind him, Sam tried to remember just exactly where he worked and what it was he did for a living.

He also wanted to go back to "The Last Resort" and show that joker at the bar that Samuel Goldman was no fool.

If only he could remember how to get there.

RICHARD CUMYN

* * * * * * *

Richard Cumyn was educated in Ottawa; Rothesay, New Brunswick; and Kingston, Ontario and now lives in Halifax, where he is active as a freelance writer. His fiction has appeared in such magazines as The Dalhousie Review, The Canadian Forum, *and* The New Quarterly. *A member of the Periodical Writers' Association of Canada, he has also contributed essays to a number of Canadian newspapers. "Ladies' Ball" was first published in* The Canadian Forum *(October 1991).*

Reminiscing about his baseball experiences, Cumyn writes, "When I was seven or eight my father produced two floppy leather gloves that had once been his father's and a pristine hardball. 'It's time you learned how to play,' he said, handing me what had once been a padded catcher's mitt. I remember thinking that I already knew how to play. I was a kid. Playing was what I did.

"So we went out beside the house. Dusk was falling and the wind coming up the Kennebecasis River from Saint John smelled like Irving Pulp and Paper. Dad showed me how to wear the baseball glove on my left hand. 'You don't put your hand all the way in,' he instructed. 'Here, like this.' On his hand it looked like a bowl stretched taut on the ends of his big fingers.

"I had to stick my hand all the way in to get the invertebrate relic to stay on my hand. The first pitch came in hard and fast. It was the arrow severing the last invisible strand of my umbilicus. It was an instant replay of that first outrageous slap that gets us breathing on our own. It was childhood's veil ripped from across my eyes, initiation, Iron John *in a spheroid.*

"I recovered, eventually got my own glove with padding. We went on to spend countless summer evenings throwing the baseball around, not talking very much, just letting the different speeds, trajectories, dances connect us. I miss that."

* * * * * * *

Ladies' Ball

Apart from passing reference, which he raised to a grudging acknowledgement at World Series time, David had neither played baseball nor contemplated its mysteries since his Little League days. Back then he had been his team's starting pitcher and had learned how to throw a bewitching change-up slider. His neighbourhood gang played sandlot ball every day after supper until the light failed and sometimes well after that. He used to oil his glove daily with Dubbin and tie a baseball in at night to form the pocket. A wad of bubblegum was permanently in his cheek. Someone was always slapping him on the back. He lived for the hustle, the chatter, the guys. He had loved batting practice and rehearsing the double play and perfecting his throw to first base. The myriad rules had been his gospel, the minutiae of statistic upon statistic his history. The ball diamond, where he had been alive and sane, was a universe of predictable outcomes. After two years of Little League baseball, he never played again. "Oh, I outgrew it," he explained to those who asked why.

That parched day in June when David and Joan moved into Clayton from the city, their next door neighbour, Grace Henderson, leaned over the fence.

"You'll be playing Ladies' Ball?" she asked, less a question than a statement of fact. Although Grace was looking at Joan when she said it, David felt just as easily that it could have included him. Grace's rural twang sent a devilish shiver through him. Ladies. The word suggested lavender, flowered hats, high tea. An antique derision resided in the word now; no young woman of his acquaintance would accept such a title as complimentary. Furthermore, knowing Joan as he did, he imagined her rolling *double entendres* around in her head the way she manipulated her jade exercise balls in one palm. Question: What happens after Ladies' Ball? Answer: Ladies' Smoke. Is the size of the bat important in Ladies' Ball or is it all in the grip? He thought he could see these sparking up behind Joanie's deep brown eyes as she smiled politely.

"I'm not really a baseball player," said Joan.

"Softball," Grace corrected her. "Come on now, none of us are that good. We're always looking for new blood. Everybody in Clayton plays."

"I don't know...but thank you anyway for asking," said Joan. David crinkled his eyes approvingly at her.

"Suit yourself. First game's tomorrow night down at the Community Centre. Why don't you just come and watch, see what it's like? We all go over to the Legion after for a cold one. Just one. We call it the One Club, but sometimes it stretches into three or four."

David decided that they needed a way to escape gracefully from Grace.

"We'll come and watch," he said. "We'll bring the girls."

They were neither of them team sports types now. Joan had played soccer as a child and had just recently discovered cycling. David was an on-again, off-again runner who played squash twice a week at noon. A friend was teaching them tai chi. They had not talked about it but David felt a tacit agreement that sports such as softball, except for impromptu games on family picnics, held nothing for them. There was something too organized about the games which required too many slavish rituals and far too much dependence on the performance of others. David had no doubt that Joan shared his contempt for the unflattering, tight uniform breeches and the peaked hat that moulds the hair into a comic mushroom cap. The way he saw it, the conformity amounted to a naive giving over of individuality, even of personhood.

The heat made sleeping impossible the next night. David suggested an evening stroll. Both he and Joan had forgotten about Ladies' Ball until the moment the four of them, Katie on David's shoulders, Joan pushing Murphy in her stroller, came within sight of the diamond. Although it was still light outside at nine o'clock, powerful floodlights had turned the softball area into a bright noon. A breeze was discernible out here beyond the buildings of the town and the players looked comfortable in their roomy half-sleeve jerseys.

"Can't we watch for a while, Daddy? Please?" pleaded Katie when it became evident to her that her father meant to skirt the ball field.

"It's too late. We're only out here to cool off."

David's pronouncement was met by protest from both children.

"We did say we'd come to watch, David. The girls aren't going to get to sleep for a while, anyway."

The bright, cold light that washed into the surrounding scrub brush and out over the road was magnetic, he had to admit. He could feel an excitement here, even though the spectators numbered only about as many as the players. There was a sense of conspiracy as if, illicitly, these people were cheating the night's stale mug.

The scoreboard showed that the teams had played four innings by the time the newcomers sat on the first tier of the bleacher behind Grace's team. They were playing a team from Byronville and were ahead by two runs. Grace caught sight of her neighbours when her team took the field and she waved. Joan waved back.

"Hey, Joan, we're short a player. You can play right field," Grace called from second base.

David expected his wife to decline politely. He was ticking the excuses off in his head: she was improperly dressed, she had no uniform, she didn't know how to play, wasn't it against the rules to bring in new players once the game had begun?

"Well, all right. Sure," she said and stood up to make her way onto the field.

"Joan, you're kidding," whispered David. "What about the girls?"

"You can take them back when they get tired," she said, a simple directive free of undertone.

"But you don't know the first thing about baseball."

"Softball, David."

Grace found her a glove and a team jersey to wear, one so large that it hung below Joan's shorts and made it look as if she was wearing nothing underneath. It drew the eye to her long, tightly muscled cyclist's legs, the soft, blonde, almost invisible hair which she had never shaved. She tied her hair back in a ponytail with a red ribbon given to her by a woman on the other team's bench.

Joan took her position in the field where she waved to them while the pitcher practised whipping her windmill windup pitches across the plate. Katie and Murphy waved and called back.

"Yay, Mom! Catch a fly, Mom. Get 'em outta there!"

The inning ended quickly with the first three batters retired without a hit. As Joan ran in from the field she slapped her glove and called encouragement to her team mates. She turned to look at her family as she passed but when David tried to signal that it was time for them to leave, she mouthed, "Okay" and waved goodbye.

"Aren't you coming?" he said loud enough for her to hear.

"I'm up to bat," she said.

"But it's way past the girls' bedtime."

"So? You've put them to bed before. I'll see you after the game."

By then the other 20 people in the stands were watching them with amusement.

"Joan, I think this has gone far enough."

"I'm having fun, David."

"Ya, the lady's having fun," said a man who hid his beer can from view behind a bear paw of a hand.

"Excuse me, but this is a private conversation," said David.

"Sure it is," laughed a woman sitting behind the beer drinker.

"Can't we stay until the end of the game, Dad?"

"No. It's bedtime. Let's go."

While he manoeuvred the stroller with the opposite hand, David swung Murphy onto one hip and led the way home, Katie sulking three paces behind him.

Bedtime was brief and spartan; he was in no mood to prolong it with the usual stories and songs. When Murphy asked about the prayer that David had forgotten to say, he mumbled something to God about granting Mommy a base hit.

"Daddy! That's not a real prayer."

"That's as real as it gets tonight. Go to sleep."

"Leave the light on."

"It's too hot for lights tonight. Just lie still on top of your sheets and think about snow. Good night."

"Daddy, are you angry because Mommy is going to be a baseball player?" asked Katie.

"I'm not angry," he said, "and Mommy is not going to be a baseball player. She's just doing this because they asked her."

The girls giggled for a few minutes until they fell asleep. David took a cold beer from the fridge and sat outside on the front porch. It was too quiet. In the distance were small sounds, like transmissions from a distant galaxy, reaching him from the aura of the playing field. One car passed in half an hour along expectant Main Street. The crickets made the most noise. Someone's television was on. He recognized the sitcom. His shirt was a wet skin in the heat.

He returned to the bedroom where the girls, breathing deeply and looking vulnerable in their underwear, sprawled on top of their bedclothes. He covered them each with a sheet and kissed them. Then he locked the house and climbed into the car. The sound of the engine kicking to life turned every secret night eye on him.

He drove, not along Main Street to the Community Centre as they had walked, but in a winding circuit through the residential section of town. The route brought him to a cul-de-sac that ended where the third base line met the ball park fence. He parked the car in the shadows and turned off the engine and the headlights.

He could make out neither the inning nor the score from where he sat. Grace's team was back in the field, Joan at her post across the outfield from him. He watched from the shadows nervously, worried about her spotting him and about the girls waking up alone in the strange house. He asked himself what this was accomplishing, whether it was devotion, wounded pride, or distrust. The crack of the bat snapped him back to attention on the game.

A pop fly arched toward Joan. She would not have to move, he reckoned.

"Just put up the glove, Joanie," he said aloud. "That's it, get it in front of the ball. No, don't move back too much. Open the mitt. Don't look away. Stare it down into the glove. Keep your eye on it."

Joan caught the ball one-handed, her head turned completely away. She seemed incredulous, at first, as she looked down at the foreign object in her glove. Then, hearing the ovation of the fans and players on both sides she began to hoot and dance. David had never seen such a look on her face. Normally she was so poised. Now her mouth and eyes filled her face. The other two outfielders ran to hug her and the three of them tumbled in a heap to the grass. Everything stopped while the celebration dance of the catch was played out. They carried Joan off the field on a litter of human arms and, when the other team failed to replace them in the field, David realized that the game was over and Joan's team had won. He got out of the car and began to walk onto the field to congratulate her.

He stopped midfield and stood waving to get Joan's attention. He called her name but already she was part of the throng heading for the parking lot behind the backstop. She did not hear and he did not repeat it. He watched her disappear into a car. The big floodlights died and with the new darkness the air seemed to stop moving again. The convoy of cars turned left one by one onto the main road back to town. After the last was gone, instead of turning back to his own car, David walked in toward home plate.

At third base, he veered toward the pitcher's mound. David thought again about Joan's catch. He had reached up involuntarily as she was waiting for the ball to fall, felt the slap in the pocket and the tug backwards on the shoulder as contact was made. He beamed. It was a beauty of a catch. His Joanie. She would be at the Legion now having her first of three or four with the One Club. He stood alone in the dark on the familiar raised mound of earth. The women of both teams had celebrated so unashamedly after the catch. Something told him that their reaction would have been just as hilarious had Joan dropped the ball.

At the pitcher's spot he stopped, squatting to sift the dusty sand through his fingers. In the dark and quiet heat, the buzz of the game still alive at the edges of perception, he felt he could disappear altogether. Desiccated, he could be added to the same dirt, indistinguishable from it. He sank down onto his left side across the mound, his left hand grasping the pitcher's rubber at his head. His cheek felt chilled against the scuffed hill of sand, the cool, packed earth of his childhood. The sting of the hardball was in his palm again. He stretched, reaching for his boyhood again, mourning the long, dry span of lapse. He was alone there and turning to dust. He missed the girls and Joan with a hollow ache. All he needed to do was pick himself up and drink them in again, he knew. But he was dead weight, unable to rise. He would stay there, he decided, until his pulse and his breathing fell in with the crickets' throb, until he had thought as long and as deep and as hard as he could about the new game, about Ladies' Ball, about irrevocable losses and edifying gains.

DONALD JOHNSON

* * * * * * *

Donald Johnson was born in 1951 and presently lives in London, Ontario. An English teacher at Fanshawe College, he has contributed short fiction to a number of Canadian literary periodicals. "Cuban Baseball: The Facts" first appeared in Matrix *(October 1992).*

"I can't remember," Johnson writes, "ever not loving baseball. I play baseball (real baseball, not slo-pitch) in an over-thirties league here in London, Ontario. As a left-hander, I am limited in the number of positions I can play; I am further limited by my age and lack of speed – therefore I play first base and, yes, I pitch. My greatest achievement as a pitcher, I believe, came when I struck out the side after having given up a lead-off triple. My favourite baseball writer is Bill James. At the moment, I am working on a few different stories, one of which involves a pennant race's effects on a marriage."

* * * * * * *

Cuban Baseball: The Facts

Fact Number One: the Acts of Contrition Michael "Bug" Jones was making during the Cuban missile crisis were sincere and plentiful, but imperfect – and therefore not very useful. Being sorry for your sins just because you were terrified of being vaporized (terrified, also, of the subsequent everlasting firestorm) was, according to Sister Clare and all of Bug's other spiritual educators, simply not up to snuff. Perfect contrition, God-loving as opposed to God-fearing, and elusive enough to Bug even during militarily placid times, was now rendered completely so by atomic terror. As things stood now, Bug really could be *truly* sorry for all his sins and not even know it, so thickly was his (if not his Maker's) judgement clouded by the filthy greys of those October skies and by his amazing nightmares. Bug had even begun to worry that all those imperfect Acts, inspired as they were by his fear of infernos both temporal and eternal, might themselves be sins. He was confused. He was in bad shape.

Fact Number Two: all Bug Jones really wanted was to be a relief pitcher for the New York Yankees. He didn't want the glory of a starter's role, didn't want the twenty-win seasons, the two hundred-plus strikeouts a year, the near-perfect and the perfect games. Bug Jones just wanted to come in with the game on the line and save the day for the good guys.

Fact Number Three: unless careless President Kennedy and Christless Chairman Khrushchev could settle this insane crisis of theirs, Bug could kiss his simple and powerful dream good-bye; he could kiss his eleven-year-old behind good-bye too.

Fact Number Four: as temperament and luck would have it, Bug was one of the few people in his Grade six class who ever bothered to read the paper or watch the news on TV. He wasn't – he couldn't be – like most of the moronic little Catholics stampeding around the rocky St. Stephen's schoolyard every day, knowing so little of the external pagan world, caring so little about its sinister convulsions. (Bug's eyes would roll in disbelief whenever he thought of a *Grade Eight* kid he knew who thought *Castro* was a *relief pitcher* for the *Tigers*.) Bug also happened to have a father who, at the outset of the crisis, had told him between swallows of bottled ale that this was *it* – that if the Russians didn't back down here, it was the goddamned end of the goddamned world.

The goddamned end of the goddamned world. Game called because of radioactive fallout. Now...now what kind of – forgive the expression, ladies and gentlemen – but...what kind of shit was that for an eleven-year-old future major leaguer to be thinking? What kind of shit – please, forgive all this unprofessional language – but what kind of *shit* was that for *anyone* to be thinking? And how was it that during that final week of the month of October, in the year 1962, a boy started thinking that his destiny might lie in litigation instead of breaking balls? Why did baseball lose its potentially greatest left-handed relief pitcher-to-be to the judicial system of a country that *still* hasn't developed nuclear weapons of its own? Michael Jones, as he is today, as he crosses the border into heart attack country, wants to know.

Let's reconstruct a bit more: the stalemate in the Atlantic still on, Moscow versus Washington, extra innings.

It was lunch time at St. Stephen's Separate School. Bug Jones had been unable to eat the squashed peanut butter sandwich and bruised Delicious crudely wrapped and packed into a used paper lunch bag by his father the night before after the eleven-o'clock news and his nightly half-dozen ales. Since the beginning of the crisis Bug hadn't had much of an appetite – today's discarded sandwich and apple weren't the first to be dumped into the lunch room's oversized garbage can. Today, though, he had been caught up with yet another whispered Act of Contrition as he exited for the schoolyard and had deposited along with its contents the paper bag itself; this would probably lead to trouble tonight with his miserly and semi-soused father. Shadowed (the sun having just escaped its cover of scudding cloudmould for the first time all week) by the monstrous air-raid siren erected two years earlier after Khrushchev had threatened at the United Nations to bury Western democracy under his pounding shoe, Bug was alone now in the schoolyard. He was bouncing a worn tennis ball against the siren's adult-tall concrete base and fielding the returns as deftly as his windbreakered torso would permit. He was waiting for Kenny Cooper, his battery-mate and best friend, to finish his lunch inside and come to assume his squat so that Bug could practise his arsenal of pitches. The World Series (won by the Yankees again) had finished late (bad weather in both the Bronx and Frisco) – in fact, had finished only a week before the monstrous Kennedy had gone on TV to change everything forever. Football and ball hockey seasons were in full flight, but fanatical Bug and Kenny continued to tote their baseball gloves to school every day. The daily routine was for Bug to pitch for half an hour with Kenny calling balls and strikes; then, for the second half of the lunch hour, Bug would throw quick, tricky grounders and towering pop-ups at and above his friend (but seldom past or over him – Kenny was a slick fielder). They were both certain – or Bug had been until Cuba had taken him over the fence – that they would be rookies together on the '70 Yankees.

Despite the coolness of the weather, Bug had never pitched better: all week that fuzzless tennis ball, its velocity electric, had been hopping, popping, dropping off invisible tables to smack hollowly into Kenny's glove. Bug was especially pleased that with his screwball, incorporated into his payload for the first time that past summer, he was now able to throw four strikes even after his imaginary batters had worked him for three balls (which hadn't been often – and Kenny was, if anything, a hitter's umpire).

Kenny's arrival was overdue. Bug thought he might have been caught by Sister Clare snapping Carolyn Conroy's bra strap from behind. (Carolyn Conroy, as far as Bug and Kenny had been able to divine, was the only girl in their class to have abandoned undershirts, or whatever it was that budding but still essentially breastless girls wore under their blouses). If so, if in fact Kenny had been caught by Sister Clare, he would probably at this very moment be heading over to the church on the other side of the school to serve out his sentence with a circuit around the Stations of the Cross, and there would be no preparation for the future today. Bug let a hard grounder slip through his legs. The ball scooted all the way to the fence behind him. As he slowly walked to retrieve it, discouragement and resignation and loneliness in every step, he began mouthing under his breath another imperfect Act.

"Oh my god, I'm so sorry!" screeches the defendant to a shocked courtroom. The trial is suddenly and luckily over, the dramatic admission of guilt coming as it does on a Friday afternoon: the false infinity of a workless weekend stretches out before Michael Jones, Crown Attorney. He'll be able to catch the Yankees, in town for the first time this year, tonight and tomorrow and the next day after all.

Unless, of course, he's nuked in his bed.

In his homeward-bound taxi, he opens his book. He reads:

> In its apparent durability, a world menaced with imminent doom is in a way deceptive. It is almost an illusion. Now we are sitting at the breakfast table drinking our coffee and reading the newspaper, but in a moment we may be inside a fireball whose temperature is tens of thousands of degrees. Now we are on our way to work, walking through the city streets, but in a moment we may be standing on an empty plain under a darkened sky looking for the charred remnants of our children. Now we are alive, but in a moment we may be dead. Now there is human life on earth, but in a moment it may be gone.

He pauses from his book, looks out and up: not a cloud of any kind to be seen. Still, in the margin of the passage he has just finished, he pencils a reminder to himself to bring an umbrella to tonight's game. At home he will read more and try to nap briefly; for now he savours the streaming warm colours of the bright city he inhabits.

"...I firmly resolve, with the help of thy grace, to sin no more and to avoid the temptation of sin. Amen."

It was his sixth Act of Contrition of the day. Bug was on a record-breaking pace: his day only half over, he would easily exceed yesterday's total of ten (his first double-figure performance). Straightening himself from a glove-handed retrieval of his ball, he happened to turn toward the school building and the green-paned windows of his second-floor classroom. The oddest image seared itself into his repentance-ridden brain: the entire row of windows was filled in by classmates, who seemed to be jostling each other for a better view of the scene below them, which, Bug suddenly realized, was populated only by himself.

Oh, and then, ladies and gentlemen...ladies and gentlemen...the horror began. The stillness of that nearly barren landscape was smashed by...it was shattered by...it was *destroyed* by the unearthly ululations of a futile, *idiotically* scheduled civil defence drill, a mindless, useless, hopeless run-through for extinction. The mammoth horn of the air-raid siren began to revolve demonically, its up-and-down shriek attacking then retreating, attacking then retreating, attacking, retreating, every three hundred and sixty degrees, ripping into and through the terrorized soul of Bug Jones, who, in its thrall at Ground Zero, had begun to run and run and run in circles of steadily decreasing circumferences until he was finally just spinning madly, around and around and around, as though trying to drill himself into the hard dry clay beneath his feet. If his horror and his vertigo had permitted anything to any of his senses, the sight of a hard, gleaming home plate would have been most welcome, most comforting.

It was Sister Clare who finally brought him down with a flying tackle, to the raucous and delighted cheers of all the school-sheltered spectators. Shit. Shit, shit, shit, shit. *Forgive me.*

Bottom of the ninth, Yanks on top 3-0, but the Blue Jays are threatening with runners on second and third, one out. The P.A.

system booms with the announcement of the Yankees' new pitcher:

"Ladies and gentlemen, your attention please...now pitching for the New York Yankees, Number Nineteen...Buuug Jones!"

His warm-up tosses are gracefully and casually executed; for the benefit of the hitter in the on-deck circle, he unloads three heaters to conclude his rehearsal for battle. He turns his back to the plate, stoops to the rosin bag, straightens to look at the still cloudless night sky beyond the stadium lights. Calmer than he has ever been – anywhere, anytime – he turns homeward to stare into the eyes of a seemingly invincible John Fitzgerald Kennedy, who is now standing straight and tall and noble in the batter's box.

After all these years, the bastard is his. Even before Bug leans in for the sign, his strategy is set inside his fail-safe brain. He shakes off his catcher's first sign for a high hard one, then agrees to the call for a screwball. Since Kennedy hits from the right side, Bug will have him thinking. Lean, lean, extend, extend. Bug winds up, throws. Ball one. "Ah, but you were tempted, weren't you, Mr. President?"

The catcher, an old and trusted ally, is now tuned into Bug's plan and right away calls for another screwball. It misses the outside corner by a hair, just as Bug wants. Ball two. Kennedy steps out of the box, taps the dust from his cleats. Bug notices that the arrogant shit doesn't even bother to look down to third base for a sign before planting himself firmly back in the box for Bug's next pitch. As always, willing to risk everything, everything, *for the glory of nothing.*

The crowd's tense, excited roar is in his ears, but Bug hears nothing. Since October, 1962, Bug Jones has never lost control...

Mega-outrage from the crowd and the opposing bench as Kennedy crumples to the dirt, limbs splayed and motionless. Somehow the umpires are able to maintain order and no retaliatory blows are struck. However, Bug must summon forth all his powers of rational persuasion in order to convince the crew chief that he is innocent of deliberately throwing at the batter and that he should therefore not be ejected. Like many of his profession, he is an adroit liar when he has to be, and so manages to stay in the game.

His condition still to be medically determined (he is alive, only that much is known), Kennedy is unconscious in the stretcher that carries him from the field.

As everyone knows, as *you*, ladies and gentlemen, know, the Cuban missile crisis was resolved with Khrushchev's capitulation to Kennedy. The overweight, bald peasant who we were supposed to believe was a madman proved to be sane after all. But why was it – why *is* it, ladies and gentlemen, that John Fitzgerald Kennedy has never been diagnosed as one of history's truly demented figures? Would we be so blindly kind, or so kindly blind, if he hadn't had his head blown apart a little more than a year after Cuba? (And, while we're on the subject – can we ever be sure that it was really JFK in that bloody convertible in Dallas? Can we?) Or – gentlemen, I'm talking to you now – would any of us ever have taken this man seriously at all, *at all*, if we didn't think he had been putting it to Marilyn Monroe in the White House during those vaunted thousand days of his? (Oh Johnny, we hardly knew ye, but Marilyn did – oh yes, Marilyn knew ye, Johnny.) Or perhaps he has escaped our condemnation because of his – ladies, what do you think? – because of his exceptionally...his exceptionally...*cute*...*smile*?

But a lunatic he was, a fact surely beyond disputation by rational, right-thinking people everywhere. Even little eleven-year-old Bug Jones had John Fitzgerald Kennedy figured out: John Fitzgerald Kennedy would have ended the world just to prove he was tough! This is the truth! Ladies and gentlemen, oh, ladies and gentlemen...how can you, or anyone, laugh at that canny little boy? Of course, his classmates, indeed, the whole St. Stephen's student body, once word got around, had a great laugh at Bug and what had befallen him but they were children, after all, and can be forgiven their innocent callousness. But here, now, we are, each and every one of us, all grown up and should see nothing funny in any of this – even if, as you must know by now, Bug managed to weather the effects of his public mortification. Thank God, ladies and gentlemen, *thank God* for the miraculously natural resilience of children...

...Fact Number...well, you, like me, might be feeling at this point a little overwhelmed by the "facts" of this case; but, please – don't doubt for even a milli-second that "facts" are of the utmost importance in the search for truth. Why, we need think only of baseball statistics (facts, some would say, at their truest and most beautiful) and their value in the determination of greatness. And it is a fact, albeit entered into the record for the first time here and now, that twenty-seven years ago next World Series, Bug Jones's tongue took over from his left arm as his primary defence against all that would threaten to belittle his existence.

The dirty habit of Sister Clare was his first test, there in the nurse's room of St. Stephen's Separate School when he regained consciousness and had to defend himself against her charge of being out of bounds when everyone else, everyone else, *all the other boys and girls, mind you*, had been paying attention to the P.A. at the beginning of the lunch hour. ("But Sister, I was *praying*," Bug protested, and he saw how his words softened her anger.) The succeeding weeks' protracted mockery visited upon him by his schoolmates (his next test) he learned to deflect by zeroing in on the vulnerabilities of whoever happened to sound the cue to "Do 'the Bug'" (as long as, of course, the dance-lover was not too renowned a schoolyard tough guy). 'The Bug,' by the way, was a popular St. Stephen's dance that autumn and early winter, and you should know that it consisted of spastically described circles accompanied by much flailing and flapping of its practitioners' arms; you should know also that it brought great delight to many. But among his many tormentors there was a surfeit of youthful crossed eyes, oversized noses, fleshy lower lips, rank body fumes, botched haircuts, and other outward peculiarities that made easy targets for Bug's outrage-inspired mouth. ("That Bug Jones – God, what a mouth on him," was the post-atomic rap on Bug). Nature, ladies and gentlemen, Nature Herself had already allowed enough mutations, genetic and otherwise, at St. Stephen's Separate School; imagine the bizarre mischief that would have been wrought by the billions and billions of radioactive particles that Kennedy and – but speculation is always an idle exercise, and besides, *there's a job to be done here.*

On the night of Bug Jones's atomic trial, his father let him do the ranting for a change while he sipped his ale and watched TV. Bug had paused for air and was about to tell him how he had put Carolyn Conroy in her place on the way home from school, but his father suddenly stopped him with a raised, beer-bottled fist, and then drained the last of another pint. He told his son to save the talk, that enough was enough for God's sake, and that if he was going to run on and run on and run on, he should god-damned well get paid for it.

"Be a lawyer when you grow up, for Chrissakes," his father told him, and then rose from his chair; on his way to the kitchen for another ale, with his back to his son, he added, his words fading along with him as he disappeared from the living room, "That is *if* you grow up – *if*, that is, this isn't the goddamned end of the goddamned world."

Bug had never much liked his father's pronouncements of life and politics, but he had never been able to disprove them, and that night in bed, after one last Act of Contrition (still imperfect, but Bug now knew that he had to take what he could get, at least until the crisis was over), he summoned to the backs of his eyelids nebulous visions of a substitute future.

Ladies and gentlemen, those are *all* the facts. No shit. Forgive me. *Forgive me this one last time.*

Finding the perfect strike zone on the squat Khrushchev will be a formidable task; the bases are now loaded (some guy named Johnson at first, pinch-running for the indisposed Kennedy) and the burly pinch-hitter, just called up from the farm and probably anxious to make an impression, won't want to look at too many pitches. Thoroughly prepared as always, Bug recounts to himself the scouting report intelligence on Khrushchev mentioning that his wheelhouse is waist-high, inside part of the plate. Bug's battery-mate also knows the facts. He signals for a fastball, knowing that Bug will not be putting as much on it as he would if he were facing someone else, if he were facing, say, an enemy. The catcher's bare hand ceases its signalling twitches; his gloved hand becomes a target that will not be touched.

Bug kicks, deals. Khrushchev swings.

It's gone. Yankees lose, 4-3. Nikita nods his thanks to Bug as he begins his trot back to where he came from.

FURTHER READING

The following listing, by author, of the first editions of Canadian literary works relating to baseball includes adult, juvenile, and children's books and chapbooks. In addition to these titles, readers should consult George Bowering's article "Baseball and the Canadian Imagination" (*Canadian Literature*, Spring 1986), which provides a brief survey of Canadian activity in the field.

For a general introduction to the genre of baseball literature, see Andy McCue's *Baseball by the Books: A History and Complete Bibliography of Baseball Fiction* (1991), Peter C. Bjarkman's anthology *Baseball and the Game of Life* (1990), and Don Johnson's *Hummer, Knucklers, and Slow Curves: Contemporary Baseball Poems* (1991), which features a foreword by W.P. Kinsella. The Society for American Baseball Research's annual *The SABR Review of Books* (1986-90) is another valuable source, as is its recently launched successor, *The Cooperstown Review: The New Forum of Baseball Literary Opinion* (information on these and other SABR-related publications is available from SABR, P.O. Box 93183, Cleveland, Ohio 44101, U.S.A.).

Useful non-fiction works on Canadian baseball include Louis Cauz's *Baseball's Back in Town* (1977), William Humber's *Cheering for the Home Team: The Story of Baseball in Canada* (1983), David W. Shury's *Play Ball Son: The Story of the Saskatchewan Baseball Association* (1986), Dan Turner's *Heroes, Bums and Ordinary Men: Profiles in Canadian Baseball* (1988), Hal G. Duncan's *Baseball in Manitoba* (1989), and Robert Ashe's *Even the Babe Came to Play: Small-Town Baseball in the Dirty 30s* (1991). Also recommended is Colin D. Howell's essay "Baseball, Class and Community in the Maritime Provinces, 1870-1910" (*Social History*, November 1989).

Bonner, Mary Graham

Base Stealer (New York: Alfred A. Knopf, 1951) juvenile novel

Dugout Mystery (New York: Alfred A. Knopf, 1953) juvenile novel

Out To Win (New York: Alfred A. Knopf, 1947) juvenile novel

Spray Hitter (New York: Lantern Press, 1959) juvenile novel

Two-Way Pitcher (New York: Lantern Press, 1958) juvenile novel

Bowering, George

Baseball, a poem in the magic number 9 (Toronto: Coach House Press, 1967) long poem

Poem and Other Baseballs (Coatsworth, Ont.: Black Moss Press, 1976) poetry collection

editor, *Taking the Field: The Best of Baseball Fiction* (Red Deer, Alberta: Red Deer College, 1990) anthology

Carrier, Roch

The Longest Home Run (Montreal: Tundra, 1993) children's book

Craig, John

All G.O.D.'s Children (New York: William Morrow, 1975) novel

Chappie and Me: An Autobiographical Novel (New York: Dodd, Mead, 1979) [Later reissued under the title *Ain't Lookin'*] novel

Godfrey, Martyn

Baseball Crazy (Toronto: James Lorimer, 1987) juvenile novel

Gordon, Alison
The Dead Pull Hitter (Toronto: McClelland and Stewart, 1988) novel
Night Game (Toronto: McClelland and Stewart, 1992) novel
Safe at Home (Toronto: McClelland and Stewart, 1990) novel

King, Thomas
A Coyote Columbus Story (Toronto/Vancouver: Douglas and McIntyre, 1992)

Kinsella, W.P.
Box Socials (Toronto: HarperCollins, 1991) novel
Chapter One of a Novel in Progress (Vancouver: William Hoffer, 1988) early version of the first chapter of *Box Socials*
The Dixon Cornbelt League and Other Baseball Stories (Toronto: HarperCollins, 1993) story collection
The Further Adventures of Slugger McBatt (Toronto: Collins, 1988) story collection
The Iowa Baseball Confederacy (Boston: Houghton Mifflin, 1986) novel
Shoeless Joe (Boston: Houghton Mifflin, 1982) novel
The Thrill of the Grass (Vancouver: William Hoffer, 1984) short story
The Thrill of the Grass (Markham, Ontario: Penguin Books, 1984) story collection

Kovalski, Maryann
Take Me Out to the Ballgame (Toronto: North Winds Press, 1992) children's book

Kusugak, Michael Arvaarluk
Baseball Bats for Christmas (Toronto: Annick Press, 1990) children's book

Moher, Frank and Gerald Reid
Sliding for Home (Toronto: Playwrights Canada Press, 1990) play

Peers, Judi
Home Base (Don Mills: General Publishing, 1991) juvenile novel

Quarrington, Paul
Home Game (Toronto: Doubleday Canada, 1983) novel

Sobol, Ken
Major League Mouse (Toronto: TVOntario, 1989) children's book

Stinson, Kathy
Steven's Baseball Mitt (Toronto: Annick Press, 1992) children's book

Verral, Charles Spain
The King of the Diamond (New York: Thomas Y. Crowell, 1955) juvenile novel
Mighty Men of Baseball (New York: American Book Co., 1955) juvenile novel
Play Ball! (New York: Simon and Schuster, 1958) children's book
The Wonderful World Series (New York: Thomas Y. Crowell, 1956) juvenile novel

Young, Scott
The Pinch Hitter and Other Sports Stories (Toronto: HarperCollins, 1991) story collection
Seven Parts of a Ball Team and Other Sports Stories (Toronto: HarperCollins, 1990) story collection
We Won't Be Needing You, Al: Stories of Men and Sports (Toronto: Ryerson, 1968) story collection

ACKNOWLEDGEMENTS

Scott Young's "Seven Parts of a Ball Team" first appeared in *Collier's* (May 6, 1950) and later in *Seven Parts of a Ball Team and Other Sports Stories*, (Toronto: HarperCollins, 1990) copyright 1990 by Scott Young. Published by permission of HarperCollins Publishers Ltd.

Morley Callaghan's "A Cap for Steve" first appeared in *Esquire* (July 1952) and is published by permission of Barry Callaghan.

Raymond Souster's "The Opener" first appeared in *A Dream That Is Dying* (Toronto: Contact Press, 1954) and is published by permission of Oberon Press.

Mordecai Richler's "Playing Ball on Hampstead Heath" first appeared in *Gentlemen's Quarterley* (August 1966) and is published by permission of Mordecai Richler.

George Bowering's "Baseball, a poem in the magic number 9" was first published by Coach House Press in 1967 and is reprinted by permission of George Bowering.

W.D. Valgardson's "The Baseball Game" first appeared in *Winnipeg Stories* (Winnipeg: Queenston House, 1974) edited by Joan Parr and is published by permission of W.D. Valgardson.

Dennis Gruending's "Chucker Chatter" first appeared in *Grain* (June 1978) and is published by permission of Dennis Gruending.

Hugh Hood's "Ghosts at Jarry" first appeared in *78: Best Canadian Stories* (Ottawa: Oberon Press, 1978) edited by John Metcalf and Clark Blaise and is published by permission of Hugh Hood.

The excerpt from John Craig's *Chappie and Me* (New York: Dodd, Mead & Co., 1979) is published by permission of Frances Craig.

Lesley Choyce's "Report from Right Field" first appeared in *Fast Living* (Fredericton: Fiddlehead Press, 1982) and is published by permission of Lesley Choyce.

W.P. Kinsella's "The Baseball Spur" first appeared in *Descant* (Fall 1983) and later in *The Thrill of the Grass* (Markham, Ontario: Penguin Books, 1984). Reprinted by permission of Penguin Books Canada Limited.

Gary Hyland's "Me and Casey" first appeared in *100% Cracked Wheat* (Moose Jaw: Coteau Books/Thunder Creek Publishing Co-operative, 1983) edited by Robert Currie, Gary Hyland, and James S. McLean and is published by permission of Gary Hyland.

William J. Klebeck's "The Picnic" first appeared (under the title "Playing Ball") in *More Saskatchewan Gold* (Moose Jaw: Coteau Books/Thunder Creek Publishing Co-operative, 1984) edited by Geoffrey Ursell and is published by permission of William J. Klebeck.

Ken Norris' "The Agony of Being an Expos Fan" first appeared in *Descant* (Spring-Summer 1987) and is published by permission of Ken Norris.

Paul Quarrington's "Home Opener, 1908" first appeared in *Descant* (Spring-Summer 1987) and is published by permission of Paul Quarrington.

Judith Fitzgerald's "How Do You Spell Relief?" first appeared in *This Magazine* (July 1987) and is published by permission of Judith Fitzgerald.

The excerpt from *The Dead Pull Hitter* (Toronto: McClelland and Stewart, 1988) by Alison Gordon is used by permission of the Canadian Publishers, McClelland and Stewart, Toronto.

Robert Currie's "How I Became a Poet" first appeared in *Grain* (Fall 1988) and is published by permission of Robert Currie.

"The Girls of Summer" is reprinted from *The Outlines of Our Warm Bodies* (Fredericton: Goose Lane Editions, 1990) by permission of Goose Lane Editions. Copyright © Pat Jasper, 1990.

Edo van Belkom's "Baseball Memories" first appeared in *Aethlon* (1991) and is published by permission of Edo van Belkom.

Richard Cumyn's "Ladies' Ball" first appeared in *The Canadian Forum* (October 1991) and is published by permission of Richard Cumyn.

Donald Johnson's "Cuban Baseball: The Facts" first appeared in *Matrix* (October 1992) and is published by permission of Donald Johnson.